Impressionists
and
Impressionism

On the cover:

Claude Monet: *Impression, Sunrise (detail), 1872. Musée Marmottan, Paris. This painting, shown at the first group exhibition in 1874, was singled out for ridicule by the journalist Louis Leroy, who ironically dubbed the group "impressionists"* (cf. page 105).

First published 1970

First paperback edition 1980

Published in the United States of America in 1980 by

𝓡IZZOLI INTERNATIONAL PUBLICATIONS, INC.
712 Fifth Avenue/New York 10019

© 1980 by Editions d'Art Albert Skira S.A., Geneva

Library of Congress Catalog Card Number: 80-5471
ISBN: 0-8478-0341-4

PRINTED IN SWITZERLAND

Impressionists

- Main Text

MARIA AND GODFREY BLUNDEN

- Documentary Notices

- Synoptic Sequence of Witness Accounts by the Painters, Their Friends, and the Writers and Critics of the Impressionist Period

JEAN-LUC DAVAL

and Impressionism

SKIRA

RIZZOLI
NEW YORK

What this book is about:

Impressionists
and Impressionism

Claude Monet: Carrières-Saint-Denis. 1872.

Thomas Couture: The Romans of the Decadence, 1847.

There is room today, in painting and sculpture—not mentioning the rest— there is room, I don't say for a great artist (great artists are welcome at all times), but for a revolution.

PIERRE-JOSEPH PROUDHON

W<small>E LIVE</small> in an age of Insurgency. A score of contemporary power seizures have made us familiar with the technique of the *coup d'état* and the ideology of the popular revolution. From the vantage point of a sophisticated century, therefore, we may look back on the career of Louis Napoléon Bonaparte with a certain detachment and even that wry amusement which comes from recognizing familiar patterns of totalitarian behavior.

Louis Bonaparte was a loner, that is, he had no party behind him, nor any popular movement. He made his bid for power by means of an alliance with the French bourgeoisie at a time when that formidable class of people was profoundly shaken by the Revolution of 1848. That revolution had written "finis" to the restored monarchy; the new Republic, the second in France's history, was becoming threateningly class conscious. The fact that he was a nephew of the illustrious Napoleon I gave Louis an edge with the popular electorate and at a critical hour he had seemed, not without a good deal of maneuvering on his part, a useful compromise leader, a compromise reflected in his title of Prince-President. It was a contradiction in terms which he soon resolved in a classic *coup d'état*, December 1851, by which means he became Emperor of the French.

Close to two hundred republican workers had been killed on the barricades while politicians and journalists were being imprisoned. In the subsequent "cleansing" of public life, ten thousand republicans were deported to Algeria, some two thousand exiled for life (not counting those, like Victor Hugo, who went into voluntary exile) and three hundred sent to Devil's Island, the "dry guillotine" of his late Uncle's regime. The hardy republican slogan, *Liberté, Egalité, Fraternité*, was erased from the walls of Paris.

The ideology upon which the Emperor planned to base his regime was one that would reflect national glory, be constantly diverting and convincingly authoritarian. The career of matchless opulence and ostentation upon which he now plunged was less a matter of self-indulgence (though it was that too) than a calculated policy of imperial grandeur, intended to inspire emulation among the rich and adoration in the minds of the irretrievably humble.

So the French saw their latest Emperor in his *voiture de gala*, a huge vehicle, all red velvet and gilding, from the center of which rose a great crowned eagle whose outspread wings sheltered the imperial occupant; or they saw their Emperor as a "man of fashion," galloping his curricle through the streets, a faint smile behind the large waxed moustache; or they saw their Emperor dancing to a barrel organ, because (popular touch) "an orchestra is so awkward," dancing the polka, the mazurka, lancers and quadrilles like everybody else; or if privileged, they were reassured to see the Emperor in white cashmere breeches, black stockings and dress sword, the long white shirtfront barred by the carmine of the *Légion*, receiving notables in the *Salon des Maréchaux*. And because he is, above all, a soldier, there are scintillating military parades: the brilliant new uniforms at Longchamp as the Emperor reviews the troops (only one in five can read): the *Cuirassiers* in their polished steel breastplates going past at the gallop; the trotting *Lancers* a veritable harvest of glittering helmets, fur busbys, shakoes

and schapkas; the artillery with its new brass cannons (the secret weapons, e.g. the deadly *mitrailleuse* and the breech-loading *chassepot*, are kept out of sight); the *Fantassins* in their long black tunics, the fezzed *Turcos* in short pants and the turbaned *Zouaves* in red pantaloons, the *Chasseurs à pied* quickstepping to Rossini's new trumpet march played by a bugle band, the little *cantinières* in colored petticoats with miniature casks of cognac swinging from their shoulders, finally the husky *Sapeurs* with bristling chin-beards, fur caps, white aprons and glittering axes (at the Alcazar, crowds going mad over Thérésa's deep-voiced: *Rien n'est sacré pour un Sapeur!*); the Emperor standing in the Champ de Mars presenting eagles to the army, as his uncle had done, or signing treaties with an eagle's quill (in the shadow of the Vendôme Column, decrepit veterans in the rags of Waterloo nodding solemn approval).

Quai des Grands-Augustins, Paris, in 1858. Photograph.

Franz Winterhalter:
The Emperor Napoleon III.

9

And because, after all, it takes two to run a palace, they see the Emperor married to tall and beautiful Eugenia Maria de Montijo de Guzman at Notre Dame de Paris; the vast nave hung with velvet, the arches banked with flowers and the aisles ablaze with candles and gold larmé, the bride wearing blue velvet with a long, lace-covered train, clusters of diamonds in her corsage, on her red-gold hair a long veil of Alençon lace under a crown of orange flowers, the high comb and diadem in magnificent sapphires; Emperor and Empress in their modest little marriage carriage with painted panels and satin cushions embroidered with the large "N" that was making its reappearance everywhere, in tapestry, silverware and on stone bridges; the Emperor and Empress receiving at the Tuileries Palace, the bedazzled guests slowly climbing the curving stairway between the rigid rows of green-and-gold *Cent-Gardes* whose tall helmets also bear the Imperial cipher.

They see Emperor and Empress setting the fashion: feminine dress weighed down with tinsel, lace, fal-lals, tulles, ribbons and artificial flowers, the crinoline which permitted women to glide across polished floors, but never to sit; their male companions of wealth and banality wearing tight trousers and wasp-waisted long-tailed coats, painted faces and circular moustaches, large watch chains, trinkets and gloves; Emperor and Empress at a *grand bal costumé*, Eugénie's lovely bare shoulders the magnet of compulsive stares.

Foreign sovereigns come to stare and wonder: the Czar of Russia, the King of Prussia, Queen Victoria (thrilled to have heard the Emperor whisper to the Empress, "*Comme tu es belle*"), the Prince of Wales, the Sultan of Turkey, gentlemen from Japan. They see Emperor and Empress dancing to the melodies of Offenbach at the Bal Mabille and the Valentino, riding together at Fontainebleau, skating on the lake at Boulogne, at boating parties, drags, shoots, reviews; the Emperor, engaged on a "Life of Caesar" while the Empress plays at spiritualism and the cult of Marie Antoinette; Emperor and Empress at the Théâtre Français to see Sarah Bernhardt in *La Dame aux Camélias,* at the Théâtre Italien to hear Adelina Patti in M. Gounod's new opera; the Emperor alone in his box to see—for the hundredth time—Hortense Schneider in *La Belle Hélène,* alone at many another voluptuous, but private, performance. This is the wine of success.

At the moment of taking power, Louis Napoleon had quoted the old French proverb: *Quand le vin est tiré, il faut le boire*—when the wine is drawn it must be drunk. The little man with the sallow complexion and dull eyes, the long cruel cheeks and the clotted moustache, had seized the cup. The opposition had been crushed. He had set the stage, he thought, for a new and glorious epoch in the history of France.

How could Louis Napoleon have known that France's lasting glory in the two decades of his rule resided not in himself, his army or his court, but in the talents of a few young people, only one of them yet of age. In the year that Napoleon tasted the totalitarian wine Camille Pissarro was twenty-one; Edouard Manet was nineteen and Edgar Degas seventeen, Alfred Sisley and Paul Cézanne were both twelve, Claude Monet eleven, Auguste Renoir, Berthe Morisot, Armand Guillaumin and Frédéric Bazille ten years old.

"Savage young revolutionaries," Zola was to call them.

The "Gilded and Voluptuous Promises" of the Second Empire

At the time of the 1855 World's Fair, Ingres was 75 years old, Corot 59, Delacroix 57, Diaz 47, Théodore Rousseau 43, Millet 41, Daubigny 38 and Courbet 36.

As for the generation of the Impressionists, Pissarro was 25, Manet 23, Degas 21, Cézanne and Sisley 16, Monet 15, Renoir and Berthe Morisot 14.

Honoré Daumier: An Excusable Error. Chickens imagining they have rediscovered the cage in which they spent their infancy. Lithograph, 1857.

*Constantin Guys: The Champs-Elysées.
Pen, wash, sepia and watercolor.*

*The Picture Gallery at the Paris World's
Fair of 1855. Woodcut.*

*Franz Winterhalter: The Empress
Eugénie and her Ladies in Waiting.*

From our vantage point in the twentieth century we have learned to recognize the factors contributing to insurgent success and longevity. We note, for example, that no insurrectionary regime has failed to exercise control over the aesthetic and intellectual life within its range. The question of free expression in the arts is no longer debated, except to prove that it does not exist; more often explicit than implicit is the revolutionary principle that the control and guidance of all forms of expression is essential to the continuing exercise of political power.

This truth was, of course, understood by the oligarchs of earlier times, some of whom countered insurrection by this means. Louis XIV, studying rebellious Paris from the security of Versailles, enlisted the Académie Française and the Royal Academy of Painting and Sculpture to capture, through the channel of honors and increment, the original and provocative minds of his long reign. Though the system was less advantageously employed by his immediate successors, it is significant that, when it came, the French Revolution, while broadening the scope of the Academy, maintained a close supervision over creative expression. Thus the ensuing popular dictatorship was able to make full use of art for its own ends; indeed, the widescreen canvases depicting the trials and triumphs of Napoleon I continue to this day to add luster to his image.

In 1791 the annual exhibition of the Académie des Beaux Arts (as it had been renamed) was thrown open, by a decree of the National Assembly, to non-members of the Academy and foreign painters. Thus inaugurated, the bourgeois age in art grew and flourished. Installed in the castles and manor houses of the disappropriated aristocracy, or building mansions for themselves, the new middle classes proceeded to decorate their status dwellings according to their own taste, leaning heavily on the Academy for guideposts to their new-found expression. Beginning with a few hundred paintings the number of exhibits at the annual exhibitions, or Salons, as they were called, had increased to thousands when Honoré de Balzac complained that "since 1830 the Salon has become a bazaar."

In great demand were the products of an art cult (there is no other word for it) called *anticomania*. Originating in the last quarter of the previous century, after the discovery of Pompeii, it had been introduced to France by the painter David. According to this system the subjects for paintings were chosen from the myths and legends of antiquity—as suggested, for example, by the classical ruins of lava-engulfed Pompeii—and told a story, usually with a moral. A perfect example of the cult is the painting, *Romans of the Decadence,* by Thomas Couture, which was awarded the much-prized gold medal at the Salon of 1847. In this competent painting the presumed reasons for the Fall of Rome are presented, as in a charade, by a number of toga-wearing models. The public loved these *grandes machines,* as they were called, and the critics who wrote for the influential newspapers described each painting, not as a painting, but as a story. The nude was also painted, but always in some mythological or archeological reconstruction. Landscapes were also acceptable, provided they depicted the mysterious Orient or some romantic no-man's-land.

"Just as in life wisdom is the loftiest expression of the soul, so tranquillity is the prime beauty of the body."

Ingres

Ingres photographed by Dolard, 1856.

There were, nevertheless, some very great painters in France. J. A. D. Ingres, born in 1780, was a superlative draftsman, preferring the carefully drawn, sculptural and stable; the pink flesh of his "Bathers" was greatly admired. Camille Corot, born in 1796, thought of himself as a purely classic artist. "What I look for is form; for me, color comes afterwards," he once said, adding, "Your feeling should be your only guide." His delicate landscapes, always finished indoors, had a lyricism and freshness which the official art did not possess. Eugène Delacroix, born in 1798, was a painter of movement, of animals and colonial soldiers; a great romantic, he found inspiration in the works of Dante, Shakespeare and Byron, but deviated from the accepted canon in his free and vigorous use of color. For the rest, the academic painters, there is little to be said, except that they were enormously popular. In the age preceding that of the camera and its reproductive media they satisfied public hunger for imagery.

It was natural, therefore, and not without precedent, that Louis Napoleon should turn to the Académie des Beaux Arts for the picture he wished to create of himself and his regime. Having based his appeal on nostalgic memories of Napoleonic grandeur, he wished to recapture the atmosphere and style of the more successful period of his Uncle's reign, that of the Directoire. As the mirror of bourgeois taste the Academy was superbly equipped, not only to reflect his image, but to provide him with the technical resources for its propagation. Behind the Academy, and at its command, were thousands of painters, sculptors, engravers, draftsmen, designers, wood and metal workers and other craftsmen. The arrival of Louis Napoleon provided work for them all. Not only were they commissioned to prepare the canvases required for the walls of his palaces, the statuary for his halls and gardens, but craftsmen and designers were needed for his furniture and tapestries, his carriages, his coinage, his plate, his (and his army's) uniforms. Not in living memory had so much canvas been put under paint, so much paint put in pots, so many frames carved and gilded, so much gold thread loomed, so much cochineal and indigo dissolved, so

Jean-Dominique Ingres: The Large Odalisque, 1814.

"Art consists above all in taking nature as a model and copying it with scrupulous care, choosing however its loftiest sides. Ugliness is an accident and not one of the features of nature."

Ingres

much marble brought from Carrara, so much bronze and brass forged. As Clive Bell has said: "In the second half of the nineteenth century, official painting, perhaps for the first time on record, certainly for the first time since Roman days, had nothing whatever to do with art."

The effect of all this industry was to make of art a vested interest. For the protection and management of this interest Louis Napoleon appointed Count Nieuwerkerke to be superintendent of the Académie des Beaux Arts and president of the jury of the annual Salon, with full powers. A page under the Restoration, a sculptor under the July monarchy, this elegant gentleman with his well-trimmed blond beard was an intimate friend of Princess Mathilde, the Emperor's cousin. Save for the influence of Ingres, Count Nieuwerkerke was sole arbiter of artistic merit in France. He made art fashionable as well as financially rewarding. The official painters such as Cabanel, Meissonier and Bouguereau, enjoyed a comfortable affluence. Their magnificently appointed and spacious studios had a great attraction for bourgeois society, gentlemen of wealth coming with their wives to see the painter at work, and perhaps commissioning a portrait.

Of the work of that small and half-starved group of outdoors painters (contemptuously referred to as the Barbizon school, after the name of the tiny village they frequented on the outskirts of the forest of Fontainebleau) Count Nieuwerkerke said: "This is the painting of democrats, of those who don't change their linen, who think that they can deceive men-of-the-world; this art displeases and disgusts me."

There was a bearded democrat among the day's painters who could not be so easily ignored. Gustave Courbet was a big gusty man who joyfully accepted the appellation "realist," conferred upon him in contempt also. Born at Ornans, near Besançon, he had been instructed in the purest revolutionary principles by his grandfather, a veteran of the Revolution of 1791. Sent to Paris to study law he had taught himself to paint by copying the old masters in the Louvre. He was a marvelous craftsman. He chose earthy or sensual subjects, such as drinkers around a table, stone breakers, winey working girls dozing on the banks of the Seine. He made notes out-of-doors, but he did all his finished work in his studio.

Courbet was often to be seen at the Brasserie des Martyrs in Montmartre which, according to the brothers Goncourt, was "a tavern of a cavern of all the great men without name: of all the bohemian little journalists; of the world of the impoverished and the unhappy." Here Courbet would take a bock or a *mazagran* (lemonade and absinthe) in the company of his spectacled friend Pierre-Joseph Proudhon, the theoretician of egalitarian socialism. Out of these discussions came the ideas, elaborated by Proudhon in his *Du Principe de l'Art,* upon which the artistic revolution would be based: "To paint men in the sincerity of their nature and customs, in their work, in the accomplishments of their civic and domestic functions, with their actual physiognomy, above all without pose, to surprise them, so to speak, in the undressed state of their consciences, not simply for the pleasure of mockery, but with the aim of general education and as aesthetic warning; such seems to me (wrote Proudhon) the point of departure of modern art."

"With Corot it is nature herself who sings and becomes her own nightingale."   Castagnary

Camille Corot: Self-Portrait, about 1835.

Camille Corot: Windmill on the Dunes. Drawing.

In 1855—four years after his *coup d'état*—Louis Napoleon felt that it was time to boast. A great International Fair was held at the Palais de l'Industrie, built for the occasion. Painting—one of the glories of France—was represented by five thousand canvases. Ingres topped the list of exhibitors with forty pictures, Delacroix had thirty-five. When two of Courbet's pictures were rejected by the selection committee, Courbet withdrew all his submissions. On a plot of ground not far from the grandiose Palais de l'Industrie he had a gallery built at his own expense, in which he exhibited forty paintings, including *The Painter's Studio* and *Burial at Ornans*, vast canvases today regarded as masterpieces. He called it the Pavillon du Réalisme.

When Delacroix paid a visit to Courbet's Pavillon du Réalisme he was alone there; the public, obedient to the Academy's will, shunned Courbet. But the works were seen by several very young painters who were not only profoundly interested by Courbet's "realism," but were inspired by the example of his nonconformity.

To his pupils Courbet said: "Imagination in art consists in knowing how to find the most complete expression of an existing thing; but never to suppose or create this thing." Naturalism in painting was Courbet's contribution to the scientific materialism of his century; by observing this dictum he believed that the artist would sidestep the traditional dogmas and recipes of official painting. Thus Courbet himself painted "the intense emotion of facts." Lesser painters, obeying his injunction, merely became slaves of the model.

"Delacroix alone has grasped the moral and human aspect of color; therein lie his achievement and his claims on posterity."

Odilon Redon

Eugène Delacroix: Arab Dancer. Pen and ink.

Eugène Delacroix: Lion Hunt, 1855.

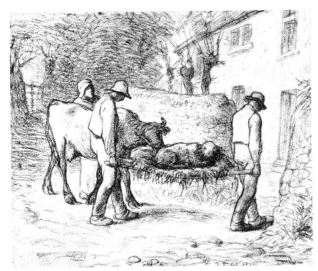

The Cry of the Earth

Impressionism can be fully understood only in the light of the progressive art immediately preceding it, the art of Delacroix, Millet, Courbet. Their influence lay not in artistic language, whose autonomy was to be so much enlarged by the Impressionists, but in their conception of a reality grasped and elaborated by the conscious mind, to the exclusion of any idealizing or mythological abstractions. Delacroix, in a Journal entry of 1853, severely criticized both Courbet and Millet, but in spite of this negative judgment he hit on the truth when he said that Millet, like the figures he portrayed, "is himself a peasant." Similarly, Delacroix's most understanding interpreter, Baudelaire, described Courbet as "a powerful workman." More and more, painters refused to withdraw into myths or ancient history, but found their heroes in the common walks of daily life. This democratic awareness of reality became the keynote of all modern art; it impinged on style and design, modifying and renewing them, and increasing their expressiveness. Millet, and Courbet even more, went beyond the realism of Barbizon because their espousal of reality was ideological and not a mere observation of natural scenes or scenery. Their example in this respect was of fundamental importance for the Impressionists, whose aesthetic and sensibility they foreshadowed in the steady advance of a now irreversible process.

Jean-François Millet: Women in an Interior. Drawing.

Jean-François Millet: Peasants Bringing Home a Calf Born in the Fields.

Gustave Courbet: The Young Stone-Breaker, about 1865. Chalk.

Millet, Rousseau, Diaz and Daubigny, the leading painters of the Barbizon school, whom Monet and the Impressionists were to meet in the 1860's, were the first artists of the nineteenth century who had no private means, who depended on their art for a living. Theirs was often a hard life, but they believed too firmly in their painting to make the least concession to the taste of the public. It was in front of their easel that they launched their social and moral revolution. As men of the people, they turned away instinctively from the classical masters to such artists as Le Nain, La Tour and Chardin, because in these painters they found a spirit akin to their own. They rejected historical and mythological painting, the whole intellectual and literary bias of the art of their time, in favor of a direct recording of human experience and everyday life.

The milieu in which they lived, the poverty which they shared with workers and peasants, imbued their work with a democratic message. For the legendary exploits of ancient heroes they substituted the modest grandeur, moving presence and age-old gestures of the peasant at work in the fields. Though revolutionaries at heart, they did not destroy the traditional spatial structure of the picture, for they dared not challenge both the subject and the manner of representing it for fear of being totally misunderstood; but they did impose on painting a new truthfulness and simplicity, a direct vision of things. A comparison of Millet's *Gleaners* with those in an old photograph shows how true to life he was. In illustrating the work of the fields and seasons, the Barbizon painters came to grips again with the problem of integrating the figure into the landscape.

With them nature lost its literary charms but regained its grandeur and silence. In their figure paintings, idealization of form gave way to a straightforward rendering of sturdy volumes.

Corot had made studies directly from nature, especially during his stay in Italy, but like the classical masters he kept these studies secret, while the Barbizon painters used theirs as sketches for studio compositions, after the example of Constable whose influence on French landscapists remained strong for several generations after the exhibition of his work in Paris at the 1824 Salon. As they made studies of Paris and its environs, Rousseau, Diaz and Daubigny came to realize the importance of light, which constantly changes the appearance of things. Their romantic temperament induced them to look in nature for an echo of their moods. In its underlying rhythms, in the renewal of the seasons and the novelty of changing light effects, landscape was better suited than any other subject to the expression of their feelings.

Curious observers of all natural phenomena, they were especially fond of spectacular manifestations, such as storms and rainbows. Into the rigid framework of classical space they thus introduced forces which transcended man, uncontrollable and inaccessible forces. In contrast with the linear gap receding toward the horizon line, there is often a violent gust of wind sweeping lengthwise across the canvas and carrying heavy clouds which project dramatic shadows onto the ground and modify local tones and the traditional aspect of things. The grass may turn vermilion or lemon yellow, the hill a tender green or violet. And man is dwarfed by the play of cosmic forces.

"I plainly see the aureoles of the dandelions and out yonder, far beyond the land, the sun flaunting its glory in the clouds. And no less clearly, in the steaming plain, I see the plow horses at work, then, in a stony place, a man hacking away whose grunts have been heard all day long and who straightens up for a moment to catch his breath. The drama is cloaked in splendor. None of it is of my devising, and this expression, *the cry of the earth,* was coined long ago. "

Jean-François Millet

Jean-François Millet: A Sower, about 1848. Drawing.

Théodore Rousseau: View of Montmartre, Storm Effect, about 1845-1848.

These four painters numbered among the official glories of the nineteenth century, among those who were awarded gold medals, the Legion of Honor and the commissions given by the State and by princes. These four pictures represent the official taste against which the genuine creators had to contend.

The scandal of the Salon reached its height under Napoleon III. In vain were some reforms made in the selection of the jury: its spirit remained the same so long as the majority of the jurymen were members of the Institut and the Academy, representatives of officialdom. In their blind conventionalism and prejudice they resisted the expression of any new ideas in art. They were the enemies of creative freedom, and things had come to such a pass that some artists were reduced to working in two manners: one tame and watered down to suit the Salon and another more bold and personal which they dared not show. The tyranny of the jury was for many a real hardship, for the Salon was then the only place where artists could exhibit their work in public. The painters who triumphed at the Salon were not necessarily devoid of talent, but they were apt to prefer slickness and conformism to truth, they had to make concessions to the prevailing taste.

To please the jury meant accepting ready-made formulas and a conventional way of seeing. The classicists assumed a tinge of romanticism in order to seem up to date; the romantics held their hand and palette in check in order to accord the customary primacy to form. Painting was reduced to illustration, and personality to technical skill.

The Renaissance conception of the picture space remained unchallenged until after the French Revolution and the resulting moral and social upheavals. Normal perspective, marking man's domination over nature, was taken for granted as the ideal and absolute system of representation. Unable to establish any new relationships between man and the world around him, academic painters contented themselves with a slightly personalized interpretation of a conventional pattern, and this inevitably meant idealizing and sentimentalizing. The picture came to be judged by the story it told, and specific pictorial values were lost sight of behind the cultural and sentimental values of the anecdote.

While in science and philosophy the nineteenth century came to grips with the phenomena of reality, official artists continued to live in a make-believe world. As photography was popularized, it confirmed the intuition of the realist painters. The evidence of photography amounted to an outright condemnation of official art, but the progressive painters striving to record their optical discoveries with the utmost accuracy continued to be treated as dangerous and vulgar revolutionaries.

Charles Gleyre gave a tinge of romantic melancholy to the idealism of David, Léopold Robert sentimentalized Poussin, Jules Breton idealized Millet, and Cormon re-echoed the sentiment of Victor Hugo in terms verging on the grotesque. But Breton's mawkishness could no more compete with Courbet's robust truthfulness than Cormon's grandiloquence with Daumier's dramatic power.

"For a painter to make a point of looking for poetry in the conception of a picture is the surest way for him not to find it."

Baudelaire

Charles Gleyre: Evening or Lost Illusions, 1843.

Fernand Cormon: Cain.

Léopold Robert: The Return of the Harvesters from the Pontine Marshes, Rome, 1830.

Jules Breton: Benediction of the Wheat in Artois, 1857.

*Gustave Courbet: A Burial at
Ornans, 1849.*

*Honoré Daumier: The
Emigrants, 1850-1855.*

Courbet and Daumier spurned anything in the way of conventions or concessions to prevailing taste. The apostle of realism, Courbet was the first artist who successfully resisted the authority of the Salon jury. It was an epoch-making event when in 1855, his masterpiece *The Studio* having been rejected by the jury, he held an exhibition of his own in a private pavilion outside the fair grounds where the official exhibition took place. This was the first retrospective devoted to the work of a living artist of the younger generation, the first assertion of independence with respect to officialdom. In his preface to the catalogue Courbet wrote: "I have studied the art of the ancients and the art of the moderns without regard to any spirit of system and without preconceptions." What he did in fact was "to elicit from a thorough knowledge of tradition the reasoned, independent sense" of his own individuality. He was the first painter to look at the present with his own eyes.

Courbet and Daumier were sturdy republicans. Recognizing the individual rights of each man, they exercised their own to the full and expressed in painting what they really felt. To safeguard this creative freedom, Daumier had to spend most of his time and energy on caricature and illustration. Self-taught, knowing nothing of the classical training of the academies, he was the first painter to rise from the ranks of the craftsmen, an individualist with a personal vision unhampered by the linear space of Renaissance art. His portrayal of human beings is convincing, compassionate, and memorable. His linework, free and quivering with life, expresses the intensity of his frank sympathy with people.

"This much must be said for Courbet, that he has contributed not a little to restore the taste for simplicity and frankness and the disinterested, absolute love of painting."

Baudelaire

"The imagination recruits its strength in nature, and there it seizes on real forms which it then raises into new allegories."

Thoré-Bürger

Gustave Courbet: The Painter's Studio, 1855.

Courbet's contemporaries were shocked by the realism of his vision, and to them it did not seem odd that the inventor of realism should paint a landscape in his studio, while a nude model posed beside him and his friends looked on. Truthfulness with him was a matter of frank personal expression, but his composition continued to owe more to imagination than to realistic observation.

For Courbet truthfulness was essentially tactile. Both in his *Studio*, the last large-scale painting of the nineteenth century, and in his

Photograph of Courbet.

"To be able to express the manners, ideas and aspect of my time...in a word, to produce living art."

Courbet

"To paint a bit of country one has got to know it. I know my native countryside and I paint it. That woodland is near my home, that river is the Loue. Go and look at them and you will see my picture." Courbet

Gustave Courbet: Stream in the Forest, 1865.

20

EXHIBITION
ET VENTE
DE

38 TABLEAUX ET 4 DESSINS
DE L'ŒUVRE DE

M. Gustave COURBET

AVENUE MONTAIGNE, 7, CHAMPS-ÉLYSÉES

Prix : 10 centimes

Catalogue of Courbet's one-man show of 1855.

Gustave Courbet: Self-Portrait, detail from ▶
The Painter's Studio, 1855.

best landscapes, he tried to render with the utmost authenticity the actual texture of things; over the local tone he superimposed the quality of the texture, the sense of touch prevailed over that of sight. Without cultural prepossessions, he felt that anything that exists is worth painting, that everything has a beauty of its own, that acquired tastes are apt to impose fallacious and ephemeral hierarchies which are best evaded by the direct expression of personal feelings. A man of the soil, he liked good workmanship and dense, full-bodied pigments, changing his technique to suit the texture of each new object and not hesitating to use the palette knife and the thick creamy paints of the house painter if need be. His gesture was direct and generous, his vision clear and straightforward. But the best of his painting is in the parts rather than the whole. He concentrated on accurate details, while the Impressionists on the contrary disregarded detail, the better to record the light that unites objects. Sure of himself and proud of his originality, Courbet produced some unforgettable pieces of painting remarkable for their forthright truthfulness. He was so much concerned with touch and texture that the play of light and shade in his pictures is often inaccurate. As a positivist, he believed only in what he could measure and touch. But he freed his successors from the stale hierarchy of genres and subjects and emboldened them to see and do everything. His painting is justified not so much by his culture or talent as by the robust authenticity of his human testimony.

Courbet's preface to his one-man show of 1855:

REALISM

The name "realist" has been imposed on me just as the name "romantics" was imposed on the men of 1830. At no time have such names conveyed an accurate idea of things; were it otherwise, our works would be superfluous.

Without going any further into the accuracy or inaccuracy of a designation which, it is to be hoped, no one need be expected to understand, I shall confine myself to a few words of explanation in order to forestall any misunderstandings.

I have studied the art of the ancients and the art of the moderns without regard to any spirit of system and without preconceptions. I have no more tried to imitate the former than to copy the latter; nor has my intention been rather to aim at the pointless goal of art for art's sake. No! I have quite simply tried to elicit from a thorough knowledge of tradition the reasoned, independent sense of my own individuality.

Knowledge is power, that was what I had in mind. To be able to express the manners, ideas and aspect of my time, according to my own estimate of them, in a word to produce living art, that is the end I have in view.   G. C.

From Realism to an Objective and Poetic Naturalism

"Never have I seen so expressive a face; he laughed and looked uneasy, assuring me at the same time that his picture was very bad and that it would be a great success. I find him quite decidedly a charming man, ever so much to my liking. As always his paintings produce the impression of wild or even slightly unripe fruit."

Letter from Berthe Morisot to her sister Edma, May 2, 1869

Manet photographed by Nadar.

"An artist has got to move with the times and paint what he sees."

Manet

Edouard Manet, one of the younger painters who visited Courbet's Pavillon, saw this at once. "Too black," was his comment, which may have been a reference to Courbet's palette, or to his outlook. Though only twenty-three at this time Manet was already embarked upon a course which would take him far beyond the confines of naturalism without obeisance to official painting. Born, January 25, 1832, at no. 5 rue des Petits Augustins and baptized at Saint-Germain-des-Prés, he was the eldest of three brothers, sons of an official of the Department of Justice, a family, not rich, but solidly respectable (they owned a 150-acre estate at Gennevilliers). He had been educated first by the Abbé Poiloup at Vaugirard, then at the Collège Rollin. Uncle Fournier, his mother's brother, who had some skill with the pencil, had given the boy drawing lessons and had several times taken him, with his friend Antonin Proust, to see the King's famous collection of Spanish art at the Louvre, five hundred paintings by Goya, Greco, Velazquez and Zurbaran, alas, withdrawn after Louis Philippe's overthrow.

Auguste Manet wanted his son to enter the Navy and when the boy failed the entrance examination he sent him to sea as an apprentice. It was a fine trip out to Rio de Janeiro in the *Guadeloupe*: the young man made sketches of the ship's company and his obvious talent was exploited by the ship's quartermaster in connection with a consignment of Dutch cheese which had spoiled in the tropical heat. "Conscientiously with a brush I freshened up these *têtes de mort* which reappeared in the beautiful tints of violet and red," Manet said, years later. "It was my first piece of painting." He returned home with the sailor's inevitable souvenir of foreign ports and some equally lasting impressions. "I spent night after night," he told the painter Charles Toché (as reported by Ambroise Vollard, the art dealer), "watching the play of light and shade in the wake of the ship. During the day I watched the line of the horizon. That taught me how to plan out a sky." His rare seascapes would surprise by their authority.

After his return to Paris his father, no doubt consoling himself with the thought of the medals to be won by a well-born artist, agreed that Edouard should enter the Ecole des Beaux Arts. In 1850 Manet enrolled, with his friend Antonin Proust, at the studio of Thomas Couture (he of the Decadent Romans). "On my first day at Couture's," he told Toché, "they gave me an antique to draw from. I turned it about in every direction. It seemed to me more interesting head downwards." Couture preferred his models to be thin, because, as he explained to his students, "you can add as much as you like, whereas with fat models, the flesh hides everything and you don't know what to take off." On the model throne the male models, proud of their athletic figures, would strike poses with torso blown up and muscles flexed. One of them, Charles Alix Dubosc, who had modelled for David, Gros and Géricault, would come down among the students, clad only in his shoes and a monocle, and pass judgment on their studies of himself. Manet detested the posturing of the professional models. "Can't you be natural!" he would shout. What does Monsieur Manet want? He wants, he says, to paint not what he is supposed to see, but what he *sees*. He hates so-called "historical painting." He despises "mythology." He would paint real people.

One cold morning in December 1851, hearing gunfire in the streets of Paris, Manet rushed out to see what was happening. By chance he found himself on the barricades thrown up by the Parisian workers who were resisting Louis Napoleon's *coup d'état*. Men were falling all around him. Without much thought for his own safety the young man (he was nineteen) pulled out a drawing pad and made lightning sketches of the scene. He was seeing real people. Nor was it the last time he would bear witness to the barricades.

In spite of differences with Couture, Manet learned a great deal from his master: sharp contrasts, a way of handling pure color. Couture, a shoemaker's son, was in advance of official painting, but could not afford to reveal this, though a feeling for real life escapes in his minor work. One of the first paintings Manet did outside the school was called *The Absinthe Drinker*. His model was an old rag-picker named Collardet who posed in a brown cloak, wearing a high hat, a glass beside him and a bottle at his feet. The influence of the Spanish masters is obvious; the real influence was Couture, the technical execution boldly conforming to Couture's rule. When the painting was finished Manet invited Couture to view it. His former master said: "My friend, there is only one absinthe drinker here. It is the painter who produced this insanity." It was characteristic of Manet that he was chagrined by this reaction to his work. As he said later: "I painted a Parisian character whom I had studied in Paris, and I executed it with the technical simplicity I discovered in Velazquez. No one understands it. If I had painted a Spanish type it would be more comprehensible."

Manet quit Couture's some months after he had seen Courbet's Pavillon, having been a steady student—with some breakaways to the relaxed atmosphere of the Académie Suisse—for six years. He had already made a brief tour of the Italian galleries; he now travelled extensively, visiting Vienna, Venice, Florence and Holland.

On his return to Paris Manet took a large airy studio with another painter, Count Albert de Balleroy, and began painting vigorously. One of his first original works was modelled by a fifteen-year-old boy called Alexandre, who hanged himself. According to Zola, Alexandre was the son of very poor parents and wanted desperately to be a painter. He had got a job cleaning Manet's palettes and tidying up his studio. Looking at Manet's painting of himself, he had realized that his ambition could never be fulfilled. Baudelaire, Manet's friend at this time, wrote a poem about the boy's suicide, which he called "Rope."

Manet had met Baudelaire in the salon of a family friend, Commandant Lejosne of the Imperial Guard (nevertheless, an admirer of off-beat poetry), one afternoon in 1858. They took to each other immediately. Baudelaire's *Fleurs du Mal* had been condemned by the Imperial Tribunal the previous year, six of the poems having been censored as indecent. His aesthetic ideas were well in advance of the age; he admired Delacroix and Wagner, both considered "revolutionary" at that time; he had coined the word "modernity," to describe the efforts of a few to give expression to the contemporary world. In his review of the Salon of 1845 he had written: "To the wind which will blow tomorrow, no one pays any attention; and yet the heroism of modern life surrounds us and urges us on... He will be truly a

Edouard Manet: Portrait of Baudelaire, 1862-1868. Etching.

Edouard Manet: The Absinthe Drinker, 1859. Refused at the 1859 Salon, Delacroix alone voting for its admission.

Manet, the fascinating man of the world, and Degas, the sarcastic misanthrope, were at one in their scorn for conventions

Edgar Degas: Portrait of Manet, 1864-1865. Drawing.

"Degas admires and envies the self-assurance of Manet, whose eye and hand are sure of themselves, who sees infallibly what in the model will give him the opportunity to put forth his full power, to work at full stretch. There is in Manet a decisive resourcefulness, a sort of strategic instinct of pictorial action. In his best canvases he arrives at *poetry*, that is at the highest point of art, by what I may be allowed to call... the *resonance of the execution.*"

Paul Valéry, *Degas, Danse, Dessin*

painter, *the* painter, who will know how to draw out of our daily life its epic aspect, and make us see and understand, in color and design, how great and poetic we are in our neckties and polished boots."

Manet may have been the answer to Baudelaire's prayer, certainly his boots were polished and he invariably wore a necktie. And he loved the daily life of the boulevards, lunching often at the Café Tortoni on the corner of the rue Taitbout in the space then existing between the rue de Richelieu and the Chaussée d'Antin, in the afternoon a place to which a select society, almost exclusively Parisian, resorted, meeting friends, promenading. Talleyrand had dined there, Alfred de Musset, Théophile Gautier, Rossini were regular customers. Zola, who was certainly there, wrote: "Edouard Manet is of average height, rather small than big. Hair and beard are light brown; the eyes, narrow and deep, have youthful vivacity and flame; the mouth is characteristic, thin, mobile, a little mocking at the corners. The whole face, of a fine and intelligent irregularity, announces resiliency and audacity, contempt for stupidity and banality... We find in Edouard Manet a man of exquisite politeness and amiability, of distinguished looks and sympathetic appearance... The artist tells us that he adores the social world and that he finds a secret voluptuousness in the perfumed and luminous delicacy of the soirées..."

In those days the Louvre was crowded, not with tourists, but with hundreds of art students, easels spread and palettes loaded, all busy copying the great masters, in accord with academic rule. Walking through the Louvre galleries one day, Manet was struck by the audacity of a young man who was engraving directly on a copper plate his version of a Velazquez. "Well, my boy, you'll be lucky if you get away with it," he said.

The young man was Hilaire-Germain-Edgar de Gas, the eldest son of Auguste-Hyacinthe de Gas by his marriage with Mademoiselle Marie-Célestine Musson of Louisiana. Of French descent the Musson family had been settled at Santo Domingo before moving to New Orleans where they had profited by the growing trade with Mexico and the Mississippi valley (a great house, built of New England granite on the corner of Canal and Royal streets, was long known as "Musson's Fort"). Educated in Paris, Marie-Célestine was sixteen when she married Auguste-Hyacinthe de Gas and barely seventeen when Edgar was born. Though banking had long been the occupation of the de Gas family—shifting from Orléans to Naples during the Revolution—Auguste de Gas was less interested in money than in antique music. It was a family in which art was discussed seriously and a young man could learn something of the technique of etching from a family friend such as Prince Gregoire Soutzo. Born in Paris, July 19, 1834, Edgar had been tutored by his Uncle Henri Musson before receiving a classical education at the Lycée Louis-le-Grand. The death of his mother when he was seventeen—she was just thirty-four—left him with a permanent sense of bereavement. Shortly after entering Law School in 1853 he decided to become a painter. His father warned him that there was no money in it. "You will have to make painting your career, your existence," he said. "If the artist should be enthusiastic about art he should wisely regulate his conduct for fear of remaining a nonentity." In 1855 Edgar Degas (as he was to sign his paintings many years later) entered the Ecole des Beaux Arts under the tutelage of Louis Lamothe, one of Ingres' pupils. In fact, it was Ingres who was the young man's inspiration. During a chance meeting he had told Ingres of his ambition to be a painter. "Do lines, many lines, after nature and from memory," Ingres had said. "In this way you will become a good artist." Degas had done most of his lines from classic models in the Louvre, copying Velazquez, Rembrandt, Raphael, Giotto, Titian, Bellini and Poussin. He had tried, unsuccessfully, for the Prix de Rome, an advantage of which was several years of study in Rome. But the de Gas family connections had made it easy for him to travel in Italy where he had copied frescoes and drawings, and was greatly taken by the sixteenth century Florentine masters. His father's sister had married Baron Belleli of Florence and the collective portrait he did of the Belleli family was one of his first important works.

About the time he met Manet in the Louvre Degas was engaged on a series of large-scale historical paintings—*machines historiques*, as Manet undoubtedly called them—and it is interesting that, on completion, they were distinguished, notably a picture he called *Young Spartans Exercising*, by the fact that, instead of the muscular professional models normally employed for such paintings, Degas had recruited his youthful models from among the *gamins* of Montmartre, thus achieving a fascinating freshness of vision. It is difficult to assess the influence of Manet and Degas upon each other, they were so different in temperament. Manet liked to charm people; Degas was disdainful of notice, pitiless in his analysis of others. He considered Manet's yearning for official honors ridiculous. "The Academy! You'll never see me there!" he once said. On one point, however, they were in agreement; both were obeying Baudelaire's injunction that the great painter must "draw out of our daily life its epic aspect."

At this time Degas was a member of a convivial group which used to meet backstage at the old Opera House in the rue Le Peletier. "He finds the dancers charming," wrote a friend, "treats them as though they were his own children, makes excuses for anything they do, and laughs at everything they say. On the other hand they absolutely venerate him and the most insignificant little *rat* would give a good deal to please him." The self-portraits Degas was painting at this time may explain what the little *rats* were raving about: he was a very handsome young man. Years later Degas summed up his Opera experience in a couple of felicitous sentences: "There is something artificial about my heart. The dancers sewed it up in a pink satin bag, a slightly faded pink satin like their ballet slippers."

Another of Degas's worldly interests was horse-racing, though there is no proof that he ever made a bet. He was fascinated by movement, on the turf as on the boards. This was a quality, an illusion, which Delacroix alone among contemporary painters had captured in paint. "If the leaves of the trees did not move, how sad the trees would be," Degas once observed. At Longchamp racetrack and at the racing stables of his friend Paul Valpinçon in Normandy, Degas watched horses and jockeys in training, making successive sketches

Edgar Degas: *Study for Spartan Boys and Girls Exercising.* 1860. Pencil.

"Their friendship has been jarred by inevitable rivalry. 'Degas was painting Semiramis when I was painting Modern Paris,' says Manet. 'Manet is in despair because he cannot paint atrocious pictures like Duran, and be fêted and decorated; he is an artist, not by inclination, but by force. He is as a galley slave chained to the oar,' says Degas."

George Moore, *Confessions of a Young Man*

Edgar Degas: *Self-Portrait, about 1852. Pencil.*

Edgar Degas: Wounded Jockey, Study for the Steeplechase, 1866. Charcoal.

What, one wonders, was the fate of this steeplechase jockey? Was he killed in his fall or only wounded? It was not the human drama that interested Degas but the contrast between his inertness and the movement of the horse; for the painter it was only a subject of observation. Repudiating the pompous eloquence of the Salon painters, Degas concentrated on an objective analysis of everyday motifs. Manet, who never betrayed his feelings before the model, who painted his father or a stranger with the same expressive objectivity, set Degas the example of an art that simply recorded visual reality.

Edgar Degas: Steeplechase. The Fallen Jockey, 1866.

breaking down their continuous combined movement. Degas did not believe that movement could be suggested by a blurred edge, or in a fleeting impression. He aimed to express movement in the poise and balance of solid masses, such as horses and their riders, and he believed that this could be done only by repeated drawing in the studio: he was an indefatigable experimenter and very early adopted certain principles which became his working code. That he was successful in extracting some mysterious life essence from the banal reality of leaping horses is shown in his painting *Fallen Jockey*, in which the fallen jockey was modelled by his, later, ill-fated brother René. Visiting Degas one day the ubiquitous Vollard found him arranging a number of little wooden horses on his table. "When I come in from the racetrack," Degas explained, "these are my models. How could one make real horses turn in the light the way one wants them to?" Vollard does not seem to have realized that these model horses were among the earliest examples of another side of Degas's genius: his sculpture.

Degas, says one who knew him, was small and thin, with a high, broad and domed forehead crowned with silky chestnut hair, with quick, shrewd, questioning eyes, deepset under high arched eyebrows shaped like a circumflex accent, a slightly turned-up nose with wide nostrils and a delicate mouth half-hidden under a small moustache. He was an assiduous collector of other men's paintings who, when expecting a bourgeois visitor, would turn the paintings to the wall.

It is Henri Fantin-Latour who cries: "The Louvre! The Louvre! There is nothing but the Louvre!" This is not surprising, since his father is a drawing master in the classical tradition and the son, born at Grenoble, January 4, 1836, is enrolled at the Beaux Arts. Fantin also has a studio in the rue Visconti and works sitting on a little chair before his easel, a skull cap on his head. Degas said: "Fantin's work is always good. What a pity it is a little *rive gauche.*" Not satisfied with his first copy of an old master, Fantin copies it again and again. He is developing his own style, his own naturalism, catching the memorable moment, the poise of a head, light diffused through a window curtain. Alas, his very fine paintings are destined to become photographic; but he will leave better-than-photographic portraits of his more revolutionary friends. Meanwhile he is the catalyst who brings the painters together. "I am of your opinion," Manet writes to Fantin, "the Demoiselles Morisot are charming. It is a pity they are not men."

Berthe-Marie-Pauline Morisot was born, January 14, 1841, in Bourges, the third daughter of Edme-Tiburce Morisot, then Prefect of the Department of Cher. Prefect Morisot's father had been an architect and he himself had begun by studying architecture at the Beaux Arts, after which he had travelled in Italy, Greece and Sicily, studying art.

In 1852 Tiburce Morisot became a government functionary in Paris and the family moved to the capital, occupying a house with a big garden on the Trocadéro hill. Berthe was then eleven years old, Edma twelve-and-a-half, Yves fourteen. Knowing that their father wanted his children to learn to draw, Madame Morisot decided to give him a birthday surprise by engaging an art teacher for her daughters. This was a certain M. Chocarne whose instruction proved to be so sad that the sisters rebelled. The Morisots finally met a real artist, Joseph Guichard, a former pupil of Ingres, who approved of the sisters' revolt against the insipid teaching of M. Chocarne. Guichard began by explaining to the girls what painting was, without touching a brush. Berthe and Edma were enthusiastic.

A studio was built for the sisters in the grounds of their home at the Trocadéro, but Berthe surprised her teacher by expressing the wish to paint landscape. Guichard took the girls to see Corot who allowed them to watch him paint at Ville d'Avray, afterwards lending them some of his pictures to copy. Soon Corot was coming to dinner every Tuesday at the Morisots. In the summer of 1863 Corot sent the sisters to his pupil Oudinot, under whose guidance they went off early every morning to paint landscape between Pontoise and Auvers. Oudinot introduced them to Daubigny, the open air painter, who lived at Auvers, and to Daumier whose house was in a neighboring village. Thus, very early in her painting life Berthe Morisot was exposed to what were then radical influences in art. When the Morisot sisters wrote to Corot, asking him to join them, he wrote back: "Let us work firmly and with confidence: let us not think too much about Papa Corot; nature is still the best to consult."

But Berthe was not quite ready to stop thinking about Papa Corot. She was painting, exquisitely, in his manner. Because of this perhaps, she had no difficulty having landscapes exhibited in the Salons of 1865, 1866 and 1867. In this last Salon her landscape, called *View of Paris,* a luminously gray view from the heights of the Trocadéro was already the work of a superior craftsman.

Edouard Manet : Portrait of his Father, 1860. Red Chalk.

Two of Manet's paintings were accepted for the Salon of 1861.

The first was a portrait of his mother and father. Whereas a conventional artist might have sentimentalized the parental subject (especially as Judge Manet was obviously failing—he would die the following September), Manet treated it as a low-keyed study, predominantly black and white. The couple looks as if it had been posed awkwardly, that man and wife are not really together. Madame Manet carries a basket with some balls of wool, evidently for no other reason than to provide a note of color. Nothing is idealized: the Manets are contemporary people in a conventional background. But a friend of the family who saw the picture said: "It is lamentable for a lady like Madame Manet to have a son like that. Just look at his portrait of his parents: one would think that they were a couple of concierges."

In Manet's second painting, called *The Guitarrero,* he mixed realism with the picturesque. The model, an authentic Spaniard, is shown sitting on a bench stringing his guitar. At his feet there are several large onions and a jar. The treatment is vigorous and bold, the color being predominantly black and gray against an olive background. In the Salon *The Guitarrero* was hung badly, but it attracted so much attention that it was unhung and placed in a better position. In the official *Le Moniteur,* Théophile Gautier, poet and connoisseur of things Spanish, was enthusiastic: "Caramba! Here is a Guitarrero who has not stepped out of a comic opera, and who would cut a poor figure in a romantic lithograph. But Velazquez would have given him a friendly wink, and

Edouard Manet : The Spanish Singer or The Guitarrero, 1861. Copper Engraving.

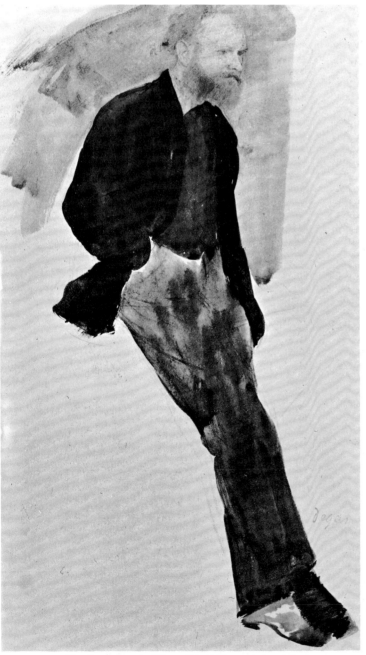

Edgar Degas: Portrait of Manet, 1864-1866. Pencil and Wash.

Goya would have asked him for a light for his papelito... There is a great deal of talent in this life-sized figure, broadly painted in true color with a bold brush..."

But in the other newspapers the critics were unanimously savage. "What poetry is there in the idiotic figure of this mule driver, in this blank wall, in the onion and the cigarette, whose combined odors have just perfumed the room!" So wrote Hector de Callias in *L'Artiste*. About the portrait of Manet's parents, Léon Lagrange wrote in the *Gazette des Beaux-Arts*: "What a scourge to society is the realist painter! To him nothing is sacred! Manet tramples underfoot even the most sacred ties. The artist's parents must more than once have cursed the day when a brush was put into the hands of this merciless portraitist." But Manet received the Salon's "honorable mention" for his Guitarrero and the general reaction had revealed that there were critics ready to defend the new trend: Astruc, Castagnary, Duranty.

Manet plunged into his work with verve and versatility, producing *Concert in the Tuileries,* a painting that was more "modern" than anything he had done up to this moment. The garden of the Tuileries, adjoining the Imperial Palace, was the afternoon rendezvous of the elegant society surrounding the Emperor's court. Here the ladies in their crinolines and the gentlemen in their long jackets and stovepipe hats sauntered about under the trees, exchanging compliments and gossip, as they listened, most probably, to the latest melody of Jacques Offenbach, played by the orchestra in the little music kiosk. Manet had visited the gardens in the company of Baudelaire and, as a vision of light and shadow in leisurely motion, the scene (to which his attention had been drawn by a sketch of Constantin Guys) fascinated him. After many preliminary studies, including likenesses of Baudelaire, his brother Eugène Manet, his friend Count Balleroy, his friendly critic, the poet Théophile Gautier, and Offenbach, he produced a shimmering canvas, dapplings of color enlivening the whole, but with every silhouette clearly delineated, an impression of life.

About this time Manet encountered the model he had dreamed of finding. She had a very pale skin, dark eyes and a good figure, if a trifle short, but she took a pose with natural ease and the understanding of what Manet was seeking. Her name was Victorine Meurent and Manet's first painting of her was as a street singer. Holding a guitar and eating cherries, she is wearing a long gray dress, gray being (a characteristic Manet note) the dominant color. But Victorine would appear in even more controversial pictures.

Manet was still fascinated by the color and liveliness of Spanish life (though he had not yet been to Spain) and when a troop of Spanish dancers came to Paris next season he found among them the models he uses in *Spanish Ballet.* But the subjects of Manet's paintings—and this was something his contemporaries did not yet understand—were seldom the identity of the sitters or the nature of the objects, but form and color. This is the sole explanation for a large painting which Manet did at this time, called *Old Musician,* which shows an old man sitting in the street, apparently preparing to play the violin, surrounded by children, an absinthe drinker and an oriental in a turban. This heterogeneous collection of objects has no conscious

But above all Degas has caught the spontaneity and intimacy of this family scene, striking in its naturalness. The composition is more closely knit, the poses more spontaneous. A dynamic progression runs from the fixity of the girl on the left, by way of the turning heads of the Baroness and her other daughter, to the father swinging around in his easychair on the right. Baroness Belleli was Degas's aunt; she showed him hospitality during his long stays in Italy, and her nephew painted this family scene as a token of thanks. Not content with an approximation, Degas made many preparatory studies for this picture, in which he was one of the first to achieve an effect of photographic immediacy.

Edgar Degas: Self-Portrait with a Green Waistcoat, about 1856.

Edgar Degas: Spartan Boys and Girls Exercising, 1860.

Edgar Degas: The Belleli Family, about 1859-1862.

Degas follows Manet in the Path of Modernity

Degas was attracted by Ingres, by the elegance and simplicity of his draftsmanship. He loved the concision of lines that render reality accurately but without detriment to the ideal beauty of the Renaissance painters. "Style is nature," Ingres liked to say, and Degas endorsed that point of view.

In 1855 Degas entered the Ecole des Beaux Arts, in Lamothe's class, but the instruction he received from that master did not answer his expectations. He preferred to consult life rather than copy feeble imitations of the ancients. His background and schooling impelled him towards traditional art; his personality, independent spirit and love of truth towards a new form of expression. In this early self-portrait he remains strongly under the influence of Ingres. Brushwork and color are subordinated to accuracy of line; keen and searching, his eye rests on things with insistent scrutiny.

History painting was then the most highly esteemed art form and Degas tried his hand at it. His picture of *Spartan Boys and Girls Exercising* brings out the contradiction between historical fiction and his taste for movement. The example of Manet, whom he was soon to meet, detached him from the academic routine and the Beaux-Arts tradition, and left him free to paint the life around him. The comparison between the *Spartans Exercising* and the *Belleli Family* is revealing. The first theme Degas took from his imagination, the second from reality. He was much more of an innovator when it came to observing than when he had to invent. In the historical subject the composition is traditional; the groups of boys and girls form the solidly planted sides of a truncated pyramid whose symmetry is all too obvious and the dynamism of the naked bodies is incompatible with this classical rigidity. In the portrait of the *Belleli Family* space is much better articulated: a broken line runs laterally across the picture and avoids the pitfalls of a central vanishing point: an inverted, asymmetrical pyramid is marked by the mother's head, the apron of the girl in the center and the upper right corner of the picture.

> "*To observe* amounts for the most part to imagining what one expects to see."
>
> Paul Valéry, *Degas, Danse, Dessin*

Edgar Degas: Portrait of Thérèse De Gas, Duchess Morbilli, 1863.

C. E. A. Carolus-Duran: Lady with a Glove (The Artist's Wife), 1869.

Artists have always grappled with the problem of rendering the visible world, and though reality does not change much from one period to another they have all given us a highly personal view of it. Yet there is a much sharper difference between artists of two different periods with a similar temperament than between painters of the same century with opposing temperaments, for the vision of space is more determinant than variations of sentiment. Degas and Manet looked with the same impartiality on appearances and movement. The portrait was the first subject which enabled them to break with idealistic make-believe, to paint modern life instead of historical subjects.

Manet and Degas, however, were not at all alike. Jacques-Emile Blanche has judiciously pointed out the contrast between them. "Degas's eye was photographic, recording exactly what he saw; then his brain corrected the proof. Degas repainted in the way that certain prose writers rewrite an initial text, correct the proofs and—by thought and will-power—confer a noble, difficult style on phrases that at first were quite banal. Manet, on the contrary, whether he covered a scrap of paper with a few touches of Indian ink or a few strokes of pen or pastel, whether he suggested by scumbling a light effect on fruit, a rose, a face, or whether he toiled for months —Manet produced in the sketch or finished work a peculiar, personal creation."

The *Lady with a Glove* was acclaimed at the Salon of 1869 and opened a brilliant official career for Carolus-Duran. He at once became a determined opponent of the Impressionists. Much later, in 1892, Pissarro rejoiced at the attacks made on Carolus-Duran in *Le Figaro* by Octave Mirbeau: "M. Carolus-Duran would make an excellent upholsterer. Herein lies perhaps the secret of his success. He does not paint women, he upholsters; he does not clothe women, he drapes them, as one would drape a door or a bed... M. Carolus-Duran does not know what a human face is. Nor does he know what painting is, in spite of all the virtuosity he displays."

Edouard Manet:

Victorine Meurent in the Costume of an Espada, 1862.

The Street Singer, 1862.

30

"Degas found in the race horse an unusual theme that satisfied the conditions which his nature and his period imposed on his choice of themes. Where could he find anything pure in modern reality? Realism and style, elegance and rigor happened to come together in the luxuriously pure being of the racing animal."

Paul Valéry, *Degas, Danse, Dessin*

Manet and Degas agreed in according less importance to landscape than to the human figure and giving priority to line over color. Both moreover were much less concerned with the study of nature than Monet and his friends. Horse racing was the first subject that took them out of doors, but given the speed of the movement it is a motif that the eye is incapable of recording with anything like photographic instantaneity; memory, knowledge and instinct had to make up for the inadequacy of observation.

Staying with his friends the Valpinçons, a family of collectors who had introduced him to Ingres, Degas began to take an interest in horses. In 1860, at Menil-Hubert near the racing stables called Haras du Pin in Normandy, he sketched their movements with increasing precision. Géricault had magisterially introduced the theme of horse racing into French painting in 1821. From 1862 Degas painted many racing pictures. In the dynamism and color of the races he found a modern subject. Two years later Manet was attracted to the Longchamp racecourse, but he was more interested in the general atmosphere and his expression of movement was less specific. In his very first racing pictures Degas showed his amazing mastery of line. The jockeys' colorful jackets and the well-dressed society women gave him the touches that brightened up his picture, just as flowers brightened up Monet's landscapes.

Edouard Manet: Races at Longchamp, 1864.

Edouard Manet: The Races. Lithograph.

Edgar Degas: Gentlemen's Race (Before the Start), 1862.

Edouard Manet: The Old Musician, 1862.

In Quest of an Immediate Expression of the Senses

"The two other pictures, the *Spanish Ballet* and *Concert in the Tuileries*, were the ones that set the spark to the powder. An exasperated art lover went so far as to threaten to take violent action if *Concert in the Tuileries* were allowed to remain any longer in the exhibition hall. I quite understand his anger: just imagine, under the trees in the Tuileries, a whole crowd, maybe a hundred people, moving about in the sun; each person is a simple, barely defined patch of color in which details become lines or dark points. If I had been there, I would have requested the art lover to stand at a respectful distance; he would then have seen that these color patches were alive, that the crowd talked, and that this canvas was one of the artist's characteristic works, the one in which the artist has most closely complied with his eyes and temperament. "

Emile Zola, *Revue du XIXe siècle*, January 1, 1867.

Zola discovered Manet through Cézanne and at once became a valiant and lucid defender of his work. On January 1, 1867, he published a long article on Manet in the *Revue du XIXe siècle*: "Here is how I account for the birth of any genuine artist, that of Edouard Manet for example. Feeling that he was getting nowhere by copying the old masters, by painting nature as seen through different eyes than his own, he quite naïvely realized one fine day that he might as well try to see nature just as it is, without looking at it through the works and opinions of others. As soon as this thought occurred to him, he took an object, no matter what, a person or thing, placed it at the back of his studio and set to work reproducing it on canvas, according to his faculties of vision and understanding. He strove to forget everything he had learned in the museums; he tried to put out of his mind the advice he had received, the paintings he had seen. All that was now at work was one man's intelligence, assisted by organs gifted in a certain manner, facing nature and rendering it in his own way. "

The public rejected Manet because of his novel themes and the original vision that justified the originality of his technique. He concentrated on directness and pattern-like simplifications, eliminated half-tones in the basic contrasts between black and white, repudiated idealism and make-believe.

Always sensitive to the currents and fashions of modern life, Manet often turned to Spanish subjects, which had become popular in Paris since Napoleon III had married a Spanish beauty. Critics accused him of plagiarizing the masters of the Spanish school, for they were at a loss how to refute or explain the novelty of his vision. Baudelaire, who encouraged Manet in his modernism, answered these attacks in a letter of 1864 to Thoré-Bürger: "The word *pastiche* is inaccurate. M. Manet has never seen Goya; M. Manet has never seen El Greco; M. Manet has never seen the Pourtalès collection. That may seem unbelievable to you, but it is true. I too have been amazed at these mysterious coincidences... Manet has heard so much about his pastiches of Goya that now he is trying to see some Goyas. "

"No, I can do nothing without nature. I don't know how to invent. As long as I went on painting as I was taught to paint, I produced nothing of any value. If I am worth anything today, I owe it to exact interpretation, to accurate analysis. "

Manet

significance, except that Manet wanted to paint them. In a sense the painting is a deliberate attack on the concept of art as a medium for telling a story or delivering a message, though Manet did not think of it in this light; he was always innocent in his role of provocateur.

With Auguste Manet's death in 1862 his son inherited a sufficient income to make him economically secure and thus he was in a different category from the young painters who admired his unorthodoxy.

In the beginning of 1863 the Académie des Beaux-Arts issued a decree, limiting to three the number of paintings an individual painter might submit to the jury of the Salon for that year. This was a blow to Manet who had completed thirty paintings since the last Salon. Many young artists were similarly disappointed and a deputation, headed by Manet and Gustave Doré, the illustrator, waited on the Minister of State, Count Walewski. They were politely received, but no change was made.

Following the precedent set by Courbet during the World's Fair of 1855, Manet decided to hold his own one-man show, an unexpected step for so young a painter and one which hinted that a bold non-conformist spirit was abroad. Shortly before the official Salon was scheduled to open he exhibited fourteen paintings at the Martinet Gallery in the Boulevard des Italiens. The critics were crushing. Paul Mantz, in the *Gazette des Beaux-Arts*, wrote of "this Parisian Spaniard's... medley of colors." Of the *Concert in the Tuileries* another critic complained that his "eyes were flayed by its colors as his ears were flayed by the music at public fairs." The power of critical rhetoric at this time may be judged from the fact that Manet, despite later successes, was never able to sell *Concert in the Tuileries*, until a friend bought it just before his death.

"With Manet," wrote his friend Antonin Proust, "the eye played so great a part that Paris has never had a stroller in her streets on whom so little was lost... He noted down in his sketchbook the merest trifle, a profile, a hat, in a word a fleeting impression, and when the next day a friend, leafing through his sketchbook, would say, 'You ought to finish this,' he would burst out laughing. 'Do you take me for a history painter?' he would say. In his mouth 'history painter' was the most scathing insult that could be addressed to an artist. 'And then,' he would add, 'to reconstitute historical figures, how ridiculous! Can one paint a man with only his hunting license to go on? The only true way is to paint straight off what you see. If you've caught it, all right. If not, then try again. All the rest is humbug.'"

Edouard Manet:

◄ The Old Musician, about 1861. Watercolor.

◄ The Spanish Ballet, 1862.

Concert in the Tuileries, 1860. Wash Drawing.

Concert in the Tuileries, 1862.

Paul Cézanne: Self-Portrait, 1865-1866.

Though the great Revolution of 1793 changed the whole face of France, both politically and socially, it failed to emancipate the twin arts of painting and literature. The Impressionist Revolution was thus a delayed part of the Revolution of 1793.

WYNFORD DEWHURST

Paul Cézanne: Apotheosis of Delacroix, about 1894.

The figures in this composition (apart from Delacroix himself, carried off by angels) are supposed to represent, from right to left, Pissarro, Monet and Cézanne (with a knapsack). One of the two other figures is Victor Chocquet. There is also a watercolor version of the same subject. Cézanne reworked this picture towards the end of his life; he can be seen retouching it in a photograph, and on May 12, 1904, he wrote to Emile Bernard: "I don't know whether my precarious health will ever permit me to realize my dream of doing his [Delacroix's] apotheosis."

URING the Second Empire the importance attached to official art, and its vast infrastructure of art-crafts and art-teaching, gave encouragement to thousands of young would-be artists. Emile Zola, the novelist, has left us descriptions of large groups of art students marching vociferously through Paris. "It was the usual thing," he says, "the band was gradually increased by the addition of comrades on the way, and then came the wild march of a horde on the war-path. With the bold assurance of their twenty summers, these young fellows took possession of the sidewalk. The moment they were together trumpets seemed to sound in advance of them; they seized upon Paris and quietly dropped her in their pockets."

And so, gathering numbers on the way, they would come swinging down the Boulevard des Invalides and across the Seine to the Champs Elysées, singing, shouting, pushing people off the sidewalks. Zola's artist-hero, Claude Lantier, is in step with the crowd. "Claude became excited. Faith in himself revived amidst the glow of mutual hope. His worries of the morning left only a vague numbness behind... Trembling with excitement he kept saying, 'Ah, Paris! It's ours! We have only to take it!' They all grew excited, their eyes opening wide with desire. Was not Glory herself looking down from the summit of the Avenue on the whole capital? Paris was there and they longed to make her theirs."

The young artists—literally thousands of them—lived in attic studios or the cellars of the old quarters of the city, most of them in a state of semi-poverty. The models who posed for Claude, waitresses and seamstresses, chalked their names and addresses on the walls of his studio and Claude would write after their names, "big brunette" or "too thin," as the case was. Standing back from one of his paintings he would say, "Parbleu, it's very black. And I can't get Delacroix out of my eye. And then the hand, that's in Courbet's manner. Everyone of us dabs his brush into the romantic sauce now and again." Sometimes, in a fit of frustration, he would dash his hand through the canvas. Occasionally Papa Malgras, the poor student's art dealer, would appear, glance indifferently at the new work on the easel and say, "Well, here's a new machine!" And then, in his dirty old redingote cape he would go poking his dripping red nose into the dusty corners of the studio, pull out an old canvas, and cry, "Twenty francs!" "Are you mad? Twenty francs?" Claude would say and then, hurriedly, he would accept, embarrassed to have to defend his work.

Rejected by the jury of the Salon, Claude would rage: "They are all daubers of penny prints! Not one among them dares to slap the bourgeoisie. Tiens! Old Father Ingres, you know, he turns my stomach with his slimy paint. Eh bien, just the same, a sacred man. And I find him very courageous, and take off my hat to him, for he doesn't give a damn for anybody, and he used to draw like the Thunder of God, reducing to the level of idiots those who now believe they understand him! After him there are only two worth talking about, Delacroix and Courbet. The rest are bastards!"

Zola's novel, *L'Œuvre*, is a firsthand account of the art world of the Second Empire. It falls down in the end because of the author's attempt to make the facts (and it is closely based on facts) fit the thesis—his contribution to the scientific materialism of his time—that "the nature of physiological man is determined by his surroundings." Zola's realism has other advantages for us. The youthful years of the chief character in L'Œuvre are so intimately and exactly those of his boyhood friend Cézanne that, in his notes for the novel, now in the archives of the Bibliothèque Nationale in Paris, Zola refers to his hero, not by the name Claude which he later invented for him, but as Paul, i.e. Paul Cézanne. Most biographers have leaned heavily on these memoirs for their portrait of the young Cézanne.

Paul Cézanne's father was of Italian origin, the family probably coming from the town of Cesana by way of Briançon. He was a hat manufacturer in Aix-en-Provence where local wool production had made felting a flourishing trade. He had contracted a liaison with one of his employees, Anne Aubert, the outcome of which was Paul, born January 19, 1839, and a daughter, Marie, born two years later. The couple were married five years after Paul's birth and produced another daughter, Rose, some time later. Meanwhile the hattery, benefiting from new techniques in steam pressing, had proved profitable enough for Louis-Auguste Cézanne to realize his dream of buying the only bank in Aix-en-Provence, which he ran, in conjunction with a minor partner, under the name of the Cézanne-Cabassol Bank.

At high school Paul had become the close friend of Emile Zola. Then Zola's mother, a widow, decided to go to Paris and her son accompanied her. After taking his baccalaureat with a "well done," Cézanne entered Law School at Aix, at his father's urging, but found law dull and dispiriting. A long correspondence ensued between the two friends. Cézanne's letters were full of jokes, rhymes, poems, Latin verse and all manner of literary conceits. On a short visit to Aix Zola sought Cézanne's collaboration in a play about Henry VIII of England, but Cézanne did not take his own literary efforts seriously. For diversion Cézanne joined the drawing classes of Professor Gibert at the local Ecole des Beaux-Arts where the students made careful studies of plaster casts of classical statuary. To his own surprise, one of Cézanne's drawings won a prize. In his next letter to Zola he confessed that he wanted to be a painter, but then followed a whole series of doubts and difficulties. On hearing of his ambition, his father said: "Child, think of the future. One dies a genius, but one eats with money."

Cézanne continued drawing, but wrote to Zola, saying that he didn't think that he could ever be an artist and that finally he would be a lawyer. Zola replied: "Be really a painter, or be really a lawyer, but don't be a being without a name, don't wear a lawyer's gown soiled with paint." Cézanne wrote back describing how he had been painting out of doors and Zola replied that if he had actually sat on frozen ground in order to paint, then painting was his vocation. At home, Cézanne became so moody and silent that his father decided to let him go to Paris, certain that he would return completely cured of his desire to be a painter. In 1861 Cézanne arrived in Paris and was joyfully received by Zola. But neither had money. Zola worked as a municipal clerk and supported his ailing mother. This was the year

A Childhood Friendship: Cézanne and Zola

Two letters from Cézanne to Zola with sketches, January 17, 1859, and June 30, 1866.

Cézanne and Zola Making Their Way in Paris

Photograph of Emile Zola at the Age of Twenty, in 1860.

"You seem to be discouraged in your last letter; you speak of nothing less than tossing your brushes up at the ceiling. You bewail the solitude that surrounds you; you are bored. Isn't this what is wrong with us all, this terrible boredom, isn't this the plague of our century? And isn't discouragement one of the consequences of this spleen that takes us by the throat? As you say, if I were with you I would try to console and encourage you."

Letter from Zola to Cézanne, Paris, June 25, 1860

Paul Cézanne: A Reading at Zola's House, 1869-1870.

that, down to his last five francs, he spent the money on having some elegant visiting cards printed, so that he would be admitted to houses where, at the right hour, there was usually something to eat. Cézanne worked on the docks, but this hardly paid for the couple of hours he spent working from the model at the Académie Suisse, not to mention food and rent. When he quit the docks in black despair, Zola tried to help out by having Cézanne paint his portrait; in all, four portraits of Zola were painted, all but one found inadequate and probably destroyed. Finally, the winter coming on hard, Cézanne went back to Aix and took a job in his father's bank.

Given the staid and costly conditions under which students prepared themselves for careers as official artists the Atelier Suisse was inevitable. It was one of several so-called "free studios" which required no entrance examination and had no distinctions to confer upon its users; but for a modest fee provided a model from which any young artist could work: 8.00 a.m. to 1.00 p.m. and 7.00 p.m. to 10.00 p.m. It was a large grimy room in a rackrent old house on the Quai des Orfèvres in the Ile de la Cité. The owner was a venerable old man called Father Crébassolles who wore a monk's habit and was reputedly a former professional model of Swiss origin. The room was furnished with a low-level divan or model throne and a number of four-legged padded stools of varying heights. The students sat or squatted on the stools with drawing boards resting on their knees. At the back of the room there was a high ledge on which a student could recline at full length and often did so, in order to sleep. The students talked incessantly, argued and sometimes threw paper pellets at each other. Father Crébassolles would continue placidly reading a book entitled *La Femme de Feu*, which he never seemed to finish. "Read to us, patron," the students would cry.

It is not certain that Cézanne ever tried to enter a Beaux Arts studio; he already had too much contempt for the establishment. At the Académie Suisse he found the company he liked and the kind of models that suited him; beats, rummies, sometimes a worker or a Negro sailor. He took them as they were, as form revealed by the old studio's dim lighting, and he drew with bold strokes of charcoal. His gutty realism, masculine and at the same time perceptive and tender, was something the age abhorred.

Among the other students at the Académie Suisse was a road laborer named Armand Guillaumin. Born in Paris in 1841, but receiving his schooling in the provincial town of Moulins, Guillaumin had been sent back to Paris at the age of fifteen to be apprenticed to his uncle, a linen draper. He had discovered the Louvre and had spent so much time there that he had neglected his work and was fired by his uncle. He began drawing and painting and to keep himself he got a job with the new Orléans Railroad Company; but he had no mind for time-tables either and was again fired. Finally he had found work with the Paris Highway Department which gave him the time to paint. His subjects were the Paris suburbs, modest, subdued and somewhat drab. He soon made the acquaintance of Cézanne; both were serious artists.

The free atmosphere of the Académie Suisse brought many visitors from the great world of art. Among them was Antoine Guillemet, a painting friend of Manet (he would model the central figure in Manet's *The Balcony*) who liked Cézanne's work well enough to intercede on his behalf with his father, as a result of which M. Cézanne paid a visit to Paris to arrange his son's affairs, providing him with a small stipend, but insisting that he enter the Beaux Arts. At the Académie Suisse Cézanne also met Francisco Oller, a Spanish painter, living and landscaping at Saint Germain. Oller took Cézanne out to paint in the countryside around Paris and it was through Oller that Cézanne met Pissarro. They had a good deal to say to each other.

The estuary of the river Seine is one of the most beautiful corners of France. Here mild weather, bearer of soft clouds and gentle rains, pushes the green fields to the very edge of the chalky cliffs which, under the chiselling wind, become columns and arches whose plinth is the foaming blue-green sea; a friendly landscape, seldom without its pattern of fishing smacks and, at that time, tall sailing vessels.

Artists like Courbet, Millet, Couture, Corot, Diaz, Daubigny and Troyon came from Paris to paint land and sea around Honfleur, on the south side of the river's mouth. They stayed at an inn on the hill above Honfleur, run by a certain Mother Toutain, over whose Sole Normande they told tall tales of sales and, when the Calvados came out, kicked the Academy around. There were a couple of resident artists, however, who were much more than fair-weather painters. Both were rough, taciturn men whose normal calling would have been the sea, had they not been so firmly anchored in its image.

Johan Barthold Jongkind was the eighth son of a Protestant pastor, born June 3, 1819, in the province of Overijssel, Holland. He had studied briefly at the Hague Academy of Art, where the landscapist Schelfhout had taught him to paint in watercolors from nature. He came to Paris, won a medal for a picture hung in the Salon of 1848 and had a couple of pictures exhibited at the World's Fair of 1855, after which he had drifted out to Le Havre where he could paint marine subjects and at the same time support himself by working around the docks. Melancholy, shy, speaking French with a strong Dutch accent, without social grace, a heavy drinker, a tall husky man with a sailor's awkwardness, he was the despair of his friends, for he was without ambition. He painted with strong vivid brushstrokes and with an engaging freshness of color. "I like this fellow," Jules Castagnary, the critic, wrote Courbet, "he is an artist to his fingertips. With him everything lies in the impression."

Eugène Boudin was the son of the pilot of the steam packet *Français*, plying the English channel ports from Le Havre. When he grew a little, he had been the cabin boy. Then his father had retired from the sea and had opened a small stationery shop on the Grand Quai at Le Havre and Eugène became shop boy. Eugène, who had made his first sketches using ship's tar for a crayon, now had pencils and paper at his disposal. One day Constant Troyon, the landscape painter, noticed one of Eugène's pictures in the shop and, through Troyon, the

The Académie Suisse

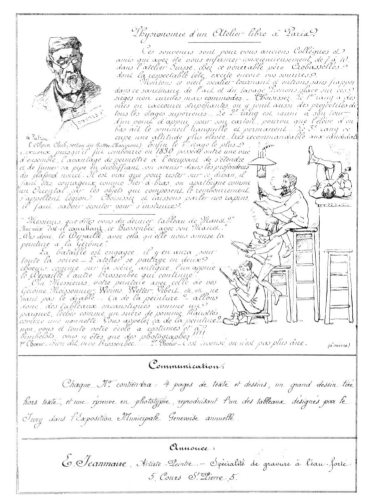

Physiognomy of a Free Studio in Paris, 1879.
Drawing by Henri Hébert.

The Académie Suisse was an independent studio where, for a very small fee, artists could work from the living model, coming and going as they pleased. The school was open from 8 a.m. till late at night. It was the haunt of all the young art students who were preparing the entrance examination for the Ecole des Beaux Arts and many other artists who were too poor to have a studio and models of their own. There Pissarro and Monet met for the first time, and there in 1861 Cézanne met Pissarro and Guillaumin.

Le Havre: Sea, Sky and Light

Monet's vocation was suddenly revealed to him when Boudin initiated him into open air painting on the Channel coast in 1858. "I confess that at first the idea of doing the kind of painting practiced by Boudin was not much to my liking. But at his urging I agreed to go out painting with him in the open air... Boudin set up his easel and went to work. I watched him with some misgivings, I watched him more attentively and then, all of a sudden, it was as if a veil had been torn from my eyes. I understood, I realized what painting could be. Thanks to the example of this artist enamored of his art and independence, my destiny as a painter opened up before me."

Photograph of Claude Monet at the Age of Eighteen, in 1858.

estuarial painters got to know young Boudin. Appreciating his natural talent they persuaded the Municipal Council of Le Havre to send him to Paris for study. Boudin spent three years in Paris and then returned to Le Havre. He had discovered that he had no desire to be an academic painter. So he went back to painting "marines" which, in lieu of buyers, were exhibited in the framing shop.

Side by side with Boudin's paintings there soon began to appear a number of clever caricatures of local personalities, signed by a schoolboy named Monet. The Monet family, originally from Lyons, had opened a grocery store in Paris where Claude Monet had been born, November 14, 1840. Five years later they had moved to Le Havre, a big thriving port where ships from all over the world docked and provisioned. Monet was, as he himself later oberved, "undisciplined from birth—they could never make me bend to a rule." At school he drew caricatures of his teachers, classmates, neighbors and friends. Soon his caricatures were so much in demand that he was able to charge twenty francs per likeness.

Young Monet was pleased to see his caricatures on exhibition in a shop window, but he did not much care for Boudin's landscapes. Inevitably they met, painter and youthful caricaturist. "Why don't you paint?" Boudin asked. On his next painting sortie he took the boy with him. Watching Boudin work, Monet suddenly understood what painting was about. Boudin said: "Everything painted directly on the spot has always a strength, a power, a vividness of touch that one does not find in the studio." The words were a revelation.

Yet Boudin was cautious enough to warn the young man that "one does not invent an art by oneself, in an out-of-the-way place, without criticism, without the means of comparison." Obviously the place to go was Paris. Claude's father wrote to the Municipal Council, suggesting that they do for his son what they had done for Boudin. But the Councillors, sensitive to Claude's gift for caricature, declined. Taking all the money he had earned from caricaturing, which his Aunt Lecadre had saved for him, Claude set out for Paris in 1859. A photograph, taken about this time, shows him in his city-going outfit: he wears dove-gray pants, a striped waistcoat, long-tailed cravat and a voluminous cape, every inch a dandy. But the eighteen-year-old face is sympathetic: fine deep-set eyes in dark shining gaze, a straight nose, a broad forehead from which the dark hair falls back in a short mane, sensual and—one guesses—mobile lips, ornamented with the downiest of moustaches and a tiny lip beard, or imperial.

Claude Monet: Caricature of Rufus Croutinelli, 1856-1858. Drawing.

Claude Monet: Caricature of Monet's Teacher, Jacques-François Ochard, 1856-1858. Drawing.

In Paris he went to see Troyon who told him: "Draw, draw incessantly." At the free and easy Académie Suisse he met Camille Pissarro who spoke of Corot and passed on Corot's advice: "Study values." Monet admired Corot too, but preferred Daubigny who painted outdoor scenes out-of-doors. The atmosphere of artistic Paris, with its thousands of painters with their conflicting loyalties and wordy ideas, may have been confusing to the provincial youth from Le Havre. Or perhaps he had just run out of money, for his father had refused to send him a sou unless he succeeded in enrolling at the Beaux Arts. At any rate when his draft number came up, his father, instead of arranging for a substitute (for a round sum a gentleman could always get some poor peasant to serve in his place—it was one of the advantages of the Empire), let young Monet be inducted into the army and sent off to Algeria. The paintings of Delacroix had over-romanticized the midnight *razzia* and the veiled odalisque; Monet contracted the statutory diseases and, with the help of his parents, was invalided out. "Two really charming years," he afterwards said. Their principal charm was that they provided Monet with a small pension which enabled him to pursue art.

Camille Pissarro was a landscape painter, "tranquilly working in Corot's style," as he himself said. He dropped in at the Atelier Suisse, to paint from the model; but also for its free and easy atmosphere and its lively conversation. He showed some of his friends there a small sketch which Corot had given him, a study full of painstaking detail. This is what Corot had said to him: "Pissarro, since you are an artist you don't need advice; above all you must study values. We don't see in the same way; you see green and I see gray and blond. But this is no reason for you not to work at values, for this is the basis of everything, and in whatever way one may feel and express oneself, one cannot do good painting without it."

Pissarro had been born, July 10, 1830, on the little island of St. Thomas (near Puerto Rico) in the Danish Antilles. His Sephardic grandfather had married a refugee of the French Revolution, first settling in Bordeaux, then emigrating to St. Thomas about 1835. Their son, Abraham Gabriel, born in Bordeaux, had married the widow of his mother's younger brother, Rachel Manzano-Pomié, born in the neighboring island of Santo Domingo. Abraham and Rachel had four sons, the youngest of whom was Jacob. When he grew up and began painting Jacob changed his given name to Camille. But for some time he still used the Spanish form of his family name when signing paintings: PIZARRO.

At the age of eleven Pissarro had been sent to boarding school at Passy, then a hamlet just outside Paris; his father warned the Principal, Monsieur Savary, of the boy's tendency to waste his time drawing. It happened that M. Savary prided himself on being something of an artist and had a relative who exhibited at the Salons. He gave Camille drawing lessons with the result that when his father recalled his son some six years later young Pissarro was already a competent draftsman. "Don't forget to draw the coconut palms," was Savary's parting advice.

Johan Barthold Jongkind: *Le Port Vauban, Le Havre, 1865. Drawing.*

Le Havre, the Outer Harbor. Photograph.

Eugène Boudin: *Boats on the Beach. Drawing.*

On his return to St. Thomas Camille worked in his father's store. It was a well-paid job, but "I couldn't stick it," he said later. He spent his spare time sketching the port and the island and soon fell in with Fritz Melbye, a Danish painter who was doing the same thing. In 1852 Melbye and Pissarro went off to Caracas where they worked at their painting until 1854, but in conditions that were very hard for Pissarro. By this time his father had become reconciled to his son's ambition to become a painter and sent him off to Paris, where he had relatives, with a small allowance to cover his needs.

Pissarro arrived just in time to see the great art show at the Universal Exposition. He was enchanted with the subtlety of Corot's landscapes and went to see the painter, then sixty years of age, in his studio on the rue Paradis Poissonnière. He also visited Fritz Melbye's brother, Anton, one of the best Danish painters at this time, exhibiting regularly at the Salons. Anton Melbye thought enough of Pissarro's talent to let him finish off the skies in some of his own canvases and taught him some other tricks of the trade. Pissarro was therefore able to endorse the paintings he now began sending to the biannual Salons, "pupil of Corot" and "pupil of A. Melbye." One of his paintings was accepted for the Salon of 1859, but was hung too high up to be seen. In 1861 his works were refused by the jury. Next year he contracted a liaison with Julie Vellay, a sturdy peasant girl.

Pissarro spent his days quietly painting Seine-et-Oise landscape. Older than most of the young men around him—ten years older than Monet—he was much beloved by them. Several were to leave sketches of Pissarro in his characteristic garb of slouch hat, painter's haversack, sensible top boots and stout walking stick. His hawklike nose is set off by a pair of mild and gentle eyes and a patriarchal beard which seems to have been always white—if we are to believe the youthful artists.

Students preparing for the Ecole des Beaux Arts were obliged to enter certain approved studios, of which Gleyre's in the rue Fleurus on the Left Bank was by far the most popular. After a long and painful beginning as a painter, Marc-Gabriel-Charles Gleyre had triumphed in the 1843 Salon with his picture, *Evening or Lost Illusions*, after which he had decided it was easier to teach painting. He was a stocky Swiss with a lisp.

His large studio was popular because it was well-equipped, spacious and Gleyre was not charging more than it cost him to cover the rent and the model's fees. He was unimaginative, unpretentious, hard-working, very regular in his habits. He had his roll and coffee at the same café every morning and ate nothing else until evening. Most of Gleyre's students were destined for other things than art and were more likely to end up, as the brothers Goncourt observed, "in the chair of the Institut, in the mouth of a crocodile of the Nile, or in the management of a photographic saloon or a chocolate shop."

According to a friend of James McNeill Whistler, who was there for a while, thirty or forty students worked from eight in the morning until noon and then for a couple of hours in the afternoon, every day except Sunday, on a living nude model, a man one week, a woman

The Young Pissarro in the Antilles

"Living at St. Thomas in 1852 as a well-paid clerk, I couldn't stick it: without thinking, I dropped everything and made for Caracas, just to snap the cable holding me to middle-class life. What I suffered is unspeakable, what I'm suffering now is terrible, much more so than when I was young, full of spirit and enthusiasm, for I feel sure there is no future before me. Yet, if I could make a fresh start, I think I should not hesitate to follow the same course."

Pissarro, about 1880

Camille Pissarro: Man with Pipe,
St. Thomas, 1852. Pencil.

Camille Pissarro: The Big Tree,
Caracas, 1854. Pencil.

the next. A bay window on the north side shed a grayish light on the model and the barn-like room was heated by an iron stove in winter. Gleyre had the male model wear a pair of short drawers when there were women students present.

Gleyre did not bother his students very much, but sometimes there was a canvas he could not pass by.

"Not bad at all, not bad at all, that thing there. But you paint too much in the character of the model. You have before you a short thickset man; you paint him short and thickset. He has enormous feet, you render them as they are. All this is very ugly."

Not bad, but not very gratifying to Claude Monet, whose painting it was. He had come to Paris from Le Havre in order to work on the figure. But Gleyre's criticism, with its reiteration of the old classical formulas, convinced him of the futility of studio work.

There were some student paintings which Gleyre felt to be beyond the reach of his criticism, and worthy only of his irony.

"Young man, you are very skillful, very gifted, but no doubt it is to amuse yourself that you paint," Gleyre said one day, pausing before a dazzling canvas.

"Why, of course, and if it did not amuse me, I can tell you that I would not do it," replied Pierre-Auguste Renoir.

A glance at the student's smock might have told Gleyre that the young man was a porcelain worker. Covered with the white dust of unglazed clay and the splashes and wipings of the bright colors which he had been employed to paint on plates, the smock was Renoir's habit for many a year; he could afford no other. He had been born in Limoges, the ceramic capital of France, February 25, 1841, one of five children of a tailor. The family had moved to Paris, taking lodgings in the Carrousel, a grievous slum in those days, but very romantic with its cracked columns and crumbling coats-of-arms. On Sundays the Renoirs went to mass at Saint-Germain-l'Auxerrois and afterwards walked along the quais as far as Notre Dame. Then the family moved to the rue Gravilliers in the Marais and it was there that Pierre-Auguste became a little Parisian. Northward ran the old rue du Temple on the sidewalks of which there was a continuous fair; on one side was the old Jewish quarter of Paris and on the other Les Halles markets, dominated by the great mass of the Eglise Saint-Eustache. Charles Gounod was choirmaster and it was he who discovered that young Renoir had a very fine voice, brought him into the choir and wanted him to become a musician. His talent lay in another direction: after his first communion he began drawing likenesses of his parents. When the time came for him to support himself he got a job as an apprentice at M. Levy's porcelain works in the rue Vieille du Temple. After a turn at the potter's wheel young Renoir was put to work in the paint shop where he showed great facility in executing the reiterated decorative motifs, shepherdesses, Imperial eagles and the like. When machine-pressed plate suddenly cut into the porcelain trade and M. Levy prepared to sell out, young Renoir proposed that the business be turned into a cooperative and that they meet competition by offering a wide variety of original designs, motifs taken from the great masters, etc., which he showed

The Studio of Bazille

In 1867 Renoir made a portrait of Bazille working at his easel and Sisley, who also visited the studio, painted the still life of dead birds on which Bazille was working. Bazille later moved into a studio in the rue de la Condamine, not far from the Café Guerbois. A painting he made of this airy well-lighted room shows, from left to right, Sisley (or perhaps it is Renoir), Zola on the stairs, Monet, Manet, Bazille himself and Edmond Maître at the piano.

Frédéric Bazille: Self-Portrait. Drawing.

Auguste Renoir: Portrait of Bazille, 1867.

he could copy at incredible speed. The effort was defeated, "by the public's love for fashionable monotony," he said later. His next enterprise had been decorating bars and bistros, at which he also showed great facility, and some pleasure, in the execution of bright broad murals. All this time he had been putting away his spare sous with the intention of entering one of the Ecoles des Beaux Arts. He had passed the entrance examinations brilliantly, in all sections, and, on the advice of his brother-in-law Leray, an engraver, had entered Gleyre's.

He was a gangling young man with a long neck in which his Adam's apple bobbed, and steady penetrating eyes. The widow's caul of his receding hair gave emphasis to his high well-formed brow, strong nose and hollow cheeks, which were often unshaved. He sometimes looked as if he needed a good meal, and probably did. His reply to Gleyre was the truth: he enjoyed painting. He had an extraordinary facility, and he liked to experiment with various techniques, and particularly with color.

"To read what was said of color by Ingres, Gleyre, Gérome and the other great teachers of the nineteenth century," says Sir Kenneth Clark, "one would suppose that it was some particularly dangerous and disreputable form of vice." Because of a certain red Renoir had used in his competition canvas for entry to the Beaux Arts, the instructor Signol had warned him: "Guard yourself against color. Be careful not to be another Delacroix." To please Gleyre, who entertained the same fear, Renoir painted a nude in the manner most esteemed by his master; caramel-colored flesh set off by bitumen, backlighting on the shoulders, a tortured expression in the face. Gleyre was delighted: here was a young man who could paint in the dramatic manner he had once practiced himself; and then he had suddenly realized that he was being made fun of. The use of color was contagious. When Gleyre discovered the young English girl in Renoir's class adding a touch of vermilion to the nipples of the figure she was painting, he cried, "Mon Dieu, it's indecent!" "I believe in free love and Courbet," said the young girl. (The best stories about Renoir are told by his motion-picture-making son, Jean, a great artist in his own right.)

Years later, speaking of his sojourn at Gleyre's, Renoir said: "While others shouted, broke window panes, teased the models and disturbed the teacher, I was always quiet in my corner, very attentive, very docile, studying the model, listening to the teacher... And yet it was I whom they called revolutionary." Just so.

A tall well-dressed young man turned up at Gleyre's one day. At first glance Renoir classed him as "the sort who gives the impression of having had his valet break in his shoes for him." Frédéric Bazille was, in fact, the son of a wealthy Protestant family with large estates at Montpellier in the south of France. Born December 6, 1841, he had studied medicine at Montpellier University, but had conceived a passion for modern painting after having seen the works of Courbet and Delacroix. His family was of the same class as the Manets with whom they were distantly acquainted. When Bazille begged his father to be allowed to take up painting, his father had agreed, with the proviso that he study medicine at the same time. Bazille lost no time coming to Paris and taking the Beaux Arts examinations.

Bazille took Renoir across to the Closerie des Lilas for a beer and Renoir soon discovered that his distinguished-looking acquaintance had the taste for verbal battle and was quite firm in his beliefs. He wanted to paint people in everyday dress in their habitual environment. "The big classic compositions are finished," he said. (He too had met Baudelaire at a party.) Bazille had a charming half-smile, blond silky hair and a well-trimmed blond beard. "A very handsome fellow," wrote Zola, "of fine stock, haughty, formidable in argument, but usually good and kind." He was to be exceptionally kind to the young men he met at Gleyre's.

Bazille introduced Alfred Sisley to his new friend. With his fair spade beard, level brows and smooth pink cheeks Sisley passed for an Englishman, which was only half true. To be sure his Kentish forebears had been engaged in the smuggling trade, but this had been converted into legal trading in South American artificial flowers and other novelties; thus his father lived in Dunkirk and his mother, Marie Felicia Sell, though born in London, lived the life of a cultivated Frenchwoman. Alfred, born in Paris, October 30, 1839, had received a French education and at eighteen had been sent to London for commercial training. Instead he had devoted himself to the study of Turner and Constable, the English painters. His parents had made no

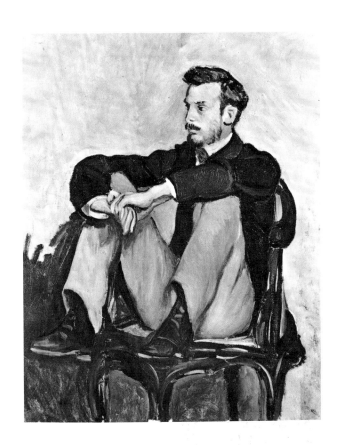

Frédéric Bazille:

Upper right: Portrait of Renoir, 1867.

Lower left: Portrait of Sisley, 1867-1868.

Right: The Artist's Studio, 1870.

demur when he had proposed taking up an artistic career. He had had the notion that he might try for the Prix de Rome, but had let it slide when he saw the competition. He was a shy, quiet young man, of whom Renoir said later: "Sisley's gift was gentleness. He was a delightful human being. He would be overcome with emotion by the pressure of a hand or even a grateful look." Sisley called his new friends his "chums," a word which gave them some amusement. One imagines Sisley blushing.

Fantin-Latour sometimes stopped by the Closerie des Lilas. On a visit to Gleyre's he had singled out Renoir as the pupil whose virtuosity harked back to the Italian Renaissance. Fantin was deeply involved in the teaching of Lecoq de Boisbaudran who had a theory about pictorial memory. It was not long before Monet joined the group and his worldly manner astonished them all. They called him "the dandy" because he wore a tailor-made suit (for which he had not paid) and his shirt had lace cuffs. Playing his part Monet once told a girl (it might have been the English lass): "You must forgive me, but I sleep only with Duchesses, or servant girls. Those in between nauseate me. My ideal would be a Duchess's servant." It was Monet who introduced Pissarro whom he had met at the Académie Suisse. Careless in dress, but not in words, Pissarro impressed them because he had already exhibited at the Salon. Speaking in a soft musical voice, he captured them with his gambit, "The Louvre should be burned . . ."

Monet had been only fifteen days at Gleyre's when the master took a look at one of his studies.

Gleyre: "It's not bad, but the bust is too heavy, the shoulders too powerful, the feet excessive."

Monet: "But I can only draw what I see."

Gleyre: "Praxiteles borrowed the best elements of a hundred models to create a great work. When one does something it is necessary to think of the ancients."

That evening Monet saw Renoir and Bazille.

"Let's get out of here," he said. "The place is unhealthy. It lacks sincerity."

Monet had been telling his friends about the advantages of painting in the open air. Corot and Courbet worked outdoors, of course, but made only sketches: their paintings were completed in the studio where Corot, for example, felt he could control his "values." And there was the Fontainebleau school, the so-called "Barbizons," some of whom were fine painters. Monet told his friends about his work with Boudin and Jongkind, in particular, about natural light and the luminosity of empty skies, qualities which could only be captured on the run. Instant painting, he might have said. It sounded wonderfully fresh and new and so the friends, Monet, Renoir and Sisley, went out to Chailly-en-Bière where they put up at the White Horse Inn on the edge of the Forest of Fontainebleau. They set up their easels in the open air. The excursion lasted only a few days, but its consequences were to be felt for a century.

A few weeks later, Gleyre, who was literally going blind, closed down his studio.

"I need not plead here the cause of modern subjects. That cause was won long ago. After such remarkable works by Manet and Courbet, no one would venture to maintain that the present times are unworthy of the painter's brush. We are, thank God, delivered from the Greeks and Romans, we have even had enough of the Middle Ages which in over a quarter of a century the French Romantics never succeeded in resuscitating. We are now face to face with the only reality, and in spite of ourselves we shall encourage our painters to portray us on their canvases, just as we are, with our modern clothes and ways."
Emile Zola, *L'Evénement illustré*, May 23, 1868.

Auguste Renoir: Self-Portrait, about 1876.

"The Painters of the New Painting"

Henri Fantin-Latour:

Self-Portrait, 1860. Drawing.

The Studio in the Batignolles Quarter, 1870.

Auguste Renoir:

Portrait of Claude Monet, 1875.

Portrait of Sisley and his Wife, about 1868.

Fantin-Latour's *Studio in the Batignolles Quarter* pays tribute to Manet's influence over the generation that followed him and emphasizes his role as leader. Progressive painters and critics were united in their ardent respect for naturalistic truth, their desire to be in step with the times, their scorn for academic pretensions. Represented from left to right are Scholderer, Manet, Renoir, Astruc, Zola, Maître, Bazille and Monet; absent were the more "countrified" painters, Pissarro, Sisley and Cézanne, who were less often to be seen in Paris. In the next decade Manet's position as leader was taken over by Monet, who is barely visible here. The public was not yet ready for this homage to Manet and certain critics continued to attack him sharply.

"In their early days, when they were still unknown and mere students, the painters who were later to be called the Impressionists were already independents, by instinct; even then they felt impelled to break with the traditional rules. The formation of the impressionist group is an interesting example of the way in which, at a given moment, when certain ideas are in the air, they may be absorbed by different men, influencing and guiding each other."

Théodore Duret, *Les Peintres impressionnistes*

Manet, An Example Rather Than a Master

Exhibited at the Salon of 1868, Manet's Portrait of Zola was praised and analyzed by the sitter himself in an article in L'Evénement illustré (May 10, 1868):

"Manet is above all a naturalist. His eye sees and renders objects with elegant simplicity. I realize that I cannot make the blind like his painting; but true artists will understand me when I speak of the faintly acrid charm of his pictures. The portrait he exhibited this year is one of his best canvases. Its coloring is very intense and has a powerful harmony. Yet this picture is by a man accused of not knowing how to paint or draw. I defy any other portraitist to place a figure in an interior with equal energy, without the surrounding still lifes detracting from the head.

"This portrait is an aggregate of difficulties overcome; from the frames in the background, from the charming Japanese screen on the left, to the smallest details of the figure, everything holds together in a bright and skillful color scheme, so real that the eye overlooks the accumulation of objects and simply sees a harmonious whole."

Edouard Manet:

Portrait of Emile Zola, 1868.

Self-Portrait with Palette, 1878.

Berthe Morisot with a Bunch of Violets, 1872.

46

A way of seeing shaped by experience and sensibility, not by tradition; a style whose keynote was sunlight and broken color, vividly recording the fleeting impression; the autonomy of painting with respect to reality; a free choice of subjects regardless of the old claims of "nobility" and "refinement"—these were the essential aspects of the art revolution called Impressionism. Each of the impressionist painters contributed to the common achievement.

Paul Cézanne: Paul Alexis Reading to Zola, about 1869.

Edouard Manet: Portrait of Stéphane Mallarmé, 1876.

Camille Pissarro: Self-Portrait, 1873.

Paul Cézanne: Self-Portrait, about 1877.

47

"The whole picture was in shades of gray. But when it was painted and I considered it successfully completed, I saw that Manet himself was not satisfied with it. He wanted to add something to it. One day when I came in, he made me take the pose he had painted me in and placed a stool beside me ... On the stool he then placed a lacquer-ware tray with a decanter, a glass and a knife. All these objects went to form a still life of varied tones in a corner of the picture, an addition he had by no means intended and I could not have anticipated. But then he added an even more unexpected object, a lemon on top of the glass on the little tray.

"I looked on rather surprised as he made these successive additions, wondering what could be the reason for them, until I realized that what I had in front of me were the workings of his instinctive and as it were organic way of seeing and feeling. Obviously the monochrome, dark-toned picture was not to his liking. It lacked the colors needed to give it the stamp of approval in his eyes, and not having included them at first he added them afterwards in the shape of a still life."

Théodore Duret, *Histoire d'Edouard Manet*

1. *Edouard Manet: Portrait of Théodore Duret, 1868.*

2. *Edgar Degas: Portrait of Edmond Duranty, about 1879. Pencil.*

3. *Edouard Manet: George Moore at the Café de la Nouvelle-Athènes, about 1879.*

4. *Edouard Manet: Portrait of Zacharie Astruc, 1863.*

The Gallery of Machines at the Paris World's Fair of 1855. Lithograph.

Honoré Daumier:
On the Way into the World's Fair, 1855. Lithograph.

What was this Salon d'Art to which all these young painters aspired?

It was, in effect, a great public entertainment, a spectacle which drew hundreds of thousands of spectators. After the World's Fair of 1855, the great empty Palace of Industry, in which the Fair had been held, had seemed a convenient solution to the problem of housing the ever-increasing number of art works chosen for the biannual exhibitions of the Académie des Beaux Arts. A huge cast-iron-and-glass structure, built on the lines of Queen Victoria's Crystal Palace (rather more fanciful than the building which supplanted it in 1900 and squats somberly on the site today) it had thirty-five galleries on several floors and an open court with a garden. A month before the scheduled opening of the Salon the great glasshouse would be invaded by an army of window-cleaners, floor-polishers and landscape gardeners. Then the days would come for the artists to bring their framed canvases and boxed marbles. Some works—for canvases of two hundred square feet were no unusual thing—would require a brigade of blue-bloused workmen to unload them and carry them up the broad stairways that circled either side of the lofty entrance.

49

The Salon in the Palace of Industry at the 1855 World's Fair. Photograph.

The Salon of 1869. The Last Day for sending in Pictures. Print by Del.

The election of the Jury which would decide which of these works would be hung was one of the chief events prior to the opening. Previous exhibitors qualified as voters, but they were grouped in about thirty different categories, such as those representing the various Beaux Arts studios, and others calling themselves, for example, the Uncompromising Young Painters, the Liberals, or the Ladies Group, etc. Each coterie drew up its list of candidates for the forty places on the Jury or Hanging Committee, as it was properly called, nominating, naturally, representatives committed to pushing the coterie's own works, but also having an eye for deals with other coteries. On voting day the lists were brought to the vast central gallery overlooking the Champs Elysées where, since it was usually early in the year, a huge fire, in which entire trees were consumed, was burning in a great ornamental fireplace. Here the lists, subject to last-minute revisions, were brought to a forty-foot-long table to be counted, re-counted and scrutinized. By four in the afternoon most of the voting lists would be in hand and while they were being called out some four or five hundred members of the various coteries and their friends would stand about, talking and laughing and raising a general uproar under the lofty ceiling. At six o'clock the assistants would bring in fuel lamps and, mistrustful of the gloom, some onlookers would crowd the long table and peer over the scrutineers' shoulders. At eight o'clock a collation of cold meats and wine would be served and the excitement would reach a climax. There would be mocking animal cries and even attempts at yodelling among the onlookers and the atmosphere would be that of a village fair. The great fire would be stoked up and its forge-like glow would illuminate the whole gallery. Then everyone would smoke their *caporal* and the lamps would become misty yellow orbs, the floor would be a mess of torn paper, corks, fragments of bread, empty bottles and some broken plates. Reserve would be cast aside and inevitably some sculptor would mount a chair and make a speech in defense of his work. Then, little by little, the people would drift away, to be replaced, after midnight, by gentlemen in evening dress and opera cloaks, coming from theater or soirée to learn the result before it was published in the morning newspapers whose reporters were to be seen dodging about the long table. Usually around one o'clock in the morning the corrections would have been entered, the final count completed and the names of the forty members of the Hanging Committee would be read out. The presence of Gustave Courbet on the Committee was the hope of all non-conformist painters and usually he was there, for his powerful genius and gentle presence could not easily be ignored.

The work of the Jury commenced next day and continued for the following twenty days. Each morning the Salon staff set up a row of paintings, resting them on the floor and leaning them against the hand rails, which reached around the entire floor of galleries. At one o'clock in the afternoon the Jury, led by the President, who carried a bell, would start off on a promenade that lasted for the rest of the day and sometimes extended late into the night. The members of the Jury gave their decisions standing and the work was got through as fast as possible, the worst canvases being rejected without a vote being taken. At times, however, discussions delayed the party; there would be a ten-minute quarrel and some picture would be set aside for the evening session. At these moments two aproned assistants would take a firmer grip on the ten-yard rope which kept the committeemen from crowding the canvases. Behind the Committee marched seventy museum-keepers in white blouses, commanded by a brigadier who sorted out the unaccepted paintings and had his men carry off the rejects in much the same manner as stretcher-bearers on a battlefield. So the Committee tramped on until late in the evening, muffled against the icy drafts in their fur-lined overcoats, without a single chair to sit upon, without respite except for the three o'clock buffet. It was usually at this sandwiches-petits fours-chocolate-cognac break that the bartering took place. Many members of the Committee carried little notebooks which they now consulted to make sure that their commitments had not been overlooked.

Then the work would begin again, but more agreeably, for they would be judging the paintings whose height was less than one-and-a-half yards and could be "passed on the easel," as the expression was. There would be chairs here and tables with paper and pens, and a good many committeemen would grow absent-minded; several would work at their correspondence, so that the President would be obliged to ring his bell in order to obtain a presentable majority vote. There were moments, however, when a gust of passion swept them and they would jostle each other and the vote, usually given by raising the hand, would take place amid such feverish excitement that hats and walking-sticks would be waved in the air above a tumult of surging heads.

Such an incident might be caused, for example, by an assistant pointing out that a painting, judged earlier and consigned to the stretcher-bearers with unanimous contempt, was, in fact, *hors-concours*, that is, outside the competition, being the work of some old classical painter revered by the Institut. "Well, fish it out, and put it among the admitted pictures," the President would say, amid the sneers and chuckles of the younger committee members. Later, facing a new painting placed on view, he might exclaim, "Now, who's the pig who painted...?" But quickly recovering himself, having recognized the signature for that of one of his friends, he might cry out, "Superb! Eh, gentlemen?" And the picture would join the ranks of the chosen, to the chuckles of some and the scornful laughter of others. From time to time they all made such blunders, and this generally caused them to cast a furtive glance at the signature before expressing an opinion. When some dubious canvas was brought forward, and inspection revealed it to be the work of a member of the Jury, there would be an exchange of signs and whispers: "Have a care, no mistake mind, it's *his* picture." Or, on another occasion, when it was a question of admitting a particularly frightful portrait, a member of the Jury would take the President aside and explain that it was a portrait of a very wealthy patron of the arts. The president might then make a great show of indignation. "You dishonor the Jury, Monsieur!" But the chances were that the portrait would get hung.

Sir,

I have recently had the honor of writing to you about two of my canvases which the jury has just rejected.

Since you have not yet answered my letter, I feel I must insist on the motives which led me to apply to you. Moreover, as you have certainly received my letter, I need not here repeat the arguments that I felt called upon to lay before you. I shall content myself with saying once more that I cannot accept the unfair judgment of colleagues whom I myself have not commissioned to appraise my work.

I am therefore writing to you to emphasize my request. I wish to appeal to the public and be exhibited even though the jury has rejected my pictures. My request does not seem to me exorbitant, and if you were to question all the painters who find themselves in my position, they would all of them tell you that they disown the jury and that they wish to take part in one way or another in an exhibition open perforce to every serious worker.

Therefore let the Salon des Refusés be re-established. Even were I to figure in it alone, I ardently desire the public to know at least that I no more wish to be confused with these gentlemen of the jury than they apparently wish to be confused with me.

I take it for granted, Sir, that you will not choose to remain silent. It seems to me that any proper letter deserves the courtesy of a reply.

Letter from Cézanne to Count Nieuwerkerke,
Superintendent of Fine Arts, April 19, 1866

Gustave Doré: Entrance of the Exhibition Hall on March 31, 1861, the last day for sending in pictures. Drawing.

After the first selection was over, the Jury rested for a couple of days while the museum-keepers rearranged the pictures. Then the work of selecting from among the three thousand rejected paintings as many canvases as were necessary to make up the regulation total of 2,500 admitted works would commence. Fighting against fatigue and striving to keep their vision clear the members of the Jury would thread their way among paintings lying like stagnant pools on the floor or leaning against endless walls.

Zola, to whose passion for documentation we owe the foregoing description of a typical Salon d'Art of the Second Empire, tells us that Varnishing Day, traditionally set aside for the artists to touch up their suspended works before the exhibition officially opened, had become a kind of fête, attended by thousands of people who had obtained free passes. Provoked by months of newspaper gossip, café controversy and ordinary curiosity, they came to the Palais de l'Industrie for the great art exhibition as they might have come to a national carnival. Processions of gentlemen decorated with the ribbon of the Légion d'Honneur, smiling and bowing to each other, art critics pretending to make notes on the margins of their catalogues, art dealers talking expertise in loud voices, professional models standing ostentatiously in the vicinity of works for which they had posed, rival painters execrating each other's works, artists' families conjecturing on the distribution of medals, elegant ladies in flowered bonnets and their escorts in long coats and silk hats, even soldiers and sailors, nursemaids and children, all were there, all guests of the "nation of artists." They entered the gigantic vestibule where the cold flagstones echoed their footsteps as in a cathedral aisle, they climbed the monumental staircases to the thirty-five glass-roofed galleries with their storied paintings of incarnadined battlefields, ennymphed forest glades, mythological nudity, bemedalled soldiers and scenes of imperial festivity. Or they strolled about the yellow-sanded paths of the ice-cold Garden Gallery where leprous marble statuary was poised against boxed trees and flocks of begging sparrows came down from their homes among the lofty girders. Or they rested on the new circular settees beneath sheaves of tropical foliage or took refreshment at the great bar under the clock. The omnipresent sound was the tramp of feet, of multitude.

The crisis came with the Salon of 1863. Expectably Cabanel's *Birth of Venus*, a recumbent nude enhaloed by cherubs, had won the Jury's plaudits and was thereupon acquired by the Emperor. But some two thousand paintings and a thousand sculptures had been refused. Their owners were in an uproar and many a paint-impregnated fist was raised in the direction of the Louvre Palace. Louis Napoleon, who had a pollster's eye for the fluctuations of popularity, decided to see for himself. Alone, except for an aide de camp, he visited the Palais a few days before the official opening and, after having viewed forty refused pictures, decided to let the public decide the issue. Despite some objections from the Academy he ordered that the refused works be shown separately, in seven spare rooms of the Palais.

The coming show—the Salon des Refusés, as it was called—

Honoré Daumier: The Last Day for Receiving Pictures.
Lithograph from "Le Charivari," February 20, 1846.

Maurice Leloir: Varnishing Day at the Salon, May 11, 1879.

Daumier:
The Public at the Salon

Honoré Daumier: This Mr. Courbet paints such coarse people . . . Lithograph from
"The World's Fair," 1855.

Honoré Daumier: In Front of Meissonier's Pictures. Lithograph from
"The Public at the Salon," 1852.

Honoré Daumier: Lovers of classical art convinced that painting is going to the dogs
in France. Lithograph from "The Public at the Salon," 1852.

Honoré Daumier: Artists Examining a Rival's Picture. Lithograph from
"The Public at the Salon," 1852.

THE PHYSIOLOGY OF THE REJECTED ARTIST

For a week we have been running into them everywhere.

There they go, slowly making their way up the slopes of Rue Pigalle or Rue d'Assas, some with a frame under their arm, others trudging behind a hand-cart on which a large canvas sways and creaks; all of them look as if they were going to a funeral. So one is not surprised to see them invariably making for the Montparnasse cemetery or the Montmartre cemetery.

What they are burying, alas, is the whole of their year's work. Not much of an effort, it may sometimes seem, but how many hopes went into it! Mediocre beauties, often enough, but what perfect satisfaction they gave their makers! Such is the life of an artist whose vanity is a source of joy when talent is wanting. Now it is all going to its resting place under the uniform epitaph: *rejected!* A blunt and meager epitaph if ever there was one, an epitaph that makes one miss the *good husbands,* the *good fathers,* the *good sons* and *good citizens* which make our cemeteries such goodly populous places.

From the Arts page of *L'Opinion nationale,* 1874

Honoré Daumier: Triumphal March.
Lithograph from "The World's Fair," 1855.

Honoré Daumier: Funeral March.
Lithograph from "The World's Fair," 1855.

promised to be very amusing. When six hundred artists withdrew their refused works, rather than have themselves exposed to public ridicule, the field, so far as the public was concerned, was left to *les rapins,* those perennial hopefuls with burning ambition and not a sou in their pockets who, Salon after Salon, put their works before the Jury hoping to eclipse the great Cabanel. It sounded like fun.

In the first hours of the opening of the Salon des Refusés on May 15—some think it an historic date—seven thousand Parisians stomped through the seven rooms set aside for the rejected paintings at the Palais, and thereafter there was never less than a thousand visitors daily. Never had an art show created so much amusement, provoked so much outright hilarity and derision, or so much scandal. Zola tells us that the rejected paintings were installed in fine style with lofty hangings of old tapestry at the doors, the "line" set off with green baize, seats of crimson velvet, white linen screens under the long skylight of the roof. At first glance the impression is identical with that of the main salon, the same gilt frames and the same bright colors, but there is a kind of special cheerfulness which the visitor does not at first realize. It is hot, a fine dust rises from the floor, there is a hubbub of conversation, some restrained laughter. The whole show is a mixture of the best and the worst styles; but from amidst the incoherent ensemble, and especially from the landscapes, all of which are painted in a sincere, correct key, and also from the portraits, there comes, says Zola, the good fresh scent of youth, bravery and passion. Sufficiently discreet at the entrance to the galleries, the laughter becomes more boisterous, more unrestrained as one advances. In the third room women cease concealing their smiles behind their handkerchiefs, while men openly hold their sides. It is the contagious hilarity of people who have come to be amused and who are growing excited, bursting at mere trifles. Each canvas has its particular success, people hail each other from a distance to point out something funny and witticisms fly from mouth to mouth; in the last gallery there is a tempest of laughter.

Its object is a painting of four figures in a shady wood, two gentlemen in the foreground fully dressed, and two women, one nude, the other standing in a nearby stream clad only in her chemise. Near the seated figures there is a basket of fruit, some food. The picture is called *Déjeuner sur l'herbe*—Picnic on the Grass.

People fight their way into the last gallery to see this picture and the laughter rises on the air, says Zola, in a swelling clamor, the roar of a tide near its fall. Eagerly they press in front of the picture, and Zola, pushing his way out of the gallery, hears their laughter behind him, "careering through the air, like a tempest beating against a cliff, the rumbling of an infantry attack."

"The idiots!" is all he can gasp, choking, he says, with grief.

The picture at which they are laughing most is, of course, to become one of Edouard Manet's most famous. Among other names signed to paintings in this Salon des Refusés were: Renoir, Cézanne, Pissarro, Guillaumin, Monet, Jongkind, Fantin-Latour and Whistler.

The big "R" stamped on the stretchers of their canvases signalled, if it did not signify, Revolution.

MANET, says Théodore Duret, "possessed a vivifying vision. In a full light everything appeared to him to glow with exceptional splendor." Jacques Emile Blanche, the portrait painter, who saw *Déjeuner sur l'herbe* when a youth (his father almost bought it for him), says that "its colors were of a vividness not easily imaginable to those who know it only in its present (pre-World War II) condition." Or perhaps it only seemed so. For the picture's initial impact in the somber mid-nineteenth century was that of a flash of lightning at dusk : the world was suddenly revealed in another dimension. This is the painting, more perhaps than any other, which led Elie Faure, the art historian, to remark that Manet "was the first man in Europe to have the audacity to lay on one light color another light color, to reduce semitones to a murmur, or even to ignore them and almost always to suppress modelling by juxtaposing or superimposing strokes bound by a line which is very firm, but which detaches from a background purged of shadows that might serve as adjuncts."

Manet's technical innovations created a furore among the academicians. But this was not the particular quality which had provoked the hysterical laughter at the Salon des Refusés, outraged the Empress and caused the Emperor to pronounce the painting "an affront to modesty." Nor was it the nudity of the female figure in the foreground—Ingres' bathers were more voluptuous, Garnier's castaway more provocative. No, the offending element in Manet's picture was the men, both wearing the everyday dress of gentlemen of the period and evidently engaged in a leisurely conversation. By this naturalistic note Manet had torn away the classical cobwebs that veiled people's identity with art ; today we can say that the hysterical laughter was provoked by the observers' sensation that, at some unguarded moment, they themselves had been under observation. Art had arrived at self-consciousness.

But the painter found a few loyal defenders among the critics. In *Le Salon* Zacharie Astruc wrote: "Manet, one of the greatest personalities of our time, is its luster, inspiration, pungent savor and surprise. The injustice committed in his case is so flagrant it confounds." And in the *Gazette de France* there appeared the unattributed remark, believed to have been uttered by Delacroix: "M. Manet has the qualities that are necessary to be refused unanimously by all the juries of the world." When Delacroix died in August that year, Manet, following the cortège, was considered by the young painters to be the new master, one who embodied their as yet diffuse feeling about what art should be.

The Salon des Refusés had failed in its purpose : in the argot of a later age it was overkill. In November the Emperor decreed a reform in the Beaux Arts organization : henceforth it would cease to be controlled by the Institut de France, nor would the Institut continue to appoint professors of art. The Salon would be held annually, instead of biannually ; only one-fourth of the Jury would be nominated by the administration, the rest would be elected by artists who had previously won medals.

The new Jury accepted two canvases by Manet for the 1864 Salon: *Incident in the Bull Ring*, and *Dead Christ with Angels*. Neither

The Salon of 1865.

Impressionism, in effect, has changed the vision of the world. In spite of all the natural and artificial obstacles, it has triumphed by its intrinsic value because it represents the moral vision of its epoch. The last of the privileged classes, the "notables," were about to disappear. From a new stratum in society the Impressionists brought their force and sincerity and integrity, their tremendous faith in their ideal, their elan of liberty. LIONELLO VENTURI

won acclaim: one critic said that the bull was puny, another that it had been painted "with an ink-well"; yet another referred to Manet mockingly as "Don Manet y Courbetos y Zurbaran de los Batignolles." Rebuking another critic who had commented on the Spanish influence in Manet's work, Baudelaire said: "Manet has never seen the Spanish masters: he could not imitate them." Manet had, of course, seen the Goya, Velazquez and Greco collection of the late Monarch, but he had never been to Spain. The criticism registered: he destroyed his bullfight picture and the following year he visited Madrid.

At the next Salon, that of 1865, official art appeared to have recovered its equilibrium. The highest award went to Cabanel for his *Portrait of Napoleon III in Ceremonial Costume*. Other successful pictures were *The Reception of the Siamese Ambassador* and *The Arrival of the Emperor at Genoa*. Among the 3,556 other exhibits were two by Edouard Manet: *Christ Insulted by the Soldiers* and *Olympia*. The Christ was a failure and Manet never again attempted a religious subject. But Olympia was a public scandal.

This picture of a slim nude girl wearing a rose in her hair and a jewel at her throat, placidly receiving a rich bouquet of flowers from a Negro maid, was another of Manet's scenes from contemporary life: *la demi-mondaine chez elle*, as one critic said, the little cocotte accepting a lover's tribute. The model was Victorine Meurent (who

LE CONSTITUTIONNEL,
JOURNAL POLITIQUE, LITTÉRAIRE, UNIVERSEL.

"With the taste for art, with that very special instinct which is the artistic faculty par excellence, the keen desire to reproduce and record external phenomena, and with a certain preconceived theoretical idea which in spite of some reservations is correct, Manet contrives to provoke the almost scandalous outbursts of laughter which attract the Salon visitors to this droll creature whom he calls *Olympia*.

"The Baroque construction of this 'august young girl' with her hand shaped like a toad causes hilarity and in some cases uncontrollable laughter. In this particular instance, the comedy results from the ostentatious pretention to produce a noble work ('the august young girl,' says the guide book), a pretention shown up by the absolute impotence of the execution; do we not smile at the sight of a child assuming the self-important air of a man? In this *Olympia* everything that has to do with line is thus irremediably condemned. The general color scheme itself is disagreeable. Only in certain parts is it accurate: in the tone of the linen, in the contrasts of sheet, shawl and flowers. But if we take M. Manet's effort seriously, we must tell him that in nature sooty shadows are rare and that he sees or at least paints no others. He takes no account of reflections and counterreflections; and it is only by studying them that he can succeed in giving his painting the harmony that nature always possesses."

A.-P. Martial, May 16, 1865

Catalogue of the 1865 Salon.

Edouard Manet: *Le Déjeuner sur l'Herbe*, 1863. Refused at the Salon of 1863.

56

The "Olympia" Scandal

"When, tired of dreaming, Olympia sleeps..."

Zacharie Astruc

Edouard Manet:

The Venus of Urbino,
after Titian, 1856.

Sketch for Olympia.

Letter from Manet
to Baudelaire, 1865.

had also posed for the nude in *Déjeuner sur l'herbe*) and the composition had been inspired by Titian's *Venus of Urbino*.

As with *Déjeuner*, visitors stood before the painting, grinning and guffawing. On the right side of the picture Manet had painted a black cat which, for some unaccountable reason, became a scandalous object. The cat provoked uncontrolled laughter; people came from all quarters of the great pavilion to see the cat. At the same time they were angry about the cat and guards were posted to prevent the picture from being damaged.

Wrote Jules Claretie in *L'Artiste*: "What is this Odalisque with the yellow stomach? A base model, picked up I don't know where, who represents Olympia. Olympia? What Olympia? A courtesan no doubt? Manet cannot be accused of idealizing the foolish virgins, he who makes them vulgar virgins..." Théophile Gautier, who had

Honore Daumier: In Front of M. Manet's Picture.
— Why is that big red woman in a chemise called
Olympia?
— But my dear, that may be the name of the black
cat.

been carefully watching Manet, now wrote in *Le Moniteur*: "Manet has the distinction of having been a danger. But that danger has now passed. Olympia can be understood from no point of view, even if you take it for what it is, a puny model stretched out on a sheet. The color of the flesh is dirty, the modelling non-existent..." Even Courbet was shocked. "It's flat and lacks modelling," he said, "it looks like the Queen of Spades coming out of a bath." Retorted Manet: "Courbet's idea of rotundity is a billiard ball."

But Olympia brought Manet to the notice of the general public. "You are as famous as Garibaldi," said Degas. It was not the kind of notoriety that Manet wanted or relished. He went off to Madrid where he had not expected to see a single Frenchman; but in the Hotel d'Europe there was a Frenchman only a few tables distant, moreover he was asking the waiter for the very dishes Manet had declined. A confrontation was in order: "You do this because you know who I am?" Manet accused. The Frenchman was Théodore Duret, a literary man, who explained that he had never heard of

Fontainebleau: The First Open Air Compositions

View of Fontainebleau Forest in 1859. Photograph by Charles Marville.

Manet. He had just come in from Portugal and was intolerably hungry. They went off to Toledo together to see the El Grecos; Duret became Manet's defender and biographer.

Manet's relationship with his parents had always been correct, but many an observer wondered whether they did not sometimes think him strange.

When Auguste Manet died in 1862 he left his fortune to be divided between his three sons. Now financially independent Edouard opened a one-man show in the Avenue de l'Alma (1867) where he exhibited fifty paintings, catalogued with an introduction, beginning: "The artist does not say to you today, 'Come and see flawless works,' but, 'Come and see sincere works.'" He also took a large apartment in the rue de Saint-Petersbourg where he installed his mother and his wife. Although Suzanne Leenhoff had been his mistress since his student days, he did not marry her until the year after his father's death. At their new house, solidly furnished in the style of Louis Philippe, Suzanne, who was an accomplished pianist, entertained their friends at musical evenings.

Of Pissarro's two pictures in the Salon des Refusés the critic Castagnary had written: "I take it he is a young man. Corot seems to be a favorite with him. A good master, Monsieur, but one on no account to be imitated." But Pissarro was already moving beyond Corot's influence, much to the old master's disapproval. He had discarded romantic subjects—haunting forest glades, etc.—and was devoting himself to the pursuit of light, in shadow as in sunshine. He had eliminated black and bitumen, brown sienna and the ochres from his palette and was leaning heavily on the new rainbow colors: white lead, light chrome yellow, Veronese green, ultramarine or cobalt blue, madder and vermilion. It took him hours to decide on the smallest details. "I do not want to make a brushstroke when I do not feel complete mastery of my subject," he said. "This is the great difficulty: without sensation nothing, absolutely nothing, is valid!" Pissarro, a thinking man, was working towards the concept of sensory perception in art, a forerunner of the revolutionary doctrine that painting is a visual impression of a scene casually encountered. He was to be the theorist of the new group of painters.

During his first years in Paris he had worked briefly at the so-called "free" studios, Isidore Dagnan's, Lehmann's, Old Picot's and the Académie Suisse, where he had met Monet and Cézanne. At these studios he drew briefly from the model, not because he aspired to be a figure painter, but for the discipline it imposed on his drawing. While painting in the countryside around Paris he had met the landscape painters Chintreuil, Desbrosses and Ludovic Piette. The last-named soon became one of his closest friends and helped him out financially. For some years after leaving St. Thomas Pissarro had continued to receive an allowance from his father, but this had finally been withdrawn, presumably because of Pissarro's steadfast refusal to enter the Beaux Arts; but also, no doubt, because Pissarro was now about thirty-five, old enough for a man to stand on his own feet. His little family (son Lucien arrived in 1863) was therefore very poor; but Pissarro never for a moment yielded to the temptation of getting a job.

The Salons of '64, '65 and '66 had accepted some of his landscapes. The titles suggest an agreeable calm (e.g. *The Marne at Chennevières* and *Banks of the Marne*), not at all in accord with their non-conformist technique. Nor did it help the artist when he ranged himself with Manet's defenders during the climactic disputes over *Olympia*, though it won Manet's friendship.

At the day's end at Gleyre's studio Monet and Renoir sometimes picked up the partially flattened tubes discarded by the other students. In this way they were able, without cost, to replenish their own palettes sufficiently to do little flower studies in the Luxembourg gardens. The zinc tube had only recently been adapted to oil paint and its effect on the development of painting was unprecedented. Hitherto, painters had mixed their own paints or they had bought them ready-mixed from dealers. As a result there was a great variation in quality and shade and, since the paints were carried in little pots, landscape painting involved the labor of carrying, not only easel and stool, palette and brushes, but a range of paint pots and solvents. Like Corot, the Barbizon painters who worked in Fontainebleau forest—Théodore Rousseau, Jean-François Millet, Virgile-Narcisse Diaz de la Peña, called Diaz—painted from nature, but finished their painting indoors: no one imagined that a painting could be finished where it had begun. Not only the zinc tube now made outdoor painting easier and speedier, but the manufacturers offered, in addition to the standard palette, an exciting range of new colors, such as, says Wynford Dewhurst, a late impressionist painter, cadmium pale, violet de cobalt, garance rose doré. The young painters were soon to discover that the new colors gave a high degree of luminosity to shadows. In his old age Renoir said: "Paint in tubes, being easy to carry, allowed us to work from Nature and Nature alone. Without paints in tubes there would have been no Cézanne or Monet, no Sisley or Pissarro, nothing of what the journalists call the 'Impressionists.' Thanks to modern chemistry the colors [still] have a vividness and richness which the old masters never dreamed of."

The young painters' first attempt to exploit the possibilities of outdoor painting ended in a few days, through lack of resources. Sisley, who had an adequate allowance from his parents, rented an apartment in Neuilly and made regular excursions in the Ile de France. Renoir returned to Paris where he destroyed *La Esmeralda*, which he had exhibited at the 1864 Salon. Once again he took up decorating pubs. "He's an artist, but he'll die of starvation," his father said. Monet soon joined him and they shared lodgings and lived on dried beans. Never in want of ideas or daring Monet proposed that they paint portraits of the local tradesmen at fifty francs a picture. After executing several such commissions Monet ordered a new suit from his unpaid tailor. "He was born to be a Lord," was Renoir's comment.

In the spring Monet left Paris for Honfleur where he began looking for "motifs" in the familiar countryside. Meanwhile Bazille

Camille Corot: In the Forest of Fontainebleau. Pencil.

Théodore Rousseau: View of Fontainebleau Forest. Drawing.

Claude Monet: Le Pavé de Chailly in Fontainebleau Forest. about 1865.

Frédéric Bazille:
Monet after his Accident
at the Inn in Chailly, 1866.

"I have only come to Chailly as a favor to Monet; but for that, I would have gone to Montpellier long ago and with the greatest pleasure. Unfortunately, since coming here we have had the most awful weather, and I have only been able to pose for him twice. Just now the weather is quite fine. If he works fast Monet will need me for three or four days; so to my great regret my departure will have to be put off."

Frédéric Bazille, letter to his parents, August 23, 1865

Auguste Renoir: At the Inn of Mother Anthony. 1866.

had sat for his medical examinations and, while waiting for the outcome, joined Monet at Honfleur. "We are staying at the baker's who has rented us two small rooms," Bazille wrote his parents. "I had lunch with the Monets, they are charming people. They have a delightful place at Sainte-Adresse... I get up every morning at five o'clock and paint the whole day until eight in the evening... I'm making progress and that's all—it's all I want." He failed in his medical examinations and returned to Montpellier. Monet wrote him: "Every day I discover more and more beautiful things; it's enough to make one go mad; I have such a desire to do everything, my head is bursting with it." This was the year that the Salon accepted two of Monet's marines, views of Honfleur. Monet's family agreed to make him a small allowance; Bazille's family agreed that their son might, without loss of dignity, make painting his profession.

Early in 1865 Bazille rented a studio in the rue Furstenberg, the tiny tree-shaded square behind Saint-Germain-des-Prés, and Monet moved in. They were visited by Pissarro, Cézanne and Courbet. Through Bazille's relative, Commandant Lejosne, the group came in contact with Baudelaire (and possibly Constantin Guys, a shy and gifted artist, now a white-whiskered sixty-three, totally ignored by the Academicians, but recently championed by Baudelaire), also Nadar, the photographer, Gambetta, then a young revolutionary, and Fantin-Latour. In April Monet was back at Chailly and wrote Bazille asking him to join him there. He had conceived the idea of making a huge painting in Fontainebleau forest. "I think of nothing but my picture," he wrote Bazille, "and if I knew I couldn't bring it off, I believe I'd go mad." Stumping excitedly about the forest Monet fractured his leg and Bazille, putting his student medical knowledge to work, had to nurse him back to health, taking advantage of his situation to make an excellent portrait of Monet in his sick bed, water dripping on his injured leg from an ingeniously suspended cask. A little later Renoir and Sisley turned up and they all went to stay at Mother Anthony's Inn at Marlotte, on the edge of the forest. "Landscape is a sport," Renoir complained, as he followed Monet about in his search for *the* "motif," though Renoir's younger brother, Edmond, was carrying most of his equipment. Finally Monet found the place he was looking for in the high lands of the forest where there was ample sunshine striking through the high roof of leaves. Here he made a preliminary study for his picture (now in the Pushkin Museum, Moscow) which shows six couples preparing to picnic in a sun-dappled grove, the large white table cloth spread, with its cold chicken and pâté-en-croûte, bottles of wine (one counts four), large loaves of bread and various fresh crudités. The ladies are in the great flowing dresses of the period, the gentlemen too are pretty well-dressed after the round-hatted high-waisted style of the time, though one, a very tall man, has taken off his coat and is reclining against the bole of a tree. It is a scene of sensuous yet decorous hedonism, quintessentially French.

Monet set about transferring this scene to a canvas thirty-three square yards in area, too big to be set up under the trees, but for which a suitable place was found in one of the outbuildings of

Mother Anthony's Inn. He had in mind a painting as large as those of Courbet, but one which would overwhelm the coming Salon by its dazzling brilliance. Bazille and Monet's girl friend, Camille, posed in turn for each of the six ladies and gentlemen. And his friends watched with amazement as Monet began laying on great swathes of pure cobalt where the sky was to be showing through the trees; and where the sunlight, spotlighting through the emerald-green leaves, fell on the picnickers' gay clothes, he painted pools of cadmium yellow, dark garance and vermilion, using Courbet's method of laying on the paint in broad brushstrokes.

"Tiens!" said Courbet, paying Monet a visit. "Here is a young man who paints something which is not angels."

It was the friendly Courbet, however, who put an end to the experiment with—so soft is the kiss of death—some well-meant advice which, having helped Monet finance the project, he felt it his right and duty to give. Monet accepted the advice and made the suggested alterations; but was then so disappointed with the effect upon his canvas that he took off the stretchers, rolled it up and, unable to pay his bill at the inn, left the canvas as surety. Recovered years later, it was found to have been ruined by damp; portions, cut out and sold by Monet, still exist.

Monet went to live at Ville d'Avray, to the southwest of Paris, where he hurriedly painted a picture of Camille wearing a green dress which was accepted by the Salon of 1866, as a result of which success his family continued to make him a small allowance. Almost immediately afterwards he set about making another outdoor painting, albeit somewhat smaller than *The Picnic*, but still large enough to require a trench into which to lower the canvas while he was painting the top portion and a pulley to hoist it out again. Courbet once more disapproved of the whole business. Camille posed for all four women in *Women in the Garden*. The painting was refused by the Salon of '67.

At the beginning of 1868, Monet, once more penniless, wrote a desperate letter to Bazille, demanding that he pay all his bills. Bazille wrote a reply in the same insulting vein, but, understanding the despair that underlay Monet's belligerency, did not post the letter. That spring Boudin arranged for a number of painters, including Monet, to exhibit canvases at an International Maritime Exhibition in Le Havre. As a result Monet won a silver medal and sold his *Camille in a Green Dress* for a useful sum. However, when the exhibition closed, the rest of his paintings were seized by creditors who sold them to M. Gaudibert, a Le Havre shipping magnate, at eighty francs apiece. Monet was painting at Fécamp and Etretat, fishing villages to the north of Le Havre, and in June he wrote Bazille: "I write these few words in haste to ask you to help me quickly. I was certainly born under an unlucky star. They have just thrown me out of the inn, naked as a worm. I've found shelter for Camille and my poor little Jean for a few days in the neighborhood. I'm off to Le Havre this evening to see if I can get something out of my shipowner. My family won't do anything for me. I don't know where I shall sleep tomorrow night." He added: "P.S. I was so upset yesterday that I did a very stupid thing and threw myself into the water, happily with no ill

Claude Monet: The Artist's Wife with a Puppy, 1866.

Letter written to Bazille by Monet after he had had to leave Camille in Paris during her pregnancy and return to his parents' home in Le Havre:

"Ah, my dear fellow, it is a painful situation all the same. Camille is such a good-natured girl and has been very reasonable about it. And on that very account she grieves me all the more. By the way, I beg you to send me what you can, the more the better: send it to me by the first of the month, for here, though I am on quite good terms with my parents, they have let me know that I could stay here as long as I like without any cost to myself, as is only right, but that if I need money I'll have to try and earn it. So please don't forget. But I have a request to make of you. On July 25th Camille will be confined; I'll be going to Paris and will stay ten or fifteen days, and I'll need money for a number of things; so try and send me a little more, if only 100 or 150 francs. Do keep it in mind, because if I don't have it I'll be in a most awkward position."

Monet, June 25, 1867

61

effects." Bazille sent him some money, but his "shipowner," M. Gaudibert, hearing of his distress, asked him to come out to his chateau and make paintings of Madame Gaudibert and himself. His problems were solved, at least for the moment.

Fontainebleau forest, according to the brothers Goncourt, was "full of impecunious, bearded young painters carrying easels." So impecunious was Renoir that he could get to Fontainebleau only by walking there from Paris, and back again. The forest was wilder then, and not without hazard. Painting in the woods one day Renoir, wearing his multicolored porcelain worker's smock, was attacked by a gang of young ruffians who might have done him injury, but for the sudden appearance of a stalwart one-legged man who beat off the attackers with his stick. The man looked at Renoir's canvas and said, "Not bad, but why do you paint so black?" It was the Barbizon painter, Diaz, himself a former porcelain worker. They became good friends and Diaz opened an account for Renoir at his paint dealer's. On another occasion Renoir was startled to hear a voice crying from the cover of the trees, "Please help me, Monsieur. I am dying of hunger." A young man appeared and explained that he was a political fugitive from Paris. Renoir took care of him, dressed him up as a painter, and he stayed with the artists for several weeks. His name was Raoul Rigault.

One of the happiest paintings made by Renoir at this time was his portrait of Mr. and Mrs. Sisley. After leaving Gleyre's Alfred Sisley had moved about the rustic suburbs of Paris—Neuilly, Batignolles—painting out-of-doors, but also working in a small studio in the rue de la Paix. Inevitably he was drawn to Fontainebleau, staying at the White Horse Inn and then at Mother Anthony's. His paintings of Marlotte still showed Corot's somber influence. He was startled to see one of Renoir's canvases, made about the time Monet was experimenting with his *Picnic.* "Are you crazy?" he said. "What an idea to paint trees blue and the ground lilac!" Soon afterward he was doing very nearly this in his own canvases. In 1866 he married Marie Lescouezec, a little brunette from Toul in the Meurthe. Renoir's painting of Marie, in her candy-striped dress, with both hands clutching the proffered arm of Alfred, in his black velveteen jacket and dove-gray pants, captures at its inception the long-lasting marital felicity of this couple.

The Fontainebleau painters filled the little forest inns which, say the Goncourts, were the scene of "noisy joyous meals at the end of the working day." Such was Mother Anthony's at Marlotte which Renoir called a "cabaret" and of which he made a painting showing Mother Anthony, his friend Le Cœur and Sisley. At Marlotte or thereabouts Le Cœur and Renoir met the sisters Clémence and Lise Tréhot, daughters of a retired postmaster. Renoir made some sixteen finished pictures, mostly of Lise, the younger sister, in a variety of poses including the nude. These were bleak years in Renoir's struggle against poverty and the critical years of his artistic development. When the relationship ended Renoir's style had attained maturity: he would be known to posterity as one of the great painters of women.

Painters and Photography

Nadar the Great. Caricature by Alfred Grévin.

Three Caricatures by Nadar:

Photography Asking for Just a Little Place in the Exhibition of Fine Arts, 1855.

The Ingratitude of Painting, Refusing the Smallest Place in its Exhibition to Photography to whom it Owes so Much, 1857.

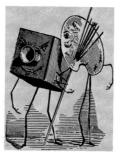

Painting Offering Photography a Place in the Exhibition of Fine Arts, 1859.

Photography made its appearance in the early nineteenth century at a time when scientists, philosophers and artists were intent on acquiring an objective and positive knowledge of reality; chemically and optically, it could have been discovered as early as the sixteenth century. Now, besides encouraging the pursuit of knowledge, it ministered to the romantic desire to arrest the flight of time and to perpetuate the memory of the past.

The first photograph had been made in 1822 by Nicéphore Niepce, whose experiments were rendered public in 1839 in a brilliant paper by the French physicist Arago, who foresaw the great possibilities of photography. That same year Daguerre showed his first metallic plates, soon to become so popular under the name of daguerrotypes; and Fox Talbot communicated the results of his experiments with light-sensitive paper.

An aid to memory and a magic mirror of reality, photography helped to educate the eye and make it aware of the variety of appearances. It did not lend itself to idealization and came indeed at a time when painters were interested in rendering reality as it is. Thanks to its low cost and rapidity, photography gradually deprived the artist of the bulk of his clientele and obliged him to abandon descriptive painting for an analysis of the phenomena of perception. After 1852 the wet collodion process replaced earlier photographic methods; it reduced exposure time and permitted an unlimited number of prints on paper. But it was not until about 1880, with the work of Marey and the use by Eastman Kodak of a dry-plate process with gelatino-bromide, that the genuine snapshot appeared.

Degas's opinion of the young painters who were searching for spontaneity in the open air of Fontainebleau forest was not very different from that of Count Nieuwerkerke, except that it was not their linen but their apparent laxity that annoyed Degas. "If I were the government," he said, "I would have a brigade of gendarmes to keep an eye out for people who do landscape from nature... I don't want to bring about anyone's death; I would insist that they load with birdshot to begin with."

He was against all that was facile. "Instantaneity is nothing but photography," he said. Photography had advanced a long way since 1822 when Nicéphore Niepce had needed forty hours to make an exposure, or even since the time of Daguerre who had needed an hour. The invention of the wet collodion plate around 1850 had reduced exposure time to a few seconds, with the result that the "snapshot" was about to pinion the world. Towards 1860 Adolphe Braun had taken his bulky camera into the country and had begun photographing landscape. His soft sepia prints of woods and fields—resembling the paintings of Corot in his later days—were proof of the fact that, then as now, photography inevitably follows the trend of popular taste. The young painters were seeking something quite different.

Degas became a passionate photographer; he liked the simplicity and the economy of the photograph, the unexpected view it sometimes gave of people and places. His analysis of movement, by

The World's Fair of 1855 gave scant notice to the new art of photography; in 1867 it was one of the major attractions of the Fair. One of the boldest experimenters was Nadar, a friend of many painters, in whose studios the first impressionist exhibition was to be held. Both portraitist and landscapist, he also excelled in aerial and panoramic views and in scenes of modern life. Photography often confirmed the painters' intuitions and helped them to break away from conventional vision with its moral and sentimental bias. A scientific instrument of knowledge, it justified Manet's objectivity as against the sentimental idealism of the Salon painters and proved how accurately the "naturalists" rendered their sensations. Photography freed the painter from any need to be descriptive or anecdotal. Henceforth he found his justification in independent creation, informed by the power of style, by his personal manner of seeing and painting.

Honoré Daumier:
Nadar Raising Photography to the Height of Art.
Lithograph published in "Le Boulevard," 1862.

Nadar: Aerial View of Paris Taken from a Balloon, 1859.
Wet Collodion.

  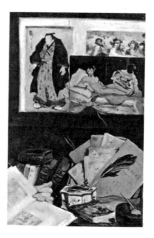

*Ando Hiroshige: Yabukoji at Atagoshita.
Print from "One Hundred Celebrated
Places of Edo," 1856-1859.*

*Hiroshige II: Kiribatake at Akasaka.
Print from "One Hundred Celebrated
Places of Edo," 1856-1859.*

*Edouard Manet: Portrait of Emile Zola
(detail), 1868.*

breaking it down into successive frames, was the precursor of cinema technique, and certain of his later paintings would make use of optical distortions resembling those obtained in film photography, the flare of a woman's skirt while dancing, for example. Yet, there is nothing less photographic than Degas's paintings.

Another historical event, the opening of the Japanese Treaty Ports by Commodore Perry in 1854, was to have even more interesting consequences on painting. Japanese craft work had made its first appearance at the Universal Exposition of 1855. A small shop, called La Porte Chinoise, opened in the rue de Rivoli and its exotic merchandise, called *chinoiserie,* was suddenly a la mode. Kimonos were worn and oriental knick-knacks began to make their appearance in the salons of the well-to-do and, consequently, in contemporary painting. Whistler began a collection of blue-and-white chinaware and Degas's friend, James Tissot, collected Japanese art. Félix Bracquemond, a young artist and engraver, discovered a volume of Hokusai prints which had been used as packing in a crate from the Orient. About the same time prints by Hiroshige and others arrived in Paris. The delicate colors and the fine drawings on silk and ricepaper excited the young French artists. Manet found inspiration in prints which were flat, without shadows or modelling. It was Degas, however, who gave these works the study and analysis they demanded. He noted with delight their rejection of the picturesque, their use of pure color in flat masses and yet the multiple gradation of values. Nothing in Degas's subsequent painting suggests that he was an admirer of the Orient, but it is from this date that his pictures sometimes make use of an audacious foreshortening of perspective, or the subject of the picture is placed off-center, or he catches the ungainly attitude of an arrested gesture. From the Japanese prints the young artists learned to treat space as a positive element in their pictures. Most interesting of all, perhaps, was the recovery of the "bird's eye view" of landscape; Monet, Manet and Pissarro learned to paint scenes looking down from balconies or rooftops.

"Admirable, this Japanese exhibition. Hiroshige is a marvelous impressionist. Monet, Rodin and I are enthralled by him. I am glad to have done my snow and flood effects; these Japanese artists are a confirmation of our way of seeing."

Pissarro, February 3, 1893

The Japanese Ambassadors in Nadar's Studio.

The Discovery of Japanese Prints and Their Influence on the Impressionists

Because of the popularity of things Japanese between 1860 and 1900, there has been a tendency to exaggerate the influence of Japanese prints on impressionist painting. Rather than a stylistic influence, they came as a confirmation of vision and design. After the opening up of Japan by Commodore Perry in 1854, both the artists and the public of the West were quickly attracted by the decorative quality of Japanese prints and artefacts. The French engraver Félix Bracquemond is said to have been the first to discover the beauty of the Japanese art style by way of some Hokusai prints which had already reached Paris by 1855. In 1862 a Madame Desoye opened a shop in the Rue de Rivoli, called La Porte Chinoise, and here Degas, Bracquemond, Whistler, Stevens and Legros discovered the strong simple design of Far Eastern art. In the prints they admired the unusual layouts, the sober and synthetic quality of the form, the wealth and purity of the tones, the clarity of the light, the originality of the pictorial effects and above all the simplicity of the means employed. Whistler, Manet, Fantin-Latour, Degas and Monet all familiarized themselves with the prints of Hokusai, Utamaro and above all Hiroshige. A pavilion at the 1867 World's Fair made Japan fashionable.

With the Meiji restoration in 1868, the emperor regained control of the country; as a result, many of the feudal nobles fled and their collections came into the market, many works being bought up by western collectors. The Japanese pavilion at the Paris World's Fair of 1878 was a great success and Japanese art was further popularized. Always responsive to aesthetic currents, Whistler, as early as 1864, began applying the lessons of Japanese taste and design. Degas, more influenced by the spirit than the form, made use of such Japanese effects as off-center design, foreshortened perspective and the form-movement synthesis, while Monet, in his last great figure painting, entitled *Japonnerie*, also fell under the spell.

Two French critics, who were friends of the Impressionists, were connoisseurs of Japanese art: Philippe Burty, who began a collection in 1863, and Théodore Duret, who after a trip around the world brought back some important works in 1873. Exhibited at Durand-Ruel's twenty years later, these works continued to appeal to the Impressionists. On February 2, 1893, Pissarro wrote to his son: "I saw Monet at the Japanese exhibition. By George, these pictures show how right we were. There are some gray sunsets which are stunningly impressionistic."

Claude Monet: Japonnerie, 1876.

James McNeill Whistler:
Caprice in Purple and Gold,
No. 2: The Golden Screen,
1864.

Cézanne Divides his Time between Paris and Aix

"But, mind you, all the pictures done inside, in the studio, will never be worth the ones done in the open air. In depicting outdoor scenes, the contrasts of the figures against the background are astonishing, and the landscape is magnificent. I see wonderful things, and I must make up my mind to do only open air things.

"I have already told you about a canvas I am going to tackle; it will represent Marion and Valabrègue going out to the motif (the landscape, I mean). The sketch that Guillemet liked, the one I did from nature, makes all the rest fall away and seem bad. I fancy all the pictures by the old masters representing things in the open air were actually done without a model, for they do not seem to me to have the truthful, above all the original look that nature provides. Father Gibert of the museum having urged me to visit the Musée Bourguignon, I went there with Baille, Marion and Valabrègue. I found everything bad. This is quite consoling. I am rather bored, work alone occupies me a little and I pine away less when I'm with somebody. The only people I see are Valabrègue, Marion and now Guillemet...

"But I tell you again, I am a little depressed, but for no particular reason. As you know, I don't know why this moodiness comes over me. It returns every evening when the sun goes down and then it starts raining. It makes me so gloomy."

Letter from Cézanne to Zola,
written at Aix, about October 19, 1866

Paul Cézanne: A Modern Olympia, 1872-1873.

In Degas, Japanese painting and the photograph combined to give his work an instantaneity and flatness, "a strangeness of design," says Clive Bell, "which was the strangeness of fact," and made him "a renderer of character of a precise and remorseless impartiality hitherto unknown."

In the 1865 Salon Degas exhibited his first picture, a medieval scene entitled: *The Misfortunes of the Town of Orléans.* It was one of his old *machines.* He had very little regard for the Salons and, unlike his impoverished contemporaries, had no need of them as a means of self-promotion. It was Zola's idea that Degas's paintings were destined to be overlooked in the great fairs or the Salons and that, therefore, he needed to exhibit with a smaller, more select group of artists, hence his association with those who were to become the Impressionists. In fact, Degas takes his place with Manet, Monet and Pissarro as one of the leading innovators of his time.

"Everything in a picture is in the interrelationships," Degas once said. "We paint the sun with the yoke of an egg. Go, put your canvas in the sun!" Only an impressionist could, at that time, have thought of the sun as a fried egg.

As soon as Zola began writing regularly for the newspapers, he toured the studios in the company of Cézanne. In this way they saw Pissarro, Degas, Renoir, Fantin-Latour, Monet and Manet (who painted a portrait of Zola) at work. Cézanne had been greatly moved by Manet's *Déjeuner sur l'herbe,* seeing it as a new approach to painting, a vision at once cool and ardent, a technique both casual and studied. He was not deceived, as many critics had been, by Manet's apparently careless brushstrokes, but saw immediately that the accidental element concealed an unprecedented virtuosity and refinement. He was critical only of Manet's color which he felt to be "poor in sensation." His awe of Manet produced a curious polarity in Cézanne: he scorned the gentlemanly mask which concealed the consummate artist in Manet and allowed him, as it were, to ambush his material; at the same time Cézanne made a profound obeisance to Manet's work by painting his own *Déjeuner sur l'herbe* and several *Olympias* (in which an hirsute, if balding, gentleman watches the sleeping odalisque being stripped of her covering by a Negro maid), a compliment as well as a comment on Manet. Cézanne's painting, previously heavy in impasto, became lighter, clearer, after he had seen the Manets.

Cézanne had not been overly distressed by public reaction to his own, or others', painting at the Salon des Refusés, but saw the Refusés as a means by which unrecognized painters like himself might continue to exhibit in public, if only, as Zola said, "to put the Academicians in the wrong." For several seasons he continued to address demands for a regular Salon des Refusés to the Academy, but without result, obviously because public reaction in '64 had confirmed public confidence in the Jury. However, in 1865, when the Jury was particularly tolerant, Cézanne's work was still refused. For the next Salon, that of '66, Cézanne prepared two oil paintings bearing the wholly irrelevant titles of *An Afternoon in Naples or Le Grog au Vin* and *La femme à la puce;* they too were rejected.

These are dark days for the young artist. He calls painting "the métier of a dog," but when he paints, he chuckles, "as if I were tickling myself." And he exclaims desperately, "I am never finished, never, never." He is gay in the morning, depressed at evening. A friend describes him as "terrible, hallucinated, like a beast in a kind of divine frenzy of hard work." Zola wrote to a friend: "Cézanne works; he affirms himself more and more in the original way of his nature. I have much hope for him. Besides we reckon that he will be refused for ten years. He seeks an opportunity of making some painting, great paintings, oils of four or five meters." To all of which Cézanne made reply: "In following the way of virtue one is always recompensed by men, never by painting."

On his allowance of two hundred francs a month Cézanne was no longer obliged to seek work, but he was often desperately hard up. On these occasions he would take an armful of his canvases and make a tour of the various dealers, ready to accept any price for them. On one of these excursions he chanced to meet his equally hard-up friend, Jean de Cabannes, called Cabaner, a talented composer who made a meager living playing piano in the cafés, jobs which he invariably lost through playing his own advanced compositions. When Cabaner asked Cézanne to show him his paintings, and immediately expressed admiration of them, Cézanne gave him the paintings, delighted to have an intelligent admirer.

When his allowance was exhausted Cézanne usually returned to Aix and lived with his family. Here his life was less disturbed and he could experiment freely without having his friends looking over his shoulder, in effect. On these trips he painted portraits of his father (reading Zola's newspaper), his mother and his sister, portraits also of his friends, Achille Emperaire, Anthony Valabrègue and A. F. Marion. He borrowed popular magazines from his sister and enlarged the illustrations, transforming them into Daumier-like paintings, often employing the palette knife after the manner of Courbet (a method held in anathema by the Academicians). He also painted some light-hearted murals on the theme of the Four Seasons which he jokingly signed in large letters, "Ingres." It was not his intention, or belief, that any of this work, save perhaps the portraits, would survive. Business had been very good for the Cézanne-Cabassol Bank and in 1859 Louis-Auguste Cézanne had bought a noble, if crumbling old eighteenth century mansion called Jas de Bouffan, about a mile out of Aix. During its restoration Cézanne took a hand in the interior decoration, painting for the walls of the salon several large panels. Later designated *Repentant Magdalene* and *Dead Christ in Limbo*, they were executed in the powerful, if heavy, style of his early allegorical painting. Discovered many years later they were lifted from the walls, framed, and after passing through several hands, were purchased by an anonymous benefactor of the Louvre for eight million francs.

They mark an important crisis in Cézanne's development. In these murals, and in similar paintings, says Roger Fry, "one sees the battle between the baroque tendencies of his visual imagination and the strong impulses in the other direction, the direction primitive and almost Byzantine of his interpretation of things seen."

Paul Cézanne: Portrait of Louis-Auguste Cézanne, the Artist's Father, 1866-1867.

"His spirits, though often in a ferment, clear up sometimes and his painting, encouraged by some genuine commissions, promises to reward his efforts; in a word, the 'sky of the future seems at times less dark.' On his return to Paris you will see some pictures that will be much to your liking; among others . . . a portrait of his father in a large armchair which looks very well. The painting is in a blond tonality and most attractive; his father looks like a pope on his throne, were it not for the 'Siècle' which he is reading [actually 'L'Evénement,' the paper in which Zola had just published his courageous articles on the Salon]. In a word, all's well and you will shortly be seeing some very fine things indeed, depend upon it."

Letter from Antoine Guillemet to Zola, November 2, 1866

Manet and His Models

When Manet's *Portrait of Eva Gonzalès* was exhibited at the 1870 Salon, the critic Laurent Pichat could write with an insolence that seems incredible now: "The female saints in the desert or handed over to the executioner were no more courageous than this young lady who has permitted M. Manet to portray her full-length in so dingy a white dress. And far from expressing her horror, she laughs at the ordeal, she smiles in the midst of her squalor as if in the midst of an apotheosis" (*Le Réveil*, May 13, 1870).

Edouard Manet: *Portrait of Eva Gonzalès*, 1870.

Manet's dislike of professional models and his bad luck with amateurs caused him to enlist his friends in that capacity at every opportunity. Madame Morisot told a friend: "He tells you this in a very natural way, that he meets people who avoid him in order not to discuss his painting with him and that, observing this, he no longer has the courage to beg anyone to pose for him." One method of overcoming the reluctance of friends to pose for him, was to agree to teach them something about his technique. In this way he obtained the services of two very distinguished young women: Eva Gonzalès and Berthe Morisot.

Eva Gonzalès was the daughter of Emmanuel Gonzalès, a journalist and novelist of Spanish extraction, who was Secretary of the Society of Men of Letters. Eva was twenty-one, a bosomy brunette whose ambition was to be a painter. Manet put on a great act, arranging a still life with flowers and holding forth, à la Corot, on values. Meanwhile Manet painted Eva in a pose in which she sits stiffly back from her framed picture, elegantly coiffured, holding her palette with little finger extended, looking away from the canvas but at the same time applying brush to it. One is reminded of a remark made by R. H. Wilenski about a picture exhibited by Eva some years later, to the effect that "it is so like Manet's paintings that it is impossible not to assume that he painted most of it": in his portrait of Eva, Manet had already made his comment on Eva's artistry.

Berthe Morisot was something very different. "Manet preaches at me," she wrote her sister, "and everlastingly holds up Mademoiselle Gonzalès as an example; she is so well behaved, so industrious, she can put a job through—whereas I, it seems, am good for nothing. He has begun and re-begun her portrait twenty-five times; she poses for him every day, and every evening he takes her face out and rubs it down with soap!" In a later letter she wrote: "All Manet's admiration is at present concentrated on Mademoiselle Gonzalès; but he cannot get on with her portrait; he is now at the fortieth sitting and the head has again been taken out."

Manet had no trouble painting Berthe. She is the dark, romantic woman—he painted her green eyes black—on the left in *The Balcony*, a picture inspired by a balcony picture by Goya, which provoked the customary storm of criticism. "Poor Manet," Berthe wrote her sister, "he told me that I had brought him luck and that he had had an offer for *The Balcony*. I should like it to be true for his sake, but I am afraid that he will be disappointed."

The painting lessons evidently continued. "To my great surprise," Berthe wrote her sister, "it seems that what I do is decidedly better than Eva Gonzalès." What did Berthe learn from Manet? "She was not his pupil," says Théodore Duret. "She adopted the new technique and the brilliant execution. These her own exceptional gifts enabled her to appropriate. In her subsequent work the scale of tones and the qualities of clarity and light were derived from Manet, but the fundamental element of her work—her feminine individuality and her personal way of feeling—remained unchanged." After meeting Manet Berthe began painting figures. In 1874 she married his younger brother Eugène.

Though the young painters may not yet have found common ground for their revolt, they soon found a common meeting place. The Café Guerbois, 11 Grand-rue des Batignolles, was easy of access from the studios in Montmartre. The Café was decorated in the contemporary, i.e. Empire, style with gilded mirrors, marble-topped tables and island hat-stands (very necessary on account of the popularity of silk toppers). The waiters wore white cheesecloth aprons and black waistcoats; somewhere back of the *caisse* there was a billiard room. In the first room of the Café, on the left side, two tables were permanently reserved for Manet and his friends. Philippe Burty and Edmond Duranty wrote novels about the place and Fantin-Latour borrowed the cast of characters for one of the group paintings, upon which his fame rests: Manet, Monet, Renoir and Bazille, together with Astruc, Maître, Scholderer and Zola. All were young, well-dressed and neatly bearded; Bazille, almost a head taller than the others, is posed like the mounted officer he was soon to become.

In the spring of 1865 Monet had had an unexpected success: two of his marines had been accepted by the Salon and were warmly praised by the critics. Because of the similarity of their names Monet's pictures were placed beside those of Manet, with the result that Manet received many of the compliments intended for Monet. Manet studied the signatures on both seascapes and thought it a joke in very bad taste. "Who is this Monet who looks as if he had taken my name and happens thus to profit by the noise I make?" he asked. The incident was made to be caricatured, as it was by André Gill, with the caption: "Monet or Manet? Monet. But it is to Manet that we owe this Monet. Bravo, Monet! Thanks Manet!" At the Café Guerbois Manet soon learned who Monet was.

Zola was a regular visitor. A short, dark, vigorous young man, he had thrown himself without reserve into the battle against official art. "You know what effect Manet's canvases produce at the Salon?" he wrote. "They burst the walls open, quite simply. All around is spread the fashionable, artistic confectioners' sweets, trees in sugar candy and houses in pastry paste, little men in gingerbread and women made of vanilla cream." The phrases are too colloquial not to have been uttered (by Zola or another) and, if uttered, where else but at the Café Guerbois! So, on Monet: "I admit that the canvas which stopped me... was M. Monet's *Camille*. This picture tells me the whole story of energy and truth." And again, on Pissarro: "Monsieur P. is an unknown man, of whom no doubt nobody will speak... I consider it my duty to shake his hand vigorously." This year, 1866, an Alsatian artist, Jules Holzapffel, committed suicide after the Jury of the Salon had rejected his painting, and a Senator, the Marquis de Boissy, joined a public demonstration in favor of reviving the Salon des Refusés. Plenty to talk about. Indeed, Zola's outspokenness was soon to cost him his job at *L'Evénement*.

In 1867 the Empire staged its last (though it could not know this) World's Fair. The King of Prussia came to see Mr. Krupp's steel siege guns on exhibition at the Champ de Mars and the Parisian crowds went for happy excursions on the new bateaux-mouche. The Jury of the great Art Show turned down the paintings of Manet, Monet,

Edouard Manet: La Parisienne. Drawing.

"Edouard [Manet] often used to say that he learned his trade over again with each picture he painted. It is this sincerity, this impressionability, that gives his work so much charm."

Berthe Morisot, *Notebooks*, 1885

Edouard Manet: Berthe Morisot with a Fan, 1874.

View of the Paris World's Fair of 1867. Print.

Following a visit to Manet's studio, Zola voiced his enthusiastic admiration for the painter's work. On May 4 and 7, 1866, he published articles in *L'Evénement* emphasizing the novelty of Manet's talent and the genuine contemporaneity of his style. The reaction was immediate: a flood of letters of protest and indignation poured into the offices of the paper, and on May 14 the editor, M. de Villemessant, announced to his offended readers that another critic, Edouard Pelloquet, had been commissioned to write three articles as a "corrective and counterpoise to M. Zola's three articles." Disgusted by this compromise, Zola resigned from the staff of *L'Evénement* and again took up the defense of Manet in a book published in May 1866, *Mes Haines.*

Zola's study of Manet was published in its entirety in the *Revue du XIXᵉ siècle* on January 1, 1867, under the title "Une nouvelle manière en peinture: M. Edouard Manet." Later that year it was reissued in the form of a brochure by the publisher Dentu.

Title page of Zola's study of Manet, published by Dentu, Paris 1867.

Renoir, Sisley, Bazille, as well as those of Courbet. Manet, like Courbet in 1855, and again this year, held his own one-man show in a wooden shack near the Pont de l'Alma, where he exhibited fifty-three oil paintings, prefacing the catalogue with the disarming observation: "M. Manet has never wished to protest... He has no pretension either to overthrow an established mode of painting, or to create a new one. He has simply tried to be himself and not another..."

At the last moment Manet put up a huge painting, calculated to incite, at the very least, a major riot. Maximilian, brother of the Austrian Emperor, had been installed on the Mexican throne largely by force of French arms; but the Mexicans, fighting a guerrilla war, had obliged the French to withdraw and abandon Maximilian who had been captured, condemned to death and, not more than a couple of months earlier, shot by a Mexican firing squad in the company of several high-ranking French officers. Manet painted the scene in his studio, using models, and obtaining a likeness of the late Emperor from a photograph. "Pure Goya," said Renoir, "yet Manet was never so much himself." Manet's inspiration had been Goya's famous painting of Murat's troops executing the citizens of Madrid, May 2, 1808, and he had given no thought to the embarrassment the picture might have created for Napoleon III. He was that innocent. Or was he?

Manet was obliged to take the picture down and it is characteristic of him that he had no further interest in it. Madame Manet rolled it up and stowed it away where it was discovered years later, ruined by damp.

Manet's naiveté was a continual source of wonderment at the Café Guerbois whose habitués tended to be politically conscious, if not downright wary. Pissarro was a socialist, in the pre-Marxian meaning of that term, and though idealistic, anarchistic and egalitarian, he could never have pretended to Manet's innocence. He was one of the few artists, beside Courbet and Degas, to have read Proudhon's *Du Principe de l'Art*. He would not have agreed with Degas's comment on that work, however: "How admirable," Degas once said, "to take a subject, hear it developed in conversation, and then write three hundred pages."

Degas was a regular visitor to the Café Guerbois and one of the more intransigent in his views. "I was, or I seemed, to be hard with everyone," he wrote later, "through a sort of passion for brutality, which came from my uncertainty and my bad humor. I felt myself so badly made, so badly equipped, so weak, whereas it seemed to me that my calculations on art were so right."

Manet and Degas once quarrelled violently at the Café Guerbois. The cause of the quarrel has been forgotten, but history remembers that each returned a painting which the other had presented to him. Degas got back his mutilated portrait of Madame Manet playing the piano; the record is not precise on what painting was returned to Manet.

Renoir had reservations about much that was said at the Café sessions. "They reproached Corot with reworking his landscapes in the studio," he said later. "They vomited on Ingres. I let them talk. I thought that Corot was right and I had my secret delight in the pretty little tummy of *La Source* and the neck and arms of Madame Rivière. In front of a masterpiece I am content to enjoy myself; it is the professors who have discovered the defects of the masters." But on the topic of music, ex-choir boy Renoir had no reservations: he was all for Berlioz against Wagner.

"Manet's show opens in two days' time. He's on tenterhooks. I'll tell you all about it in due course. It will be curious to see the opening. As for Courbet, he opens a week from today, that is next Monday. With him it is quite a different matter. Just imagine, he is inviting all the artists in Paris for the opening day. He is sending out three thousand invitations. And indeed with each one he includes his catalogue. Just to show you the way he does things, he intends to keep his shed where he has already installed a studio for himself on the upper floor, and next year whenever we please he will let it to those of us who would like to hold an exhibition there. So let's work hard and we'll turn up there with things above reproach."

Letter from Monet to Bazille, May 21, 1867

Courbet's One-Man Show at the Rond-Point de l'Alma, Paris, in 1867.

Edouard Manet: View of the Paris World's Fair, 1867.

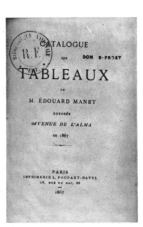

Fearing that his work would be rejected at the World's Fair exhibition of 1867, Manet followed Courbet's example and held a one-man show in a wooden pavilion erected at his own expense at the corner of Avenue de l'Alma and Avenue de Montaigne, where he exhibited fifty pictures. In the preface to the catalogue he justified his attitude and explained why he took this step:

REASONS FOR HOLDING A ONE-MAN SHOW

Since 1861 M. Manet has been exhibiting or trying to exhibit.

This year he has decided to show the whole of his work directly to the public.

When he first showed at the Salon, M. Manet obtained an honorable mention. But afterwards he found himself too often rejected by the jury not to feel that if ventures into art are a contest, at least the fight must be fought on equal terms, in other words one must be allowed to show what one has done.

Otherwise the painter would be too easily locked inside a circle from which there is no escape. He would be forced to stack his canvases away or roll them up in a garret.

For admission, encouragement and official rewards are, it is said, a warrant of talent in the eyes of part of the public, which is then predisposed in favor of works accepted and prejudiced against those refused. But on the other hand the painter is told that it is the spontaneous reaction of this very public which motivates the cool welcome given to his canvases by the different juries.

Finding himself in this situation, the artist is advised to wait.

To wait for what? For there to be no more jury?

He has preferred to let the public settle the matter.

The artist does not say to you today: "Come and see flawless works," but "Come and see sincere works."

The effect of sincerity is to make these works seem like something in the nature of a protest, whereas in fact the painter has only tried to render his impression.

M. Manet has never wished to protest. On the contrary, it is against him, to his great surprise, that the protesting has been done, because a traditional system of teaching has laid down the forms, methods and aspects of painting, and those who have been schooled in such principles admit no others. From this derives their naïve intolerance. Nothing that departs from their formulas can have any merit, and so they become not only critical but actively hostile.

To exhibit is the vital issue, the *sine qua non* for the artist, for after several viewings people soon get used to what may have surprised and even shocked them. Little by little they understand and accept it.

Time itself acts on pictures with an imperceptible polisher and smoothes away the original asperities.

To exhibit is the way to find friends and allies for the fight.

M. Manet has always recognized talent wherever it is to be found and has no pretension either to overthrow an established mode of painting nor to create a new one. He has simply tried to be himself and not another.

Moreover, M. Manet has met with widespread sympathy and he has come to see the extent to which the judgment of genuinely talented men is becoming more favorable to him day by day.

For the painter, then, it is only a question now of winning over this public which is supposed to be inimical to him.

May 1867

Edouard Manet: *The Execution of the Emperor Maximilian, 1867. Lithograph.*

Some of the Café regulars were wonderfully picturesque. Nadar, a giant of a man who wrote and drew superbly, had made sensational balloon ascents, but was to be known to posterity for his excellent photographs, including portraits of the young painters. Villiers de l'Isle-Adam, bearer of an aristocratic name, was a writer with a little yellow beard, his white hands agitatedly emerging from his shrunken sleeves. Stéphane Mallarmé, a high school teacher of English, who wrote exquisite and obscure poems was often there. "If you would only write just once as you would write for your cook," Berthe Morisot implored him. "But I would not write differently for my cook," said Mallarmé. Constantin Guys, an artist of a previous generation, was a sometime visitor. In its freshness and lightness his work was a premonition of the coming age of painting, of which Baudelaire had warned the academicians: "Modernity, this transitory, fugitive element, metamorphoses of which are so frequent (e.g. in Guys), you have no right to treat it with contempt." It was probably at the Café Guerbois that Courbet made the oft-quoted remark about his own paintings: "They're so beautiful, it's stupid."

Cézanne did not often come. "All those people are *salauds*," he said. "They are as well-dressed as notaries." He did not like the animated atmosphere of the Café and he particularly distrusted Manet because of his impeccable dress, his doe-skin gloves, silver-topped cane, silk hat and polished shoes. But one day his friend Cabaner brought Cézanne along to the Café Guerbois. He is wearing a huge black felt hat deformed by age, and a long overcoat, once

Poster of the Manet Exhibition held in New York in 1879.

The first impressionist exhibition in the United States took place in March 1886, organized by Durand-Ruel and sponsored by the American Art Association in New York. But the first canvas of the new French school to be seen in the United States was Manet's *Execution of Maximilian*, brought to America by the French singer Madame Ambre (of whom Manet had done a portrait) and her impresario Gaston de Beauplan. For political reasons Manet was forbidden to exhibit the picture in France, but it was shown in November 1879 at the Clarendon Hotel in New York and the Gallery Building in Boston. The event was heralded by considerable publicity. But press and public showed little interest, and the idea of a further exhibition in Chicago was abandoned.

The attitude of the critics was reflected by an article in the New York Herald (November 29, 1879): "Manet is the apostle of French naturalism in painting, as Zola is in literature... The faults of his work are many and it is sadly inaccurate... it will appeal more to the artist and the art lover than to the general public, as the work of an original man who goes against conventions."

The Café Guerbois

"The meetings at the Café Guerbois, with painting in light tones and bright colors represented by Manet, and the technique and procedure of open air painting represented by Claude Monet, Pissarro and Renoir, were to have fruitful results. From those meetings sprang the powerful development of art which was soon to go by the name of Impressionism. "

Théodore Duret, *Renoir*

Edouard Manet: Paris Café (Café Guerbois?), 1869. Pen and Ink.

"It wasn't until 1869 that I saw Manet again, but we became close friends at once, as soon as we met. He invited me to come and see him each evening in a café in the Batignolles district where he and his friends met when the day's work in the studio was over. There I met Fantin-Latour and Cézanne, Degas who had just returned from a trip to Italy, the art critic Duranty, Emile Zola who was then making his début in literature, and several others as well. I myself brought along Sisley, Bazille and Renoir. Nothing could be more interesting than the talks we had, with their perpetual clashes of opinion. Your mind was held in suspense all the time, you spurred the others on to sincere, disinterested inquiry and were spurred on yourself, you laid in a stock of enthusiasm that kept you going for weeks on end until you could give final form to the idea you had in mind. You always went home afterwards better steeled for the fray, with a new sense of purpose and a clearer head. "

Monet

black but now weathered to a sickly green, with buttons all the way down to his ankles. This he unfastens and with a galvanic movement of his sturdy shoulders casts it off. He then takes a severe hitch at the red belt holding his baggy trousers, a movement which reveals his blue socks, and then stands black-bearded, a little stooped and agitated by a tremor of nervous worry habitual to him, his large laced boots planted firmly on the ground. He squeezes hands all round, but when Manet extends his firm white hand, Cézanne looks up and says, "No, I cannot shake hands with you, Monsieur Manet, for I have not washed for eight days. " Then Cézanne sits in a corner, appearing to ignore the general conversation and keeping his opinions to himself, until some particular remark offends him, and he goes off without a word of farewell.

In the early months of 1870 Manet and the critic, Edmond Duranty, quarrelled at the Café Guerbois. The cause may have been a Duranty anecdote about a man, standing before Manet's picture *The Music Lesson,* saying with a shudder, "What a debauch!" (A story Duranty took great pains to explain away in a subsequent issue of *Paris Journal*.) Manet demanded an explanation and on not receiving a satisfactory reply, slapped Duranty. Only a duel could assuage such an insult and so the two friends soon found themselves face-to-face, rapiers poised. According to Zola, who was Manet's second, both antagonists were ignorant of the art of fencing, but attacked each other with such intrepidity that the rapiers were twisted into the semblance of corkscrews. Manet, having pricked Duranty's breast, was considered the winner. They remained the best of friends.

Alas, that national tempers were not so easily assuaged that fatal year. The Café Guerbois outlasted war, occupation, siege and revolution, but never again boasted so brilliant a company. Remade over into the Brasserie Muller it succumbed to the demolishers within living memory and a "One-Price" store now occupies the site.

The new railroad which brought Saint-Germain to within twenty minutes of Paris also brought out the Parisians, the young men and women who could not afford carriages and had not yet discovered the velocipede. Monsieur Fournaise's restaurant, a wooden platform built out from the river bank at Chatou, where guests, sitting on backless forms before long plank tables, dined in the open air under a blue canopy, was called La Grenouillère, not because the place literally resembled a frog pond, but because, says Jean Renoir, this was *argot* for the young women, the little grisettes, who came there with their athletic young men for summer weekends. Renoir went there because the place was in the popular style and "the frogs" and their sweat-shirted partners often posed for him without recompense.

Monet and Camille came to live at Bougival, a little further downstream, not because Monet needed models, but because the river at this point was broad enough to support regattas, rowing races and other colorful marine events. His rejection by the 1869 Salon had been a severe blow, but Shipowner Gaudibert had advanced a sum sufficient for him to take a cheap summer rental. He tried to drum up commissions, by writing to an influential friend, saying,

"I'll do anything at all for any price." He wrote Bazille, asking for money with which to buy paints and, on not receiving a prompt answer, wrote again: "Dear friend, would you like to know how we lived during the eight days I have been waiting for your letter? Well, ask Renoir, who brought us some of his own bread, so that we should not die. For eight days, no bread, no wine, no kitchen fire, no light. It's appalling."

Desperation seems to have liberated their brushes from all formalistic restraint, for it is in the pictures they made here that the particular technique of applying paint to canvas in vivid strokes, commas and dots, which future art historians would define as the "impressionist style" got its start. In fact, it was the water, the soft rolling ripples caused by the rowing boats and the deep moving reflections of sun and tree-shadows which completely absorbed them. They had to work fast and without much cogitation, but being now thoroughly versatile painters, accustomed to "instant" brush-work, at ease in the open air, they captured the color and gaiety of the aquatic and gastronomic revels. The oarsmen and the "little frogs" are there; Lise is there and we catch a glimpse of Camille's old striped dress. There are probably no more unselfconsciously hedonistic paintings to be found anywhere since the age of Pompeii.

Monet, finally running out of paint, rages against Bazille: "There's nothing for me to do except break my head against a wall . . . I have indeed a dream, a picture of bathing at Grenouillère for which I have made some bad sketches, but it's a dream." Said Renoir: "We don't eat every day, yet I am happy in spite of it, because, as far as painting is concerned, Monet is good company."

As Kenneth Clark has said: "The riverside café of La Grenouillère is the birthplace of Impressionism."

Bougival
Early Ventures in Open Air Painting

"In the vicinity of Paris there were also places to be found whose attraction lay not only in the beauty of the site but in the pleasant outings that took place there and the merry crowd of pleasure seekers. There was a time, beginning about 1848 and ending about 1885, when the banks of the Seine from Asnières and Argenteuil to Bougival and Marly were thronged with young people from Paris. There they were free to amuse themselves. They could go boating, swimming, dancing. On Sundays, visitors of all sorts, even the placid bourgeois, would come out that way to enjoy the fun. There was no Parisian at that time who was not familiar with the region, having frequented it himself or heard about it from those who did frequent it."

Théodore Duret, *Renoir*

Charles-François Daubigny: *Train and River Boats. Pen and Ink.*

View of Bougival. Lithograph.

View of La Grenouillère. Print.

"Here indeed is a good opportunity to draw up a rational and historical theory of the beautiful, in contradistinction to the theory of a unique and absolute beauty; and to show that beauty is always and inevitably of dual composition, although the impression it produces is one; for the difficulty of detecting the variable elements of beauty in the unity of the impression does not make it any less necessary to include variety in its composition. Beauty is made up of an eternal and invariable element whose quantity is extremely difficult to determine, and of a relative, circumstantial element deriving in turn, or all at once, from the period, from fashion, morality, passion. Without this second element, which is like the amusing, titillating, appetizing envelope of the divine cake, the first element would be indigestible, unappreciated, ill-adapted and ill-suited to human nature."

Baudelaire, *The Painter of Modern Life*

Gustave Courbet: *The Hammock*, 1844.

Camille Corot: *Landscape at Mornex, Savoie*, 1842. Drawing.

"The painting is attractive in every way: accuracy of effects, a delicate range of colors, unity and vividness of impression, excellent distribution of light. This art looks so simple, yet how rare it is, how rewarding to study! It would have been impossible to put more candor than this into a theme whose entire charm stems from light. "

Zacharie Astruc describing Renoir's *Lise* in his review of the 1868 Salon.

An early work, Courbet's *Hammock* was one of his first masterpieces. Here he entered the new field of *open-air figure painting*, the theme over which Manet and the Impressionists were to fight their battle against academicism. Breaking with convention, Courbet preferred a girl's unsophisticated charms to the artificial allurements of goddesses and muses. An outline quivering with sensuality chisels the languid figure of the sleeping beauty and sets it off from the dark landscape which acts as a foil to the subtle transparency of the clothes. In the *Déjeuner sur l'herbe*, Manet, on the contrary, veiled his feelings behind the cool intentness of his scrutiny. The odd and unexpected group of figures, a female nude and two well-dressed gentlemen talking by a stream, gave the picture a provocativeness that made the modernity of his vision pass unnoticed. It was left for the Impressionists not only to integrate the figure into its natural setting but to make it share to the full the radiant life of nature. In this drawing by Pissarro the human presence is swallowed up in the landscape, but already Monet and Renoir had achieved a new harmony between man and his milieu. Renoir's *Lise* is sensorially very close to Courbet, but the full, metamorphosing glow of natural light makes all the difference between him and his great predecessor.

Camille Pissarro: Under the Trees, 1862. Drawing.

Auguste Renoir: Lise with a Sunshade, 1867.

Frédéric Bazille: Family Reunion, 1867.

Frédéric Bazille: Study for the Family Reunion, 1867.

Picnic on the Grass, Women in the Garden, Family Reunion—such themes as these enabled Monet and his friends to arrive at a new harmony between man and nature. The latter no longer appears as a mute and indifferent setting or a sentimental backdrop re-echoing the moods of romantic heroes; warm, welcoming, alive, it has become a source of bountiful enjoyments and relaxation. The country, for Millet a place of unrelieved hard work, became for the Impressionists a wide world for happy outings on fine days.

With his *Déjeuner sur l'herbe* (Picnic on the Grass) Monet aimed at producing the first figure composition painted entirely in the open air; but the canvas proved too big, the subject too complicated and the weather too unsettled for him to realize his ambition. In 1867, however, he succeeded in doing so with his *Women in the Garden*. Here the direct study of nature brought home to Monet the importance of light, of its elusive shiftings and variability. He accordingly renounced the traditional chiaroscuro treatment of volumes and successfully integrated figures into landscape by means of unified lighting. By placing his models in the shade of the trees instead of standing them against a background of leafage, he achieved a new unity of lighting in which cast shadows join harmoniously with natural shadows. Already the sharply impinging light filtering through the trees breaks up surfaces and alters the color of things. Monet had discovered his true subject: light.

The generous and inseparable friend of Monet and Renoir, Bazille was led to tackle the same themes as his friends. He joined them on their painting excursions to Chailly in Fontainebleau forest, and he bought *Women in the Garden*, thus helping to tide Monet over a period of desperate poverty. Returning to the family home at Montpellier during the summer of 1867, Bazille attempted a similar picture. The southern light was warmer and steadier than that of the Ile de France, but he came to the same conclusions regarding the coldness and transparency of shadows. Like Monet, he replaced gray with blue in the folds of the girls' white dresses. His line is more classical, his respect for volumes greater, but he could not resist breaking up the shadows that dapple the foreground.

"Unable to venture on a large composition, I have done my best to paint as simple a subject as possible. Moreover, to my thinking, the subject matters little, provided my work is interesting from the painterly point of view. I have chosen the modern period, because that is the one which I understand best, which I find most alive for people living now..."

Frédéric Bazille, letter to his parents, early 1866

"Everything is bright and tender, and each figure is a living presence, glowing with the beauty of the day and hour, an hour arrested for the future. Henceforth this moment of life caught unawares will keep its charm, these immobilized gestures will testify to the grace of these vanished figures amidst the masterpieces of art. These four women in white so different from each other, these flowers, this verdure, this bit of blue sky—this is youth and springtime."

Gustave Geffroy, Claude Monet

James McNeill Whistler: In Bright Sunlight, 1857-1858. Etching.

Claude Monet: Women in the Garden, 1867.

Monet intended his *Déjeuner*, which he was preparing for the 1866 Salon, as the manifesto of open air painting. In order to get the benefit of natural lighting, he planned to paint the picture as much as possible out of doors. In the spring of 1865 he chose a suitable clearing in Fontainebleau Forest and asked Bazille to join him there; but a leg accident obliged him to postpone his project until the following year.

Monet's boldness aroused the curiosity of his friends, and they came out to see this ambitious attempt to replace studio work by a direct confrontation with nature, studied idealization by the observation of ephemeral phenomena. Everybody gave him advice, especially Courbet whom he admired. But he was vexed at this interference. Above all, his work was delayed by unsettled weather and he realized he would not be able to carry his analysis as far as he had hoped. A few days before the Salon opened, he abandoned the canvas; it was later divided into three parts.

Le Déjeuner sur l'Herbe

Monet's *Déjeuner sur l'Herbe* is one of the key works in the evolution of painting. For the first time an artist set out to paint a figure composition in the open air, on the spot, in order to recreate the setting in all its immediacy. In trying to execute so large a canvas out of doors he met with many difficulties and setbacks. "At that period he embarked on his big picture, the *Déjeuner sur l'Herbe*, now cut up into several pieces, but still so fine in its figure grouping. The scene is set in Fontainebleau Forest, and Monet resolutely brought all the power of his youthful art to bear on representing figures just as they appear out of doors, in their green and leafy setting. Here was a real revolution in the practice of painting, and one that wholly justifies the name of Open Air School given to the painters who followed the same principle of observation as Monet ... This vast picture is still in his studio on the day I write these lines, and I hope it will only leave his studio for the Luxembourg and then for the Louvre, its natural home, for it marks an epoch in the history of painting, as well as being an extraordinarily fine and energetic affirmation of a talent seeking its way and finding it," wrote the great friend of the Impressionists, the critic Gustave Geffroy.

A few years after Monet, Cézanne took up the same theme, which he later treated twice again during his impressionist period. But the version made in 1869-1870 is particularly interesting since it so clearly reflects Cézanne's character. Perpetually at odds with himself, dissatisfied and tormented, he seems almost bewildered by the magnitude of the task he has set himself. And by a typically southern reflex, he takes refuge in irony. He takes an ironic view of his own temperament, which he knows to be violent and impassioned, and of his theme: this picnic on the grass, a sort of Embarkation for Cythera of the bourgeoisie, seems to him to reflect a "joy of life" which he knows is a mirage. Many years later, when he painted his *Bathers*, an incomparable cosmic recreation, he fully and completely achieved his pictorial conception of the harmony and interfusion of figures and nature.

1. *Claude Monet: Fragment of the Déjeuner sur l'Herbe, 1865-1866.*

2. *Claude Monet: Le Déjeuner sur l'Herbe, 1865.*

3. *Henry Peach Robinson: Women and Children in the Country, 1860. Composite Photograph.*

4. *Claude Monet: Le Déjeuner sur l'Herbe, 1866.*

5. *Claude Monet: Le Déjeuner sur l'Herbe, 1865. Sketch.*

6. *Paul Cézanne: Le Déjeuner sur l'Herbe, 1869-1870.*

4

5

6

Comparison between the initial sketch and the painted version of his *Déjeuner sur l'Herbe* shows the progress made by Monet. In the drawing the natural setting remains classical. In the painting the artist replaces the luminous gap of the woodland path by a clearing; avoiding recession and cleaving to the surface, he contrives to render light harmoniously and evenly by filtering it through the dense foliage. Struck by the difference in tone and value between lights and shadows, he adopts a flickering brushstroke, not hesitating to break up a plane of shadow by a few touches of sunlight.

It is interesting to compare Monet's *Déjeuner* with a contemporary photograph of picnickers. The painter contrives a snapshot, while the photographer tries to vie with classical art. The long exposure time emphasizes the volume of figures and light is solidified in a violent contrast; above all, the composition, spiraling up from the three little girls seated on the rock, keeps to the most elementary recipes of the Ecole des Beaux Arts. Monet handles the subject more freely, catching his figures in relaxed attitudes and merging details into the dynamic harmony of the light. While one seems to have photographed a sculptured group, the other captures something of the very breath of life.

"...some Dazzling Seascapes..."

Summer holidays at the seaside became popular with the affluent classes under Napoleon III. But neither Corot nor Courbet—in spite of the latter's success with the fashionable crowd at Trouville and Deauville—allowed any trace of this society atmosphere to appear in their seaside compositions. Corot continued to render the poetic, sentimental light which he carried within himself; Courbet found in the sea a marvelous contrast between majestic power and bold textural effects. Whistler, for his part, though a professed follower of Courbet, whom he accompanied to Trouville in 1865, nevertheless recorded in his seascape an aristocratic vision tinged with aestheticism.

Self-taught and independent-minded, Boudin painted the Channel beaches as he found them, peopled with elegant strollers. He saw that light continually changes the color of things; he found in parasols and summer dresses the spots of color that brightened up the picture and set the grays vibrating. Monet introduced Jongkind to him in 1862. The Dutchman was already an experienced seascape painter whose watercolors had an atmospheric delicacy, a limpid coloring and a sureness of hand unrivaled at that time. The example of his two elders confirmed Monet in the bold handling which close observation of the motif gradually prompted him to adopt, and reassured him as to the accuracy of his sensations.

James McNeill Whistler: Harmony in Blue and Silver: Courbet at Trouville, 1865.

Gustave Courbet: Calm Sea, 1869.

Camille Corot: Rocks on the Seashore, 1870.

Eugène Boudin: Beach at Trouville, 1863.

Johan Barthold Jongkind: Beach at Sainte-Adresse, 1863. Watercolor.

"One is too much preoccupied with what one sees and hears in Paris, however strong-minded one may be, and what I do here will at least have the merit of resembling nobody else because it will simply be the impression of what I alone have felt." Monet, Le Havre 1868

CLAUDE MONET:

Upper left: Seaside Terrace near Le Havre, 1866.
Summer visitors enjoying the sunshine on a flowered terrace overlooking the sea, with its passing ships, while two flags flap in the wind: here Monet combines an open air theme with a vivid impression of a happy day.

Lower left: Hôtel des Roches Noires at Trouville, 1870.
From this time on, in many such open air scenes as this Trouville picture, Monet concentrated on the problem of rendering the vibration of light and this became in effect the real theme of his work. As here, he treated the subject in a less descriptive manner, conjuring it up rather by rapid, allusive touches.

Upper right: Jetty at Honfleur, 1864.
First exhibited at the Salon of 1865, this seascape attracted notice and favorable comment. The critic Paul Mantz, reviewing the Salon in the *Gazette des Beaux Arts*, wrote of Monet's "bold manner of seeing things and compelling the spectator to focus his attention on them."

Lower right: Beach at Sainte-Adresse, 1867.
The study of the sea light revealed to the impressionist painters the importance of the atmosphere, of that evanescent spray of humidity without which light would be invisible. Monet returned each year to the Channel coast, painting the scenes to which he owed his first successes.

La Grenouillère

"In despair. I sold a still life and could then work on for a while. But as usual I've had to call a halt for lack of colors. I alone will have nothing to show for this year." Monet wrote these words on the 25th of September 1869, only a month after he and Renoir had painted their pictures of the Grenouillère. His poverty was such that he gladly accepted the bread Renoir brought him whenever he came to see him. But there is no trace of despair in his painting, which glows with the wealth and variety he had discovered in nature. During this trying summer the ties binding Renoir and Monet were strengthened and they often worked together out of doors. Monet, with his incomparable eye, had already arrived at the observations and procedures which were to crystallize in the impressionist style. He was the leader and pacemaker, and working with him Renoir freed himself from the ascendancy Courbet had gained over him. The two friends painted their pictures of the Grenouillère at the same time, side by side. Monet here stands on the threshold of Impressionism, about to master the last technical inventions which would enable him to record his sensations faithfully and freely. The Impressionists were not in search of any ready-made formula. They were genuine creators with a fresh perception of the world. From 1865 to 1872 they made a series of observations which led them step by step towards a new way of painting, a new mode of expression, for what they had to say had never been said before. They groped their way forward into the unknown, guided not by good taste or studio recipes but by the truth of their own sensations.

"Bougival, the landscape studio of the modern French school."
The Goncourt Brothers, *Journal*

The Bathing Place of La Grenouillère on the Island of Croissy.

Claude Monet: La Grenouillère, 1869.

Inauguration of Bougival Bridge on November 7, 1858.

Auguste Renoir: The Boat, 1867.

It is fascinating to compare these canvases by Monet and Renoir. Monet saw that light is color, that it overlays local tones with warm gleams, and that its absence cools down those tones. By dint of painting directly from nature he had learned to work fast, and his observation of light reflected on water had led him to use an ever freer, more flickering brushstroke. He realized now that his "divisionism," this dense pattern of small touches of color applied in separate strokes, was the only way of rendering the colors he saw before him. While it is easy to shade off any tone towards black or white, it is impossible to mix certain colors chemically without altering them. Seeking to convey with his paints the luminous intensity of the world, he emphasized complementary colors with forceful insistence.

Renoir's vision is gentler, more sensitive, and more poetic. While Monet steps up contrasts, Renoir softens them down in an all-pervading harmony of subdued and silvery colors.

Auguste Renoir:
La Grenouillère, about 1869.

Claude Monet:
La Grenouillère, 1869.

"And there he goes along the roads in the neighborhood of Paris. He is engrossed in the pleasure of painting what he sees, of giving way freely to his emotion, of passionately being a painter of truth. He works on the still completely rural slopes of Montmartre, where there are trees, hedges, fields and animals... Nothing stands between his youthful sensibility and nature. He paints her just as he sees her, in the emotion he receives from her."

Georges Lecomte, *Pissarro*

Camille Pissarro: *The Versailles Road at Louveciennes, 1870.*

Montmartre

Alfred Sisley: *View of Montmartre, 1869.*

The Heights of Montmartre before the Construction of the Sacré-Cœur Basilica, about 1869. Photograph.

Armand Guillaumin: *Montmartre, 1865.*

For Sisley and Pissarro the work of Corot continued to be a living example, but they gradually moved beyond it. They shared the modesty of their old master, who used to say: "Mine is only a small flute, but with it I try to strike the right note." Both of them consistently aimed in their painting at sound pictorial design and an overall harmony of form and color.

The technical inventions of Pissarro, Sisley and Guillaumin are less spectacular than those of Monet; they are no less effective and authentic. Living in the country—even Montmartre was then still quite rural—they had not been prompted to develop the bold free brushwork that Monet had arrived at by studying the reflections of light on water. But they too felt the need to achieve a more accurate rendering of atmosphere, without any intrusion of the picturesque or anecdotal.

Pissarro was a delicate and skillful recorder of the play of light and the beauty of even the most ordinary scenes; the full savor of a season, of its light, its warmth, its odors, is conveyed by every stroke of his brush. In 1903, shortly before his death, he confided to a journalist interviewing him at Le Havre: "I see only patches of color. When I begin a picture, the first thing I try to do is to fix the color scheme. Between this sky and this ground and this water, there is necessarily a relation of colors, and therein lies the great difficulty of painting. What interests me less and less in my art is the material side of painting (lines). The great problem is to bring everything, even the smallest details of the picture, into agreement with the whole, in other words to work out the color harmony."

Sisley and Guillaumin, the latter especially, worked in a more descriptive idiom. They had not yet given up values for color. But the pulsing life of nature, its light, wind and warmth, was already beginning to break up the rigid framework of traditional vision.

Site of a Pitched Battle between Communards and Versaillais, 1871.

The very existence of Impressionism which transformed nature into a private, unformalized field for sensitive vision, shifting with the spectator, made painting an ideal domain of freedom; it attracted many who were tied unhappily to middle class jobs and moral standards, now increasingly problematic and stultifying with the advance of monopoly capitalism.

MEYER SCHAPIRO

RANCE likes palaces in profusion and builds them without knowing to what use they will be put," wrote Eugène Pelletan in his *Nouvelle Babylone*. "They have built a palace at the Louvre and lodged antiquity there; another in the rue de Bourgogne and there they lodge the Corps Législatif; another at the Bourse and there they lodge the speculators; another at the Hôtel de Ville, and there they lodge M. Haussmann; another at the Luxembourg and there they lodge the Senate... Above all the palaces Paris carries in the sky her innumerable cupolas; a cupola at the Panthéon, for sheltering the candidature of dust for immortality; a cupola at the Invalides, to cover up some wounds; another at the Val de Grâce, to cover sickness; another at the Institut for covering up compliments." In a cautious way M. Pelletan was saying that a town-planning upheaval was going on in Paris which neither Baron Haussmann, who was its instrument, nor the Senate, the Legislative Assembly, the Institut de France, the University, nor any other institution dared acknowledge. The Emperor had quietly ordered a city clean-up of a special order.

There was some excuse for this: the old gaslit city was jampacked with traffic. Carriages of every conceivable kind, horse-riders and pedestrians crowded its narrow streets, a traffic recently augmented by some hundreds of horse-drawn buses, velocipedes and tricycles, not to mention the steam locomotives pushing ever closer to the city's heart. Two million people were living in Paris, yet there were windmills on Montmartre, fields at the Trocadéro and rural scenes beyond the Arc de Triomphe. Under the royal windows at the Louvre palace there was a flea market with benches and stalls, heaps of old iron; aviaries of birds, guinea pigs on straw, squirrels on wheels and all manner of people and beasts making a prodigious din. At Haussmann's command it all vanished overnight and in a miraculously short time the palace appeared with a curious brood of statues on the balustrade of its portico.

The rue de Rivoli was prolonged and the boulevard de Strasbourg built over the rubble of old buildings; a road was driven through the Luxembourg gardens, displacing the Medici Fountain and destroying the Tree of Liberty, cherished relic of the great Revolution; suddenly new roads proliferated in all directions, "shafts to nowhere," someone said. Then it was noticed that all the new roads led to, and from, the great military barracks that encircled the city, that they were, in the words of a distinguished historian of the period, "marvelously accessible to air, light and infantry." As Eugène Pelletan observed: "They have demolished Paris because the February (1848) Revolution has shown that no honest government can subdue in one blow a million souls, in this roiling skein of streets and lanes, impasses and galleries where a dozen paving stones, one on the other, and behind the paving stones, some blouses, the first (republican) guards, the first secret society, can halt for a day, two days, even three days, all the infantry, all the cavalry, all the artillery, all the gendarmes of Paris."

The replanning of Paris had been carried out without regard for the people who were displaced. They received a printed notice to quit and if they had not moved out by the time the wreckers arrived they were forcibly evicted. Tens of thousands of Parisians were suddenly homeless, many of them already impoverished by sweat-shop conditions; but the clean-up hit everybody, including intellectuals like Professor Pelletan who could not afford an apartment in one of the tall new buildings with which Baron Haussmann was lining his new boulevards and was obliged to move out to the suburbs among the vegetable plots.

"France contains, according to the Imperial Almanac, thirty-six millions of subjects, not including subjects of discontent," wrote Henri de Rochefort in *La Lanterne*. A string of similar *bons mots*, progressively stronger in tone, brought the crimson-bound *La Lanterne* a hundred thousand readers and Rochefort a term in prison and, finally, exile.

The Goncourt brothers were concerned about the 120,000 cocottes (professionals), cocodettes (amateurs) and grisettes (beginners) who plied their trade in Paris, some like Anna Desloins and Cora Pearl, decked out in diamonds, but the vast majority now without a bed to their backs. "Never has the gangrene been so profound," wrote the brothers in their famous journal. "The most elevated arts have been travestied by ignoble buffooneries. From the Madeleine to the Bastille there is not a café where absinthe is not softening the brain towards maniacal fury."

Paris seethed with revolt, but the system of police informers, spies, stool-pigeons, provocateurs—that professionalism which has ever distinguished the Sûreté—kept the Emperor well informed. Finally, it was not the internal, but the external, situation which brought disaster.

Like most dictators it was in the field of foreign policy that Napoleon made his fatal mistakes. A posture of bellicose nationalism leans on glorious feats of arms and the laurels of foreign victories. Thus, in 1849, the French had invaded Italy, thwarting her desire for union with Rome, making a friend in the Vatican, but an enemy of the Italian people. In 1865 Napoleon had annexed Cochin China, a business that was not to finish in his century (the same could be said of his Suez Canal Company). In 1854, by joining Britain and Turkey in the invasion of the Crimea, he had made an enemy of the Czar and had offended Britain by leaving her out of the peace settlement. In 1859 he had invaded Lombardy where, on the basis of a much-publicized battle, he had made a quick peace which still further offended the Italians. In 1864 he had taken advantage of America's Civil War to install a puppet on the Mexican throne, and had then stood by while his puppet was executed by a Mexican firing squad. Thus, the Emperor had not a friend in the world when, finally and inevitably, he had accepted war with an observant Germany.

The Salon of 1870 had surprised everybody. With the exception of Monet and Cézanne all the young painters were represented. Responding perhaps to currents of uncertainty, the Academy had agreed that every recognized artist had the right to vote for his choice of jurymen for the selection committee. The Café Guerbois had immediately nominated its own panel of jurymen which included Courbet and Manet, Daumier and Daubigny, Corot and Millet. But only Daubigny and Corot had been admitted to the Jury. However, the

In the Streets and Boulevards of Paris

Edouard Manet: In a Cab. Drawing.

Edouard Manet: Queue in Front of the Butcher's Shop. 1871. Etching.

choice of works for exhibition had showed an extraordinary liberality towards the young painters, compared with previous years.

Cézanne had waited until the last moment before bringing in his entries. These were: *Reclining Nude*, which paid no court to conventional ideas of feminine grace, and a portrait of his paraplegic friend Achille Emperaire which made no attempt to hide the shrunken legs beneath the handsome head and powerful torso; and, being painted in hard and bold colors, was a challenge, not merely to the genteel Jury, but to the world at large, and perhaps posterity.

On the whole the young painters had occasion to congratulate themselves: despite continuing adverse press criticism their work was being exhibited and seen by thousands of people. The intelligence that France was at war with Germany was discouraging, but not overwhelming: France had been at war with half-a-dozen countries in the last twenty years and the army's battle record was as brilliant as its uniforms. But the news, six weeks later, that the Prussian armies had broken the French line at Sedan and that Bonaparte had surrendered and was a prisoner of war came as a stunning shock.

Hundreds of thousands of Parisians milled about the boulevards. Tricolors were raised and cockades worn; orators of every stripe delivered vehement speeches to which people listened in a dazed manner. The *Marseillaise* was sung and so was the *Chant du départ*. Newspapers were snatched from the hands of vendors and the city hummed with false rumors. A coalition Government of National Defense was formed and announced the creation of a National Guard for the defense of Paris. Both Degas and Manet joined up, their social status obtaining them commissions. Manet was disappointed to find that his superior officer was the painter, Ernest Meissonier, one of the stalwarts of the Academy, as uncongenial in as out of uniform.

A fortnight after the fall of Sedan the Prussians arrived before Paris, taking up positions opposite the system of forts which encircled the city. An attempt by the revolutionary parties to seize power was foiled; the government appointed General Trochu to govern the city and General Vinoy to command its forces. Léon Gambetta, whose revolutionary fervor had turned to republican ardor on the fall of Napoleon, was ballooned out of Paris with the mission of reassembling the dispersed French forces in the south and the west of France for the relief of the capital.

About two months after the Germans had closed their iron trap a gallant effort was made to break out of the besieged city. A large force under General Ducrot struck out to the east of Paris with the objective of reaching the Marne, then swinging southward and effecting a junction with the French army that had been hurriedly assembled on the Loire. For three days there was heavy fighting in the region of Champigny where Manet, riding dispatches between Paris and Ducrot's staff, saw action for the first time. The breakout failed at great cost to the inexperienced French forces, the battlefield being, in the words of an English correspondent, "an indescribable bloody mess with the brave women of Paris administering succor to the wounded and dying." Any hope there may have been of effecting a

Leveling the Approaches to the Boulevard Malesherbes, 1864. Photograph.

Hippolyte Bayard: The Roofs of Paris from Montmartre, 1842. Photograph.

As a result of industrial development the population of Paris doubled during the first half of the nineteenth century, and living conditions in the overcrowded city became alarmingly unsanitary. In 1853 Napoleon III accordingly ordered Haussmann, prefect of the Seine, to modernize Paris, whose present-day aspect is largely of his creation. Haussmann put through new thoroughfares and widened old ones, enlarged and improved the parks, provided a new water supply and a gigantic system of sewers, erected new buildings, bridges, railroad stations and the central markets. These transformations, while they met the requirements of modern life, were nevertheless governed by an absolutist conception of power: the wide new thoroughfares brought light and air into the city, and eased the flow of traffic, but they also facilitated the intervention of the army in the popular quarters where rebellion smoldered.

junction with Ducrot's army and that of the Loire, had already been thwarted by a German army, commanded by the Crown Prince of Prussia, which had forced the army of the Loire into retreat. It was in this retreat that Bazille was killed.

While negotiating Napoleon's surrender at Sedan, Bismarck had accused the French of being "a nation irritable, envious, jealous and proud to excess." Pointing out that in the previous two hundred years French armies had made war on Germany no less than thirty times, he told a French general: "It seems to you that victory is properly reserved to you alone." On January 18, 1871, at Versailles—seat of the former kings of France—King William of Prussia was crowned Emperor of Germany, before a glittering cohort of his jackbooted generals. At the end of January the armistice went into effect and a general demobilization was ordered. Manet went to join his family near Bordeaux and immediately began painting. Degas remained in Paris, spending much of his time at the Morisot house.

A new government, headed by Adolphe Thiers, was set up at Versailles and entered into peace negotiations with Bismarck. Meanwhile the citizen army in Paris—the Federals, as they were called—refused to disband. Towards the end of February the Thiers government signed a convention with Germany which provided for an unprecedented indemnity and a limited occupation of Paris. The convention was denounced by Gambetta and a few days later the German troops, goose-stepping down the Champs-Elysées in their spiked helmets and shining breastplates, were received in utter silence. The effect of this humiliation—as Bismarck may have calculated—was to cause the Federals to go into active rebellion. By this time a force of some 300,000 men, they seized the artillery, elected their own command and ordered the election of a city government committed to resistance. In the sixty days of its existence the Commune of Paris passed out of the control of simple patriots and into the hands of revolutionaries whose ideas and aims went beyond the city's defense. It seemed to these men that the moment had come for redressing all the evils and injustices of the Bonapartist regime: the political repression, the police system, the crushing poverty and prostitution, the uncontrolled commercialism and the irresponsible military adventures. As the situation progressively got out of hand power was exercised according to the only precedents within their knowledge, those of the revolutions of 1793 and 1848: that is, by dispensing death with that insouciance which would attend their own inevitable destruction. Nothing the Communards did, however, could match in scale or ruthlessness their own suppression. All the cruelty, malice and chagrin of the class of people accurately described by Bismarck was expended on the Communards and the unfortunate Federals. Manet, who returned to Paris with the Versailles troops, made several vivid sketches of the summary executions at the barricades. They have a curious resemblance to the sketches he made as a youth, during the 1851 *coup d'état,* and also to Goya's famous painting of the executions carried out by French troops in Madrid, which had inspired Manet to make his painting of the execution of Maximilian. Or perhaps the banality lies in the act itself.

Ernest Meissonier:
Sketch, 1870.

Ernest Meissonier:
The Siege of Paris, 1870 or early 1871.
Sketch.

Edouard Manet: The Barricade, 1871. Lithograph.

After the Prussian breakthrough at Sedan, Monet decided that the time had come to quit France. Before taking the Portsmouth packet he left some paintings at Pissarro's house in Louveciennes. Within a few days, however, Pissarro also decided to leave Paris. Louveciennes, lying on the main road to Paris from the northwest, was a predictable German objective. Pissarro stacked away his canvases—some hundreds of them, his life's work—and took his little family to his friend Ludovic Piette in Mayenne, near Le Mans, but this hardly seemed safer; and so, probably with some financial assistance from Piette, he too crossed La Manche.

In London Monet visited Daubigny, an expatriate of slightly longer standing. Moved by Monet's evident distress Daubigny told him about a young French art dealer named Paul Durand-Ruel who had fled Paris with his stock of pictures and was now in business in New Bond street. Durand-Ruel bought several of Monet's paintings for three hundred francs apiece. "I must sell a lot of your work here," he said. Pissarro and Julie, arriving in London shortly before the birth of their third child, were received in the house of Phineas Isaacson whose wife was Pissarro's half-sister; here they were soon married. Pissarro also visited Daubigny and, by the same connection, sold a picture to Durand-Ruel and contacted Monet. "Monet and I were very enthusiastic about the London landscapes," Pissarro later wrote. "Monet worked in the parks while I, living at Lower Norwood, at that time a charming suburb, studied the effects of fog, snow and springtime. We worked from Nature and later Monet painted in London some superb studies of mist. We also visited the museums, studying the watercolors and paintings of Turner and Constable."

Monet and Pissarro were represented by two pictures in the French section of the International Exhibition at South Kensington in 1871, probably through Durand-Ruel's efforts. The paintings they entered for the Royal Academy exhibition were "naturally turned down." The "naturally" was an echo of their habitual treatment by academies; not Constable or Turner, but Dante Gabriel Rossetti was the ruling fashion in English art and, quite recently, after a short visit to Paris, had given it as his opinion that "the new French school is simple putrescence and decomposition."

Pissarro wrote Théodore Duret that he was returning to Paris as soon as possible. "Yes, my dear Duret, I shall not stay here as it is only when you are abroad that you realize how beautiful, great and hospitable is France. What a difference here! You only get disdain, indifference, and even rudeness; among one's own confreres jealousy and the most selfish mistrust. Here there is no such thing as art; everything is treated as a matter of business."

Arriving in Paris a short time after the German withdrawal, Pissarro had difficulty recognizing his house at Louveciennes. During his absence it had been taken over by a German supply unit which had used it as an abattoir. Oxen, sheep and pigs, slaughtered and hung for skinning, had saturated the ground all around the house with their blood. The German butchers, in order to preserve their feet from this sanguineous quagmire, had carpeted their pathways with Pissarro's (and Monet's) canvases.

Bazille had obtained his commission in the 3rd Zouaves through his friend, Prince Bibesco, ordnance officer on General du Barail's staff. After a brief sojourn in Algeria for training he had taken the field in that belated action under Generals Aurelle, Chanzy and Martin de Palliers, which had had some initial success in the region of Orleans and then deteriorated, because, according to a staff report, its forces were "made up of men who knew how to get killed, but not of soldiers." Renoir had declined Prince Bibesco's help in the same direction, but had accepted Bazille's suggestion that he enlist in a cavalry regiment, despite the fact that he had never ridden a horse. Sent to Bordeaux for training, Renoir had painted a portrait of his commander, and one of the commander's wife, who, he afterward said, "was soon more revolutionary in her ideas about art than I was." When his commander was transferred to Tarbes to supervise the training of cavalry remounts, Renoir went along with him and soon became an accomplished rider. However, during an epidemic of dysentery, he was taken ill and might have died like hundreds of other soldiers, had not an uncle brought him to Bordeaux.

With the armistice and the general demobilization, Renoir thumbed his way to Paris where he learned of the death of Bazille. During the withdrawal the tall, easily-targeted young officer had, it seemed, been the victim of a sniper's bullet on an icy road at Beaune-la-Rolande, about twenty miles south of Fontainebleau forest where they had spent so many happy and expectant days.

Renoir had entered Paris during the confused period between the peace negotiations and the setting-up of the Commune of Paris. At Louveciennes, where he stayed with his sister and her husband, the

"Papa will find Paris in a most surprising state of excitement, one that is certain to end badly. I was unable to go to Victor Noir's funeral because of the drenching rain that fell that day, and also because I was posing for a picture by Fantin, one of my friends. But on the outer boulevard I saw all the people pass by who were going to it. There was not a single worker left in Paris. Had it not been for Rochefort, two hundred thousand men (at least) would have been peppered with grapeshot. Mark my words, all this will end badly, it is no longer a joke, there is a widespread irritation which will set the guns firing at the first opportunity, which will not fail to appear."

Frédéric Bazille, letter to his mother, January 1870

A Barricade in the Rue de la Paix during the Commune, 1871. Photograph.

Edouard Manet: The Civil War, 1871. Etching.

engraver Leray, there were lively discussions; his sister proposed that he meet Louise Michel, who had suddenly emerged as the champion of women's rights. "Clemenceau will introduce you," his sister had said. Instead, Renoir went to see Courbet, who had accepted the post of Director of Art under the Commune and was busy stowing away the city's art works, paintings, statuary and books, in places that would be safe from the shelling; he was far outside the bitter political struggle which was changing, almost daily, the composition of the Commune and the command of its army.

Renoir took his paintbox and easel and, ignoring war and revolution, began painting his old love, the Seine. It was a strange occupation in a besieged city and he cannot have been overly surprised when a couple of Federals mistook him for a Versailles spy. A crowd gathered and someone shouted, "Throw him in the Seine!" The Federals took him to Commune security headquarters at the Hôtel de Ville where, with that facility which distinguishes revolutionary regimes, his fate might have been settled in a matter of minutes by the red-sashed Chief of Security, had not Renoir suddenly recognized him. He was the young runaway Renoir had sheltered in Fontainebleau forest. Reminded of that occasion, Raoul Rigault embraced Renoir, led him past a double line of guards, with arms at the present, to a balcony overlooking the Place de Grève where there was a great concourse of people. "Now, fellow citizens," shouted Rigault, after having introduced Renoir as a painter and one of themselves, "Let us sing the *Marseillaise* for Citizen Renoir!" Rigault gave him a pass which enabled Renoir at any time to enter or leave the Commune area, warning him, however, not to show it to a Versailles guard or it would cost him his life.

"Good people, the Communards," Renoir told his son, Jean, many years later. "They had good intentions. But you don't play Robespierre all over again. They were eighty years behind the times. And why burn the Tuileries? It wasn't much, but at least it was less sham than a good deal that came afterwards."

Renoir had spent his earliest youth in the shadow of the old unreconstructed Tuileries.

One of the first acts of the National Defense Government had been to appoint a commission of artists to take care of the city's art treasures, museums and public monuments. Elected president of the Commission Courbet had proposed the destruction of the Vendôme Column. Then surmounted by a statue of Napoleon I wearing the laurels of a Roman Emperor, with a spiralling bronze sheath (made from melted-down Russian and Austrian guns, captured at the Battle of Austerlitz), on which was engraved, in imitation of Trajan's Column in Rome, the picture-story of Napoleon I's triumphs, the 150-foot column was considered an intolerable reminder of Bonapartism. Though the idea tickled Courbet there were more urgent things to be done, such as storing the Louvre treasures and sandbagging the city's monuments, like the Arc de Triomphe, to protect them from Prussian shells. In the meantime the National Defense Government had been replaced by the Commune, and though Courbet was then

Edouard Manet: Portrait of Courbet, 1878. Pen and Ink.

RÉPUBLIQUE FRANÇAISE
LIBERTÉ, ÉGALITÉ, FRATERNITÉ.

ÉLECTIONS
A LA COMMUNE

SCRUTIN DU 10 AVRIL 1871

Les Membres du Comité électoral du 6ᵐᵉ arrondissement, par déférence pour le suffrage de leurs concitoyens, recommandent à leur choix, pour l'élection à la Commune, le citoyen

COURBET

qui a obtenu le plus grand nombre de voix après les élus du 26 mars, et lui adjoignent le citoyen

ROGEARD

Le Comité électoral républicain du 6ᵉ Arrondissement.

Paris.—Typ. Rouge frères, Dunon et Fresne, rue du Four-Saint-Germain, 43.

Poster for the Elections to the Commune, 1871.

RÉPUBLIQUE FRANÇAISE

N° 128   LIBERTÉ — EGALITE — FRATERNITE   N° 128

COMMUNE DE PARIS

La Commune autorise le citoyen G. COURBET, nommé en assemblée générale Président de la Société des Peintres, à rétablir, dans le plus bref délai, les Musées de la Ville de Paris dans leur état normal, d'ouvrir les galeries au public et d'y favoriser le travail qui s'y fait habituellement.

La Commune autorisera à cet effet les quarante-six délégués qui seront nommés demain *Jeudi, 13 avril*, en séance publique à l'École de médecine (grand amphithéâtre), à *deux heures précises*.

De plus, elle autorise le citoyen COURBET, ainsi que cette assemblée, à rétablir l'Exposition annuelle aux Champs-Élysées.

Paris, le 12 avril 1871.

La Commission exécutive,
AVRIAL, F. COURNET, Ch. DELESCLUZE, Félix PYAT,
G. TRIDON, A. VERMOREL, E. VAILLANT.

IMPRIMERIE NATIONALE. — Avril 1871.

Poster of the Commune, 1871.

Courbet and the Commune.
Photograph.

Courbet's Membership Card
of the Federation of Artists
created during the Commune.

able to institute one of his favorite reforms, the suppression of the Académie des Beaux Arts, its salons and schools, the socialist moderates of the Commune like himself were fast being elbowed out (or shot without trial) by the Blanquists, Hébertists and Jacobins.

There is no record that Courbet took a strong stand against the terrorist acts of the Commune, but it is certain that he was profoundly moved by the summary execution of his friend Gustave Chaudey, whose brief tenure as Mayor of Paris had not met with Rigault's approval. On May 11, 1871, Courbet resigned his post. He was present, however, when, on May 16, the Vendôme Column was brought crashing down amid a flutter of tricolors and the sound of the *Marseillaise*. The next day, belatedly perhaps, Courbet broke completely with the Commune.

On May 21 the Versailles troops entered the city, splitting into two main columns, taking the right and the left banks of the Seine, and advancing towards the Hôtel de Ville. The Federals fought them street by street, from one cobblestone barricade to the next, receiving and giving no quarter. In the Commune's last hours Rigault shot a number of hostages, including Archbishop Darboy, and some of his supporters put fire to the symbolic institutions of Napoleon III's reign: his residences, the Tuileries Palace and the Palais Royal, the Royal Mint, the House of the Legion of Honor and, finally, to their own fastness, the Hôtel de Ville. In the army's mopping-up operation the survivors of the Federals and the Workers' Battalions were flushed out of the catacombs of the Left Bank, the cemetery of Père Lachaise and the cellars of Belleville, brought to drumhead courts, tied together in groups of ten, in some cases, and mowed down by mitrailleuse: the Seine below Lobau barracks literally ran red for days. Camille Pelletan, who made a careful study of the matter some years later, says: "The re-entry of the government in Paris was marked by a massacre of twenty or thirty thousand Parisians, according to some, of seventeen thousand, according to others." The regular army of more than one hundred thousand men suffered 873 dead.

Courbet was arrested a week later in the house of a friend and imprisoned at Versailles. During the next three months he was moved from one crowded jail to another while the military tribunals went through thousands of cases. When Courbet's turn came, military justice had been appeased to some extent and all charges against him were dropped, except that of complicity in the destruction of monuments. As a result he received a comparatively light sentence of six months on the routine charge of having assisted in the disaffection of the troops. His health had broken down; a part of his sentence was served in hospital and he was afterwards allowed to make several paintings while under detention. Monet and Boudin paid him a visit, finding him thin, white-haired and looking very old.

Returning to Ornans, his birthplace, Courbet made two paintings which he sent in to the next Salon. Both were summarily rejected. "Courbet must be excluded from exhibiting," said Ernest Meissonier, the new panjandrum of official art. "It is necessary that henceforth he shall be dead to us." His pictures were removed from public exhibi-

95

The New Louvre and the Tuileries. Photograph by Martens.

View of the Fires in Paris on the Nights of May 23 and 25, 1871. Lithograph by Deroy.

Daniel Vierge: The Fall of the Vendôme Column. Drawing.

The Vendôme Column Overturned, May 16, 1871.

tion. The pronouncement provoked protests from the liberals, but the official artists were furious over the leniency shown towards Courbet. Shortly afterwards the National Assembly passed an act declaring Courbet responsible for the destruction of the Vendôme Column and demanding that he meet the cost of its restoration. Faked photographs showing Courbet shaking hands with the destroyers of the Column were circulated. A bill for 323,091 francs was presented to him and preparations were made to seize his property and personal effects. Courbet fled to Switzerland where he had some difficulty finding a place to live—the Swiss were not anxious to have so notorious a "Communard" in their midst—but he eventually settled down at La Tour-de-Peilz, near Vevey, where he found some lesser Communard exiles already in residence. He continued to paint and people from all over the world came to visit him, including Rochefort who had escaped from imprisonment in New Caledonia. In 1877 some paintings which the government had seized in lieu of payment of its bill—among them his portrait of Proudhon and his family—

"*If only I can remember what the sun looks like!*"

Courbet, on entering his cell at the Sainte-Pélagie prison, 1871

Gustave Courbet: Execution at Sainte-Pélagie, 1871. Drawing.

Rue de Rivoli, 1871. Photograph.

Gustave Courbet: Courbet at Sainte-Pélagie, 1871. Drawing.

were auctioned off at the Hôtel Drouot for the sum total of ten thousand francs. The contemptible bids satisfied Meissonier: the government case was terminated and Courbet was free to return to Ornans. Broken in health the old painter could not be moved; a month later he was dead.

Thus, to be called a "Communard," as the young non-conformist painters often were at this time, was not a meaningless pejorative.

After his adventure with the Communards, Renoir went to stay with the Sisleys who had rented a little house at Louveciennes. Sisley's father, whose portrait Renoir had painted, had died after a long illness, leaving Sisley without any further means of support. It could not be said that Sisley was faced with the decision of looking for employment: he knew only how to paint. One of the very few paintings he made that year is a double portrait of his children, Pierre and Jean, working at their lessons, a work possibly due to Renoir's influence, for Sisley never again made a serious attempt at figure painting.

Renoir himself was mainly occupied with obtaining portrait commissions. Lise posed for a picture which may have been a wedding present, for she shortly afterwards married Georges Brière de l'Isle, a young architect, and did not again see Renoir, though she treasured his letters and other memorabilia, destroying them some years after his death and before her own demise in 1922. Through his friend Le Cœur, Renoir got a job decorating the ceilings of Prince Bibesco's new mansion, but the friendship with the Le Cœurs seems to have foundered as a result of a compromising *billet doux* which Renoir had addressed to sixteen-year-old Marie Le Cœur.

"There he met Pissarro, and during a visit to the National Gallery both were very much struck by Turner's pictures. This bewitching artist, at once visionary and naturalistic, seeking now the unreal in the real, now the real in the unreal, could not but incite them to strive after a more vibrant coloring than the delicately shaded harmonies in gray of Corot and Boudin, than the rich but heavy impastoes of Courbet. This was not an invitation, but simply another step forward, a decisive one however. Turner may have been for them what Constable and Bonington had been for Théodore Rousseau, Paul Huet, Cabat, Daubigny and to some extent Corot himself. All had been stimulated, but not subdued, by these two admirable English naturists. "

Arsène Alexandre, *Claude Monet*

Unfit for military service and badly in need of money, Monet left Camille and his son Jean in Normandy on the outbreak of war and went to England, a neutral country where he hoped to be able to work and to sell his pictures. There he ran into Daubigny, who introduced him to his own dealer, Paul Durand-Ruel, who had opened a gallery in Bond Street. This meeting was decisive: in Durand-Ruel the Impressionists found a dealer who believed in them and several times went to the verge of bankruptcy for their sake.

In his memoirs Durand-Ruel tells of this first meeting with Monet: "It was in my London gallery at the beginning of 1871 that I made the acquaintance of Monet. I had already noticed some of his work in the recent Salons, but had had no opportunity to meet him, since he was almost never in Paris. He was brought to me by Daubigny, who thought highly of his talent. I immediately bought from him the pictures he had just done in London. "

Fleeing Louveciennes before the advancing Prussians, Pissarro too went to London. He submitted some canvases to the Royal Academy exhibition, the English equivalent of the French Salon, but they were rejected. He then applied to Durand-Ruel, who bought some pictures from him and gave him Monet's address in London. So through Durand-Ruel—"But for him we would have starved in London, " wrote Pissarro—the two friends were reunited and went out painting together, studying rain, snow and fog effects. Years later Pissarro confided to the English painter Wynford Dewhurst, who was writing a book on *Impressionist Painting, Its Genesis and Development*: "The watercolors and paintings of Turner and Constable, as well as canvases by Old Crome, certainly had some influence on us. We admired Gainsborough, Lawrence, Reynolds, etc., but were most impressed by the English landscapists, who were nearer to our own experiments in open air work, in light and fleeting effects..."

Extracts from Dewhurst's book were published in *The Studio* early in 1902. Irritated by the excessive importance attached by Dewhurst to the English influence on Impressionism, Pissarro wrote to his son Lucien on May 8, 1902: "This Mr. Dewhurst doesn't understand what Impressionism is all about. He sees it only as a technical device and mixes up the names; he thinks Jongkind inferior to Boudin. That can't be helped. He also says that before going to London Monet and I had no conception of light; yet we have studies that demonstrate the contrary. He makes no mention of the influence of Claude Lorrain, Corot, the whole 18th century, especially Chardin. But what he doesn't realize is that Turner and Constable, while they taught us something, showed us in their works that they had no understanding of the analysis of shadow, which in Turner's painting is simply used as an effect, a mere absence of light. As far as tone division is concerned, Turner proved the value of this method among methods, although he did not apply it correctly and naturally; besides we derived from the eighteenth century. "

Monet and Pissarro in London

Like Monet, Pissarro made several trips to England, in 1871, 1890, 1892, 1897 and 1899. During his very first stay there, he turned, almost instinctively, to the countrified themes which he had treated so often and so lovingly in France, scenes with village houses glistening in the cool light that follows a rainfall. Pissarro "contrives to render the fresh charm of England's aristocratic landscapes," wrote Charles Saunier in the *Revue indépendante* in 1892.

In London, in June 1871, Pissarro received a letter from Duret describing the desolation of Paris under the Commune. Pissarro answered a few days later in an equally despondent vein complaining of the general indifference his work had met with in England: "Here there is no such thing as art; everything is treated as a matter of business. As far as sales go, I have got nowhere. Apart from Durand-Ruel, who bought two small pictures from me, my painting does not catch on, not in the least; wherever I go it is the same tale ... Perhaps I shall be back at Louveciennes shortly. I have lost everything there; out of fifteen hundred canvases about forty are left."

Camille Pissarro: Snow at Lower Norwood, 1870.

Claude Monet: Westminster Bridge and the Houses of Parliament, 1870.

Camille Pissarro: Dulwich College, 1871.

Under the pressure of events Monet went to England for the first time in 1870. He made a second trip in 1891 and returned to London several times between 1899 and 1904, when he executed a long series of pictures whose central theme was the Thames. During his first stay he painted in Hyde Park and did views of the Thames in a spirit fairly close to certain Whistlers, thus showing once again the astonishing community of outlook and research that links the painters of this period.

◀ *J. M. W. Turner: Burning of the Houses of Parliament, 1834.*

◀ *John Constable: The Bay of Weymouth.*

After the War

"They came back from London more determined than ever to paint only with the colors of the prism and to juxtapose on their canvases all the tones that their sensitive eye could detect in an impression of nature. One can imagine the enthusiasm and zeal with which, at the Café Guerbois and in the studios where they met each other, they told their friends about their discoveries and reflections. And their friends, who themselves were striving by trial and error to express their sensation of these color phenomena, were delighted to have this confirmation of their perceptions and experiments. Their palette was refined and brightened up even more."

Georges Lecomte, *Pissarro*

Claude Monet: The Studio-Boat, about 1874.

Paul Cézanne: Four People Sitting in a Park, with a Parasol and Baby Carriage, 1872-1895. Pencil.

"How do you like painting women?" Renoir was once asked. "Naked," was his answer. But this often led to misunderstandings of the kind which, on another occasion, caused him to say sternly: "I've known painters who never did any good work because, instead of painting their models, they seduced them."

He was a gaunt, raffish young man, wary and deadly serious, so thin that the peasants who saw him working in the fields used to say, "He could kiss a goat between the horns."

Monet did not immediately return to Paris after the war, but went to Holland, either at Daubigny's call or in his company. Though generally classed with the "Barbizons," Daubigny had close links with the marine painters like Jongkind and Boudin. He had built himself a small studio on a flat-bottomed boat which he poled about the Seine and the Marne, from which he made paintings directly from nature. He was probably very much at home on the broad waters of the Zaandam, just to the north of Amsterdam, where Monet also made some paintings, though vastly more colorful. Immediately on his return to Paris, Monet went back to Argenteuil and began looking around for a boat with enough beam to provide him with a small floating studio and possibly living space. In the course of this search he came in contact with Gustave Caillebotte, a young man of twenty-four whose father had just left him a large fortune. Caillebotte, who owned several racing skiffs and was something of a boat buff, helped Monet find and fit out his floating studio. Monet made a picture of his boat lying at its moorings, but Manet, who paid him a visit, went one better and made a picture of the boat with Monet at work in it. Evidently a shallow craft, propelled by oars, it had a high cabin on its after part in which we see Camille comfortably seated. Monet in a white smock and straw hat squats in the bows under a striped awning. Before him is a painting, one of those many made in this boat—did it have a name?—not the least of which are those of the new iron bridges which were being thrown across the Seine and the Oise and which, seeming quaint to our eyes, were then the essence of that modernity for which the young painters were reaching.

Gustave Caillebotte became so interested in Monet's project that he himself took up painting. Some of his pictures seem to have been made, not only in Monet's boat, but in Monet's manner also.

Pissarro found a new home at no. 22 rue de l'Hermitage at Pontoise, near the confluence of the Seine and the Oise, where he remained for the next ten years. Here his little daughter Minette died and here his second, third and fourth sons, and another daughter were born. Vollard says that Madame Pissarro had to till the ground herself to provide for her family. Pissarro's mother and his sister seem to have been on hand a part of the time. And there were always friends. "Guillaumin has just spent several days at our house," Pissarro wrote Duret. "He works at painting in the daytime and at his ditch-digging in the evening. What courage!"

It was during this period, says Lionello Venturi, "that Pissarro developed his exquisite style, the perfection of values of tones, steadily reducing the importance of the subject." He also experimented with the figure, introducing shepherdesses and milkmaids into his paintings, to the consternation of his friends, who were afraid that he might begin to sentimentalize the bucolic life in the manner of Millet. "But Millet is biblical," retorted Pissarro, "and I am only Hebrew." Nevertheless, he dropped the human figure and continued to concentrate on the "sensations" of light in landscape.

Cézanne turned up at Auvers-sur-Oise, not far away. He was in Aix-en-Provence when France fell. As soon as the National Defense government had announced its intention of assembling a southern army for the relief of Paris, Cézanne had gone quietly to the little fishing village of L'Estaque, near Marseilles, where he had remained until the end of the war. "I did a lot of painting," he told Vollard, who was curious about what he had done there. It seemed a sufficient explanation. On his return from the South he had been accompanied by Hortense Fiquet, his sometime model and companion, and they had lived for a time in a little apartment near the Halle-aux-Vins, where a son had been born, and named Paul.

Pissarro was a little astonished at the turn Cézanne's painting had taken since their last meeting. He did not call it biblical (though he could have done so), but wrote Duret: "When ever you want a five-footed sheep, Cézanne will be able to supply you, for he has some very strange studies of things he has seen as no one else ever saw them."

Cézanne's friend, Dr Paul Gachet, whom he had met at the Café Guerbois, had been a surgeon-aide-major in the National Guard during the War—"Doctor Gachet of the Ambulances," as he was called. He had recently bought a fine house on a hillside overlooking the Oise valley where his wife and children lived while the Doctor, a homeopathic specialist, attended his practice three days a week. Cézanne lived at the Gachet house while painting the Oise landscape. He worked simultaneously on two subjects, one for the morning and one for the afternoon, going out every day at regular hours. He also had alternative subjects for gray and sunshiny days. Madame Gachet often arranged vases of flowers which Cézanne painted. When Pissarro saw the finished products of these excursions he was not thinking of five-footed sheep when he wrote Duret: "Our friend Cézanne raises our expectations, and I have seen, and have at home, a painting of remarkable vigor and power. If, as I hope, he stays some time in Auvers where he is living, he will astonish a lot of artists who were in too great a hurry to condemn him."

Duret notes that "it was at Auvers that Cézanne began painting in the open air . . . (He) invented an individual coloration, so harmonious in what may be called its violence that the others profited by it. At this period Pissarro introduced a brilliant range of color into his landscapes, suggested by Cézanne."

Dr Gachet bought Cézanne's *Olympia* and a number of other paintings, including one of Hortense, a dark short-haired girl, lying asleep, half nude, with the sturdy infant Paul tugging away at her breast.

Pissarro and Cézanne. Photograph.

"Cézanne came under my influence at Pontoise and I came under his. You remember how Zola and Béliard lashed out at us about this. They thought that painting was invented out of nothing and that an artist was original when he resembled no one else. What is curious to note in this exhibition of Cézanne's at Vollard's is the kinship between some of his Auvers and Pontoise landscapes and my own. To be sure, we were always together."

Pissarro, letter to his son Lucien, November 22, 1895

Degas in New Orleans

"I shall certainly be back in Paris in January. To vary my voyage, I intend to go by way of Havana. The French liners call there. I am eager to see you again at my place and to work in familiar surroundings. Nothing can be done here, it's in the climate; nothing but cotton, people here live for and by cotton. The light is so strong that I have not yet been able to do anything on the river. My eyes need so much care that I dare not expose them to any risk. A few family portraits will be my sole effort; I could hardly avoid doing them and would certainly not complain about it if it were not so difficult, if the arrangements did not seem so insipid and the sitters so restless. But never mind! I shall have had the trip and not much more than that. Manet, more than I, would have seen some fine things here. But he would not have done any more work. One can love and apply to art only what one is accustomed to. By novelty one is first captivated, then bored."

Letter from Degas to Henri Rouart,
written from New Orleans, December 5, 1872

Edgar Degas: The Cotton Office at New Orleans, 1873.

The war had exhausted Degas. He complained of eye trouble, due, he thought, to exposure while on duty during the icy nights of the siege. When, late in 1872, his brother René returned to France from New Orleans, he had no difficulty persuading Edgar to pay the American branch of the family a visit. The four months Edgar spent in New Orleans were memorable in many ways. He found his Uncle Michel Musson, his deceased mother's brother, living with René's family in a huge mansion on The Esplanade, with all the appurtenances of ante-bellum splendor, save that the slaves were now servants. "Nothing pleases me so much," wrote Degas in a letter, "as the Negresses of every shade, holding little white babies—Oh! so white—in their arms: Negresses either in white mansions with fluted columns or in orange-gardens, ladies in muslin in front of their little houses, steamboats with two funnels as high as factory chimneys, and the contrast between the busy, so-well-arranged offices and this immense black animal force, etc, etc. And the pretty pure-bred women, the charming quadroons and the well-built Negresses."

The Musson-De Gas household was full of pretty women and it was perhaps the only time in his life that Edgar gave a thought to family on his own account. "It is something to be married, to have nice children," he wrote. He was probably thinking of his sister-in-law, Estelle, whose fourth child, Jeanne, was born shortly after his arrival and for whom Degas was godfather. Estelle had been married at the age of eighteen to Captain Lazare David Balfour, heir to the great Fall Back plantation in Louisiana, who had been killed at the battle of Corinth. Shortly after having met her cousin, René De Gas, Estelle had gone blind, but, against the opposition of her father, and after obtaining an episcopal dispensation to do so, Estelle had married René.

His most famous American painting, *Cotton Office in New Orleans,* tells the rest of the sad story. The old gentleman teasing a piece of raw cotton is his Uncle Michel Musson, Estelle's father; the bearded gentleman reading the *Times-Picayune* is Edgar's youngest brother, René; the figure leaning against the window on the extreme left is his brother Achille. When their father Auguste-Hyacinthe De Gas died in Naples early in 1874, the affairs of his bank were in a disastrous condition, due in a great measure to the financing of René's New Orleans venture into cotton margins. Achille tried to hold off the creditors by arranging for René to refund principal and interest by installments; but the post bellum depression had finally hit New Orleans and the "busy, so-well-arranged" Cotton Office was close to bankruptcy. One of Auguste De Gas's creditors, the Bank of Anvers, sued the De Gas sons for 40,000 francs, which precipitated the total collapse of René's affairs. Edgar and Achille agreed to repay their father's debts in monthly installments.

Daniel Halévy is correct in saying that it was family financial misfortunes which suddenly changed Degas's outlook on life and art. "He could not endure the stain on the honor of the family," Halévy says. He was also suddenly without the private income which had enabled him to live the life of a man-about-town. He gave up his pleasant house in the rue Blanche and rented a studio at the foot of an alley off the rue Pigalle. This was the time when the boulevardiers said of him: "Degas would like to see his reflection in a boulevard window, in order to give himself the satisfaction of breaking the plate glass with his cane."

He had ceased to be an artist wealthy enough to disdain the dealers. Nor was he any longer wealthy enough to choose his own models. He gave up painting race horses and turned to his own neighborhood for models who would pose for very little or nothing. It is to this circumstance that we owe his laundresses and his working girls taking a tub in a small room.

After the debacle of 1870 the French army needed to be reminded of worthier traditions. That apparently was the reason why ex-Colonel Meissonier painted the huge canvas depicting Napoleon I coolly surveying the Battle of Friedland as the breast-plated cavalry, or cuirassiers, went charging into action. Ex-Captain Manet visited the exhibition and a little crowd gathered as he stood before the painting. "It's good!" said Manet. "It's really good! All steel except the breast-plates." (*Tout est en acier sauf les cuirasses.*) The crack went the rounds of the salons, for Manet was having the success he had always longed for. He was finally famous *and* popular.

Shortly after the end of the war Manet and his wife had toured Holland and on his return he had painted a picture which was not only accepted by the Salon of 1873, but was given the best place on the line. It was a portrait of the engraver, Bellot, an habitué of the Café Guerbois, who is shown with jolly rubicund face and long pipe sitting at a café table beside a glass of beer. *Le Bon Bock* seemed to strike a chord in the public heart. Copies of it would soon decorate the beer halls of France; it would be the subject of a popular revue; Bellot himself would enjoy a vicarious fame. But there were still people who begrudged Manet his success; "Manet has put water in his bock," said Critic Albert Wolff. "Not water," said Painter Alfred Stevens, "that's pure Haarlem beer." He meant that it had been painted in the manner of Frans Hals.

Manet's success merely underlined the failure of the other young painters to obtain notice of their work. And "young" was a relative term: Pissarro was 43, Degas almost 40, Monet, Renoir and Sisley, approaching 35. The "painters of the new painting," as Duranty called them, would soon be middle-aged. Monet proposed that they hold a joint independent exhibition at their own expense. He had made the suggestion before and it had been rejected because the group had not wanted to appear to be running wild; the buyers they wanted were, of course, moneyed and, by definition, respectable. This time, however, Monet's suggestion found support from Pissarro and Degas. Citing his experience with a similar venture twelve years earlier Pissarro proposed that they form themselves into a cooperative association such as—and he quoted chapter and paragraph—the Bakers' Union of Pontoise. His socialistic outlook demanded an orderly approach to the problem; but Renoir would have none of it. Nor would Renoir stand for a meaningful, i.e. pretentious, name for the organization. Thus they called themselves the Société anonyme

A Manet Success at the Salon

Edouard Manet: Le Bon Bock, 1873.

Exhibited at the 1873 Salon, this picture represents the engraver E. Bellot, a habitué of the Café Guerbois. Founder and president of an association known as Le Bon Bock, he launched, in February 1885, an illustrated weekly called *L'Echo des Brasseries françaises;* on the masthead of the paper Manet's picture was reproduced.

Twenty-one painters have conceived the idea of forming a company for the purpose of organizing free exhibitions, with neither jury nor honorary rewards, where each member can show and sell his works. A committee has been formed which has at once appealed to painters, sculptors, engravers and lithographers, and already the adherents are forty in number. The money question has been solved with the help of monthly contributions, and the Company was able yesterday to open its first exhibition in Nadar's former premises in the Boulevard des Capucines, which are admirably suited to a show of this kind. *Article on the exhibition in* Le Gaulois, *April 18, 1874*

Catalogue of the first impressionist exhibition.

If you like, we shall speak today of the first exhibition. Although it is a small show as far as the number of canvases goes, it is intended as a protest and this personal character gives it a very special flavor. For these artists profess to have no further recourse to the official exhibition and to forestall the decisions of the jury, decisions which are admittedly taken for the benefit of the majority.

The leaders are three artists of whom I have occasionally spoken and who at least have the undeniable merit of pursuing their aims single-mindedly. This very single-mindedness imparts to all three of them a common aspect whose initial result is to bring out the *procedural* side of their painting. At first sight there does not seem to be much difference between M. Monet's pictures and those of M. Sisley, or between the latter's manner and that of M. Pissarro. Looking a little more closely, you soon learn that M. Monet is the most skillful and most daring, M. Sisley the most harmonious and most timorous; M. Pissarro, who in fact is the inventor of this painting, the most real and most naïve. But we must not linger over these nuances. What is certain is that the vision of things affected by these three landscapists in no way resembles that of any previous masters; that it has its plausible sides and asserts itself with a conviction which makes it impossible to dismiss it.

If one had to define this vision of things, one might say that it is above all *decorative*. Its sole aim is to record an *impression*, leaving the quest of *expression* to those concerned with line. Complete works of art are a combination of both, and this point in itself is enough to put this interesting but narrowly conceived venture in its proper place.

Armand Silvestre, review of the exhibition in l'Opinion nationale, *April 22, 1874*

des peintres, sculpteurs, graveurs, etc.—The Limited Company of Painters, Sculptors and Engravers. The charter, dated December 27, 1873, names the following foundation members: Monet, Renoir, Sisley, Degas, Berthe Morisot, Pissarro.

Pissarro made a strong case for the admission of Guillaumin and Cézanne. The prosaic (today we might say the proletarian) nature of Guillaumin's pictures was against him, but it was agreed that he should be admitted. None questioned the worth of Cézanne, but his strange provocative paintings were certain to be labelled revolutionary. Degas had his private reasons for seeking a wider and more profitable market for his work and he did not want to be hindered by any "revolutionary" fuss. In agreeing to Pissarro's nominees, Cézanne and Guillaumin and one Béliard, Degas proposed his aristocratic friend the Viscount Lepic and his young friend Rouart. Nor did he stop there, but

Claude Monet: Impression, Sunrise, *1872.*

went on enlisting orthodox artists, such as de Nittis, Legros, Bracquemond, while his colleagues in the group brought in Boudin, Jongkind and yet others for a total of thirty exhibitors.

The problem of a location was settled when Nadar, the photographer, gave them the use of his spacious duplex on the corner of the Boulevard des Capucines and the rue Daunou. As a last effort at camouflage, Degas proposed that they call themselves "the Capucines," i.e. the Nasturtiums; but the others would have none of it. The catalogue was prepared by Renoir's brother, Edmond, who complained to Monet about the monotony of his titles, in which Monet seemed to take little interest. When Edmond asked him for a title to a misty sunrise at Le Havre, Monet said, "Why don't you just call it 'Impression?'" Edmond did just that.

The show opened, April 15, 1874, and drew 175 visitors the first day (entrance: one franc, catalogue: fifty centimes) and thereafter averaged a daily attendance of about 130 to its close a month later. The artists' friends wrote some wise and intelligent comment in obscure journals; the pompous critics either did not come or peppered their reviews with phrases such as "this laughable collection of absurdities," or "the most absurd daubs," or "Messieurs Monet, Pissarro and Mlle Morisot appear to have declared war on beauty." Berthe's mother asked Guichard, her old teacher, to give her a private report. "One certainly finds here and there some excellent fragments," wrote Guichard, "but they all have more or less cross-eyed minds."

The exhibition was a natural for the funny magazines. *Charivari* sent along Louis Leroy who spoofed the show in a manner which only now seems irreverent. His piece pretends to report the reactions of an Academy medallist on viewing the various exhibits. Before Monet's *Impression, Sunrise*, the Medallist says: "Impression—I was certain of it. I was just telling myself that, since I was impressed, there had to be some impression in it... and what freedom, what ease of workmanship! Wallpaper in its embryonic state is more finished than that seascape."

Charivari's light-hearted kidding was evidently seen by Jules Castagnary, one of the old Café Guerbois set, who put the record straight a few days later in *Le Siècle*: "...The common concept...is the determination not to search for a smooth sensation... Once the impression is captured, they declare their role terminated... If one wants to characterize them with a single word that explains their efforts, one would have to create the new term of *Impressionism*. They are impressionists in the sense that they render not a landscape, but the sensation produced by a landscape..."

It was clever of Castagnary to turn a joking journalistic gag-line into a meaningful appellation. The trouble is that posterity tends to endow the child with the attributes of the name.

Elie Faure found it appropriate: "For the first and only time in the history of painting the name given to the movement is well applied, at least, if one limits it to the works of Monet and Sisley, to the larger part of Pissarro's work and to the first efforts of Cézanne and Renoir. It is the flashing visual sensation of the Instant, which a long and patient analysis of the quality of light and the element of color in their infinite changing complexity permitted three or four men to seize." R. H. Wilenski also accepts *Charivari's* coinage: "The impressionist painter is always concerned to persuade us that his subject is his visual impression of a scene accidentally encountered and that he has made it a point of honor to accept everything as it chanced to appear at the particular moment when he happened to be there..." Kenneth Clark thought that they might justly have been called "sensationalist," and spoke of their "rainbow" palette.

It is hardly surprising, therefore, that a quasi-scientific theory should have emerged concerning impressionist "technique." This held that the painters had laid on their brilliant colors in a manner designed to produce a prismatic effect in reverse, namely, that adjacent colors on the canvas would, at a certain distance, merge in the observer's eye to produce a different and more luminous tone. The theory of "retinal fusion," as it was called, was exploded some twenty-five years ago by Professor J. Carson Webster of Northwestern University. Professor Webster borrowed a number of paintings by Monet, Pissarro, Renoir and Seurat from the Art Institute of Chicago

LA PRESSE

In all fairness, it is important to make a distinction in approaching the exhibition in the Boulevard des Capucines: while there is much that is deserving of the heartiest encouragement, there is much too that should be strenuously contested. The first is entitled to all our praise, the second must be rejected out of hand; the latter contemptible, the former worthy of every interest.

This is not the first time that artists have banded together in an association in order to free themselves from administrative tutelage. Some fifteen years ago an initial venture was made: two hundred artists joined together in the Boulevard des Italiens to exhibit their works and sell them directly to art lovers. Some interesting exhibitions were held and the public had already found its way to the exhibition of the Société Nationale des Beaux Arts when the hostility of those in charge of the fine arts led to the breaking up of this association.

Today the new association of artists will only meet with sympathy on behalf of the fine arts administration, which has officially stated that from next year on it will no longer take charge of the art exhibitions.

I realize that many people look with terror to the coming of a time when artists, left to themselves, will have to attend to the organization of their annual exhibition, draw up their own regulations, select their jury, accept or refuse the works to be exhibited, award the prizes or at least forward to the administration the list of artists recognized as the most deserving.

The joint-stock company of artist-painters has settled these difficult questions in the simplest way; it has done away with the jury, done away with prizes. Will this utter absence of regulations be a good thing? Only the future will give us the answer to this question.

and subjected them to a series of exhaustive tests which showed that their colors did not merge in the eye of the observer. Professor Webster's conclusion was that the painters had intended that their brilliant colors should be seen as such, and close at hand, and not in distant diffusion.

If the word "impressionism" has any precise meaning, it applies, as Faure has said, to only two or three of the painters and then only to their work at certain periods. Custom alone justifies its use in regard to the founders of the movement.

When the management committee of the Limited Company of Painters etc. presented its balance sheet there was a credit of less than a thousand francs. Berthe Morisot, Degas and Boudin had sold nothing; the total sales of Sisley, Renoir and some others amounted to only 3,600 francs.

France was in the depths of an economic depression. The huge indemnity imposed by the Prussians was being met by foreign loans and much of the material damage sustained during the siege and insurrection was being rapidly repaired. But the economy had been dangerously hurt by the previous two decades of imperial extra-vagance, peculation and uncontrolled commercial exploitation. MacMahon, the "hero" of Sedan, had been elected president of the Republic (France's Third), but the monarchists, many and powerful, were maneuvering for an Orleanist restoration. Meanwhile there was inflation, unemployment, and bankruptcy for many small traders, with, this being France, always the fear of another revolution. The Commune had frightened all classes of people and the Impressionists had become identified—no one knew how, unless it was their beards— with the Commune.

This possibly was the reason for the unprecedented scenes of protest and insult which attended the auction of seventy-three paint-ings, the residue of the recent exhibition, at the Hôtel Drouot, March, 1875. According to Durand-Ruel, who was present in the capacity of expert, there were howls of scorn and derision as the canvases were held up and paraded round the floor by the auctioneer's clerk, about twenty each by Renoir, Monet and Sisley, and a dozen by Berthe Morisot. When the bidding failed to get beyond the level of 150 francs the artists bought their paintings back. Unable to see his *La Source* go for 110 francs, Renoir withheld it from sale. Monet's epochal *Impression* went for something less. Berthe Morisot got the best prices, up to 480 francs for one picture.

But the Impressionists had not been altogether without defenders. Gustave Caillebotte, Monet's boating friend, helped push up the bidding and got one or two canvases for himself. And another buyer, completely unknown to the artists (he had not even visited their exhibition), Victor Chocquet by name, bought one of Monet's paint-ings of Argenteuil, and wrote Renoir that very evening, asking him if he would do a portrait of Madame Chocquet.

Camille Pissarro: Entrance to the Village of Voisins, 1872.

107

Charles-François Daubigny: Frontispiece for the Durand-Ruel catalogue, 1845.

While the Impressionists continued, in the face of the blindest and most commercial resistance, to pursue their conquest of light, the movements preceding or paralleling their own were continuing, or hanging on beside them or existing within themselves, without anyone's perceiving the fact. This was the inevitable consequence of the social disassociation which was advancing with them. Between the solid construction of the artists who came forth from the Revolution and its romantic expression and the infinite fragmentation of the researches which were now being attempted, there was the same distance which separates the moral idea of the bourgeois conquest from the needs which it had itself created. Corot, Daumier, Millet, Courbet and Puvis de Chavannes though living seemed to have been dead for years. All that was new, all that was unexpected or personal, they called Impressionism, to express their hate or love for it. ELIE FAURE

PAUL DURAND-RUEL was already forty years of age when he began dealing with the Impressionists; it was a relationship that was to last a further fifty years. He was the son of an art dealer who, at the time of Louis Philippe's enthronement, had introduced the young painters Delacroix, Decamps and Corot—the "great school of 1830," as it was called. Born the following year, Paul had been brought up in the hushed atmosphere of the Restoration; an ardent Catholic, he had first wanted to be a soldier, then a missionary priest. Succeeding to his father's business, shortly after the Bonapartist coup, Paul had championed the works of Delacroix and Corot against those of Winterhalter, the saccharine German who was the Emperor's favorite. Ignoring official Bonapartist art, Durand-Ruel had taken up the Barbizon painters, becoming exclusive agent for several of them and almost bankrupting himself by buying the total production of Théodore Rousseau.

According to Renoir, the streak of nonconformity in Durand-Ruel had its roots in the family's loyalty to the Bourbon monarchy. Long afterwards Renoir said: "We need a reactionary to defend our painting which the Salon crowd said was revolutionary. At any rate Durand-Ruel was the one person who didn't run the risk of being shot as a Communard."

Renoir was not speaking lightly. After the War of 1870 and the Commune of Paris, it was generally expected that France would adopt a constitutional monarchy on the British pattern. In 1873, when Napoleon III, following an operation for stone, died in England, a concerted effort was made by the French monarchists to put the legitimist Count of Chambord on the throne of France. When the aging Thiers was forced to resign that year the monarchists maneuvered successfully to install Marshal MacMahon as stand-in president, pending the time it would take to adopt a monarchial constitution. Their plans were set back, however, by Chambord's obstinate refusal to accept the tricolor as the national flag, in place of the traditional white flag of the kings of France. Seizing upon this quirk as an indication of Chambord's intention of exercising full monarchial powers, the republicans were able to press through the National Assembly three vital constitutional laws which effectively reduced the role of the chief executive to that of a conciliator. Supposedly "pragmatic and temporary," these laws, despite ruthless attack by the monarchist parties, remained on the statutes, progressively anchoring power in the bicameral National Assembly, leaving the way open for the later adoption of universal suffrage and other democratic procedures. The Impressionist struggle for public recognition exactly paralleled this political development, an integral, if perhaps unconscious, part of the republican ethos.

As Durand-Ruel tells it, his first Impressionist tie-up was with Monet, "a solid and durable man who, it seemed to me, would paint tirelessly for more years than I had given myself to live." (This was true: Monet, still painting, would outlive Durand-Ruel by four years.) Two years later Durand-Ruel had become Renoir's dealer and had then "entered into relations" with Pissarro, Degas and Sisley. "Ah, a villainous moment for painting," he said later. "If I had not been, in a word, nourished in the trade, I would not have survived the battle against public taste that I had entered into ... They looked upon me as a madman, hallucinated! They had given me credit for standing up for the beautiful Delacroix's and Corots (against Winterhalter), but to hear me now praising the Monets and Renoirs, that showed a complete lack of common sense fully deserving of public insult! Yes, in 1875, precisely, when I organized at the Hôtel Drouot the first sale of paintings by Monet and Renoir, which I had taken care to present in superb frames. There, during the sale—that was a beautiful row, as one says now—ah, how we were sneered at, and principally Monet and Renoir! The public shouted and called us shameless idiots. Some paintings were sold for fifty francs because of the frames. I withdrew a great many myself. Afterwards, I was all but carried off to the insane asylum at Charenton. Happily I was on good terms with my family. "

He had come back to France after the War full of optimism. Stopping by the studio of the popular Alfred Stevens he had seen a couple of paintings which Manet had left there in the hope of interesting one of Stevens' buyers. Durand-Ruel had bought them on the spot and next morning he had gone to Manet's studio where he had bought his entire stock of paintings—twenty-three canvases— for the sum total of 35,000 francs. Manet had hastily rounded up paintings which he had loaned to friends; Durand-Ruel bought these also. (Next day, at the Café Guerbois, Manet had sat down at his table, saying loudly: "Who is the painter who cannot sell fifty thousand francs worth of pictures in a year?" "It's you!" cried his friends. "Not true!" exclaimed Manet triumphantly. That same week he had taken a large studio in the rue de Saint-Pétersbourg.)

Full of confidence in the future, Durand-Ruel had included fourteen Impressionist paintings (by Degas, Monet, Sisley and Pissarro) in a lushly illustrated catalogue advertising his stock of three hundred paintings, which included the Manets. Armand Silvestre, who wrote an introduction to the catalogue, said of the Impressionists: "What should hasten the success of these late-comers is the fact that their pictures are painted in a singularly gay scale." Of the Manets, he said: "The moment has come for the public to be convinced, enthusiastic, or revolted, but not astounded." The catalogue also listed seven canvases by Courbet, including some he had painted while in prison. In view of the shattering prejudice against the anti-Bonapartist Courbet, extending in part to the Impressionists, one can only assume that Durand-Ruel felt that France was on the eve of a royalist renaissance in which a truly refined and detached, i.e. aristocratic, taste would prevail, or else that he was a very brave man.

Brave is the only word for the exhibition of modern French painting which he now held in London: thirteen canvases by Manet, nine by Pissarro, six by Sisley, four by Monet, three by Degas and one Renoir (an early *Pont des Arts*). It must have been a rare and wonderful exhibition, a beacon shining through the Victorian smog; but it went unnoticed. Though repeated in succeeding years, the upper classes were not yet buying Impressionists.

"Just as my father had had some difficulty in imposing the great school of 1830, that of Delacroix, Decamps and Corot, so I too ran the same risks in trying to sell the pictures of Monet and Renoir."
Interview with Durand-Ruel by Gustave Coquiot
in *Excelsior*, November 28, 1910

Auguste Renoir: Mademoiselle Jeanne Durand-Ruel, 1876.

LES
CONTEMPORAINS
JOURNAL HEBDOMADAIRE
ADMINISTRATEUR : M. DUFFIEUX, 15, FAUBOURG MONTMARTRE, PARIS. — UN AN : 6 FR.

EDOUARD MANET

Un quatuor courbé
Porte, en plein air, Manet sur sa large palette. | Il reçoit fièrement de chacun la courbette.
Mais qui pense à Courbet? F. C.

Manet, King of the Impressionists. Caricature by Alfred Le Petit.

Manet Featured on the Front Page of "L'Eclipse", May 14, 1876.

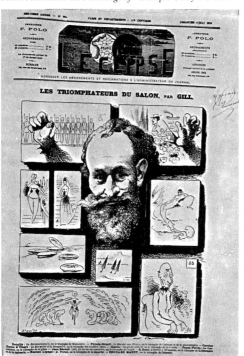

The last of the "pragmatic and temporary" constitutional laws had been adopted in July 1875, after a long and difficult passage through the legislature. The struggle between the monarchists and the republicans entered a new phase, distinguished by ruthless political in-fighting.

The Impressionists chose this moment, April 1876, to hold their second group exhibition. The front pages of the rightist newspapers had been blazoning republican animus for months past and no doubt the back-of-the-book editors were delighted to have an opportunity of affirming their solidarity in the cultural columns. What, they evidently asked themselves, could be more characteristic of the "anarchy" and "discord" that was ruining the country than these "impressionists" who ignored the rules of taste and decorum? And (it might easily have been said) had not one of their number been hailed as a comrade by that reddest of all Communards, Raoul Rigault? Whether the critics thought through their reaction to the Impressionist exhibition hardly matters: they, in fact, reacted with all the exacerbation of men whose social position is threatened, and in a measure out of all proportion to the numbers and influence of the Impressionists.

Edmond Duranty published *La Nouvelle Peinture* on the occasion of the second group exhibition in 1876. It was the first book dealing with the new movement. A novelist and short story writer, previously associated with Courbet, Duranty had launched a periodical called *Le Réalisme* in 1856. A friend of the Impressionists, above all of Degas, he took an active part in the Café Guerbois gatherings. In his book he criticized official painting with irony and insight and showed that the "new painting" was firmly rooted in the great tradition.

Title Page of "La Nouvelle Peinture" by Edmond Duranty.

Durand-Ruel's resources had been all but exhausted by his investment in the Impressionists, but, probably because he had so many of their paintings already framed, he allowed them to use his galleries, 11 rue Le Peletier, for their second exhibition. With Cézanne and Guillaumin abstaining (they were not handled by Durand-Ruel), there were 24 works by Degas, including *Cotton Office in New Orleans* and *Absinthe*; 18 by Monet, including *Beach at Sainte-Adresse* and *Snow Effects at Epernay*; 17 by Berthe Morisot, including *The Ball, Awakening, The Toilette*; 15 by Renoir, including *Nude in the Sun* and his portrait of Bazille; 12 by Pissarro, mostly Pontoise landscapes; 9 by Sisley, mostly views of Argenteuil and Louveciennes. Among the fifteen other exhibitors was Monet's boating friend, Gustave Caillebotte, who showed several competent paintings.

"Here is a new disaster..." wrote Albert Wolff in *Le Figaro*. "Five or six lunatics, one of them a woman, a group of unfortunate creatures seized with the mania of ambition, have met... to exhibit their works. Some people burst out laughing in front of these things—my heart is crushed by them. These so-called artists describe themselves as the intransigents, the impressionists; they take canvas, colors and brushes, carelessly throw on some tones and sign the thing. This is the way madmen at Ville-Evrard [an asylum for the insane] bring in stones from the road and think they have found diamonds. A frightful spectacle of human vanity working itself up to the point of dementia. Try to make M. Pissarro understand that the trees are not violet, that the sky is not the color of fresh butter, that in no country does one see such things as he paints and that no intelligence can accept such lunacies! As well spend time making a madman, who believes that he is the Pope, understand that he is living in Batignolles and not the Vatican. Try to make M. Degas see reason: tell him that in art there are some qualities having a name: drawing, color, execution, control, and he will laugh in your face and treat you as a reactionary. Try to explain to M. Renoir that the torso of a woman is not a mass of decomposing flesh with green and violet patches denoting the state of complete putrefaction in the cadaver! There is also a woman in the group, as in all famous bands; she is called Berthe Morisot and is curious to observe. With her, feminine grace manages to maintain itself in the midst of the ravings of a frenzied mind..."

Berthe Morisot had difficulty restraining her husband, Eugène Manet, from challenging Wolff to a duel.

A few days later *Le Figaro* added injury to insult: "It seems that art doesn't always soothe the mind. Yesterday the policeman guarding the gallery was obliged to expel an over-nervous gentleman who, in front of the paintings, the color of which offended him, was seized by an epileptic fit. It was quite a job to bring him back to his senses." And again, a few days later: "Yesterday, coming out of the exhibition, a poor fellow was arrested for biting people."

An anonymous writer in *La France* said: "The impressionists have assumed the right to follow no rules whatsoever... without taking into account common sense and truth... Their models look as if they had been taken out of the Morgue... It is unhealthy..." In the *Constitutionnel* Louis Enault posed the question about Monet: "I don't know where he has seen these landscapes he reproduces, but I doubt if he ever found their model in nature." In *Le Soir*, Bertall, the cartoonist, wrote: "At the rue Le Peletier there is a branch of the house of Doctor Blanche [a well known alienist]. They mostly admit painters here. Their madness is harmless. It consists of copying their canvases in the most incoherent colors. A series of which paintings they have framed magnificently and at great cost, for all the patients of this madhouse are affluent, housing their works in well-lighted and conveniently disposed rooms... These people have a pleasant aspect, they are dressed with care and sometimes elegantly. They are gentle and polite, they are called the Impressionists." In *Le Soleil*, Emile Porcheron asked: "What is an impressionist? The matter is delicate and requires some reflection. As far as we are concerned an impressionist is a man who, without knowing why, feels the need to devote himself to the cult of the palette and who, having neither talent nor the necessary study to obtain a serious result, contents

N° 4.　　Prix : 15 centimes.　　28 Avril 1877.

L'IMPRESSIONNISTE

JOURNAL D'ART

Paraissant tous les Jeudis

En vente : 15, rue du Croissant, 15　　|　　Administration et Rédaction
ET DANS TOUS LES KIOSQUES　　　　|　　22 BIS, RUE LAFFITTE

Scieurs de long, croquis de M. SISLEY, d'après son tableau.

Front Page of the Art Journal "L'Impressionniste" of April 28, 1877.

In the first issue of L'Impressionniste *(April 6, 1877), an art magazine published every Thursday, Georges Rivière replied to the insulting article in* Le Figaro.

To the Editor of *Le Figaro*:

When a few years ago [in 1874] a group of artists sharing the same views had the idea of holding an exhibition outside the official Salon, it is common knowledge that the newspapers heaped insults on these revolutionaries who were seeking in art something that no one had suspected. At that time the newspapers had the scoffers on their side; this painting was quite different from the painting one saw every day and the public let itself be taken in by the ill-natured gibes directed at young men who were said to be acting like fools.

The second exhibition [in 1876] was greeted by the same exclamations from the press. M. Wolff, who pretends to be a connoisseur, could not find abuse enough in his fertile brain for these artists courageously struggling against hard luck. The public however, seeing how insistent these painters were in the pursuit of their experiments, looked at their works more closely, and the impressionists emerged stronger from this second trial, supported by a large number of remarkable men.

In 1877 the exhibition is having an immense success; on Wednesday everybody responded eagerly to the invitation of the exhibitors. Many people have taken to their work, and so on Thursday morning it was very sad indeed to read the ridiculous and odious criticisms levelled at the impressionists. Except for *Le Rappel, L'homme libre* and a few others, the papers were unanimous in their recriminations.

himself with making loud publicity in favor of his school, and giving the public some paintings the value of which is no more than the frame which surrounds them."

In *Le Pays*, Georges Maillard pretended to strike a balance: "Basically they are, I believe, discontented people, radicals of painting who, not being able to find a place in the ranks of the regular painters, have constituted a society, have flown some sort of revolutionary flag, and have organized an exhibition... For the most part their canvases would make a cab-horse rear... There is here a brutality of brushwork, a madness of execution and an insanity of conception which is absolutely revolting; it would make one fall into despair if one were not splitting one's sides laughing."

The boulevards were not all that amused, or interested. Four issues of *The Impressionist*, a slender sheet in which Georges Rivière defended the impressionist approach to painting, went almost entirely unsold. Dumped at the shop of a former Durand-Ruel employee who had opened a small importing business, the unsold copies were finally used to reinforce leaking bags of plaster.

Nor was Manet immune from critical malice at this controversial moment. His picture of a man and a woman in a boat, painted at Argenteuil where he had watched Monet at work, exhibited at the '75 Salon, had been attacked for its "scandalous colors." At the '76 Salon his two pictures were thrown out, *Le Bien Public* reporting a member of the Jury saying, "Enough of this. We have given Manet ten years to turn over a new leaf. He has not done so, on the contrary he grows worse. Let's reject him." Manet invited the public to come and see the rejected pictures at his studio, causing *Le Français'* critic, Bernadille, to ask: "Why didn't he favor the exhibition of his brothers and friends, the Impressionists, with his two paintings? Why does he act the lone wolf? This is ingratitude. With what luster wouldn't the presence of Manet have endowed that coterie of artistic rogues..."

The critics probably realized that the painters were immune to their shafts. The references to the expensive frames, the well-lighted gallery, coupled with the running theme of lunacy, suggested the target they were aiming at. Durand-Ruel, a businessman, had much to lose from being publicly designated a candidate for Doctor Blanche's lunatic asylum, a man hallucinated by bad art, a class renegade. When the Impressionists, despite all criticism, decided to hold their third exhibition the following year, Durand-Ruel's fine rooms were not available.

The durability of the amended constitution was tested towards the end of 1876 with President MacMahon's choice of Jules Simon as Premier. France waited tensely to see how far Simon, who had a reputation for compromise, would yield to MacMahon's intention of standing down in favor of the Count of Chambord. Meanwhile the Impressionists prepared for their third exhibition, the resourceful Caillebotte finding a large empty apartment in the same street as Durand-Ruel's gallery, for which he advanced a month's rent out of his own pocket. This time they adopted their given name: they called it the Impressionist Exposition. Degas and Renoir protested ("Impressionism—a word I loathe, " Renoir always said), but were overruled; Degas, however, succeeded in having the group agree not to attempt to exhibit at the Salon; and if none protested against Cézanne continuing his old feud (he still campaigned for a regular Salon des Refusés) it was because his case was hopeless. There were eighteen exhibitors with a total of 230 works on view, among them Renoir's *Swing* and his *Moulin de la Galette*, Cézanne's *Bathers* and *Impression after Nature*, Monet's *White Turkeys* and *Gare Saint-Lazare*, pictures of dancers, café scenes and women making their toilette by Degas, Sisley's *Flood at Marly*, and other landscapes by Pissarro, Guillaumin and Caillebotte.

The exhibition opened its doors at the beginning of May. On May 16, 1877, the Republic had its greatest crisis since the War. MacMahon dismissed the wavering Simon and installed the royalist de Broglie as Premier with a cabinet of rightist businessmen, pending general elections later that year. The test of the liberal constitution had come and the rightists had prepared for it by a coalition of Legitimist and Bonapartist factions in a Party of Order, whose principal campaign cry was that the country was in danger of falling into the hands of the "Reds." (The contemporary phrase was *Le spectre rouge*.)

Political tension took the sting out of the critics' writings and many were too busy politicking to comment at all. Théodore Duret says that the exhibition "gave rise to outbursts of laughter, contempt, indignation and disgust." Roger Ballu, a Beaux Arts critic, wrote: "Monet and Cézanne... It is necessary to have seen them to imagine what they are... When children amuse themselves with a box of colors and a piece of paper, they do better. "

Predictably sales were few, and the artists decided to hold a public sale of their paintings at the Hôtel Drouot immediately after the close of the exhibition. Each picture as it was brought forward by the auctioneer's helper, was received with groans and passed around, from hand to hand, turned upside down. (This joke, says Duret, had emanated from *Le Charivari* which maintained that in the impressionist landscapes the line of the horizon was indistinguishable, earth, water and sky being equally amorphous, etc. The joke had found its way into the music halls where an impressionist dauber was represented as being incapable of finding out which was the top and which the bottom of a canvas he had just smudged with paint.) At one point, during the sale, the painters were all but physically attacked by groups of people who addressed them as Communards, Gambettists, Democrats, etc. When one among the mob called Berthe Morisot a *gourgandine* (harlot), Pissarro promptly punched the man in the face. There does not seem to have been any doubt that the painters were the object of an organized political attack.

The sale at the Hôtel Drouot realized 7,610 francs for a total of 45 canvases, a considerable number being withdrawn by the painters. At Durand-Ruel's gallery there was a fifty-years retrospective, Corot, Delacroix, Rousseau, etc. Durand-Ruel was on the verge of bankruptcy.

LA RÉPUBLIQUE FRANÇAISE

Exhibition of the Impressionists (signed Ph.B., i.e. Philippe Burty), in *La République française*, April 25, 1877.

Though generally greeted by jeers and anger, this exhibition nevertheless continues to attract the public... The first impression nearly always produces a movement of keen surprise... The word "impressionists"... fails to characterize them. They are in particular impressionable people. Without going into a discussion of method which would certainly weary our readers, we may say that these artists seek on the whole to record the general aspect of things and people, their character disengaged from conventional aspects; and that in actual practice they aim at bright colors and proclaim the uselessness of black and opaque tones. Is this something to laugh at or be indignant about? Certainly not. It is only a peculiar development of what Corot had sought after in abandoning outlines, in constantly breaking up shadows by more or less emphatic shades of gray.

These works are too thoroughly marked by a set purpose for them yet to be accepted by the public for a long time to come. Yet they have their buyers, and these are not just anybody. As pictures they offend... When in place and as decorations, they have a brightness and a frankness of effect which are undeniable. They will not for a long time yet force the door of the official exhibitions. They will, however, make their way into them as if by infiltration...

The genuine impressionist landscapists are Messrs. Claude Monet, Cézanne, Pissarro and Cisley [sic]. Their landscapes, which cannot be confused when looked at attentively, have for us one unforgivable defect: they reduce the tree to the state of a bodiless wraith, they take these trunks, these branches which have a beauty of their own just as the human body and limbs do, and give them the unjustifiable stiffness of a telegraph pole or formless twigs...

M. de Gas also paints for the fastidious, and of course with more accent and vehemence... He has chosen [in his pastels] some odd corners of Parisian life: the boulevard cafés, the café-concerts on the Champs-Elysées, the wings and ballet rehearsal rooms at the Opera. He enters them as a man endowed with feeling, wit and mocking observation, as a prompt and skillful draftsman. His work is light and subtle, of salient originality. The present Salons are too starched and formal to accept his sensitive studies, which correspond in literature to neat and pointed short stories.

M. Renoir is very impressionistic, but to characterize him better one would have to call him "a romantic impressionist. " Of an extrasensitive temperament, he always shrinks from overstating things. With a few added touches to emphasize what is stable in a *Ball at Montmartre* [i.e. the *Moulin de la Galette*], the chairs, benches, tables, he would give their true action to dancing or talking groups, their quivering spots to the rays of sunlight, and on the whole he would set a stamp of reality which as it is it fails to achieve.

Paul Cézanne: The House of the Hanged Man, 1873.

Camille Pissarro: Portrait of Paul Cézanne, about 1874. Pencil.

Cézanne Sitting in Pissarro's Garden at Pontoise in 1877, with Pissarro Standing on the Right. Photograph.

"We were always together, but what is certain is that each kept the one thing that counts, his sensation."

Letter from Pissarro to his son Lucien

After the war, which he spent working quietly at L'Estaque on the Riviera, Cézanne returned to the neighborhood of Paris where he rejoined Pissarro, who had just come back from England. With Hortense Fiquet and his son Paul, only a few months old, Cézanne settled at Pontoise in 1872 near his friend, then in the fall of that year moved to Auvers-sur-Oise where he lived for the next two years. There he began a series of pictures—the *House of the Hanged Man* is one of them—which remain among the most famous of his impressionist period.

The presence of Pissarro, an inspiring personality, solid in his affections, large-hearted and broad-minded, was a great comfort to Cézanne and a strong catalyst in the evolution of his art. Beside Pissarro he felt the need to discipline his restless, excitable temperament. Discarding the overwrought colors that verged sometimes on a melodramatic emotionalism, he turned now towards the rendering of the sensations aroused in him by nature and the working out of a corresponding pictorial form.

His friendship with Pissarro was solidly based on mutual esteem. In a letter to his mother written in 1874 he said: "Pissarro has been away from Paris for about a month and a half, he is in Brittany; but I know he has a good opinion of me who," he characteristically added, "have a very good opinion of myself." The rest of this letter

throws light not only on his personality but on the line of research which he was following up. "I begin to find myself stronger than all those around me and you know that the good opinion I have of myself has been arrived at with my eyes open. I always have to work hard, but not to achieve a slick finish, which attracts the admiration of fools. And this finish that the vulgar appreciate so much is only a matter of handiwork and makes any picture resulting from it unartistic and common. I try to complete what I begin only for the pleasure of making it truer and more accomplished."

Pissarro, for his part, admired Cézanne's work and some of his own landscapes show the impact of their common preoccupations. His more earthy temperament, however, more attuned to the daily sights and sounds of nature, impelled him to study landscape as a means of conveying, by rapid touches, the ever-changing pattern of light and shadow which, in his hands, becomes a hymn to life. "You have a profound and intimate sense of nature, and a power over the brush that makes a fine picture by you something absolutely sound and four-square," Duret wrote to him in 1873. Into his art Pissarro projected a moral view of the world, even when the subject was no more than the play of light on a wall through the branches of a tree.

114

Camille Pissarro: Red Roofs. Village Scene. 1877.

"I felt that my mind was being emancipated in the very days when my eyes were emancipated."

Camille Pissarro

"Meanwhile come and have a look in the garden of the people here. You will see an attempt to create from scratch a wholly modern art, wholly imbued with our surroundings, our feelings and the things of our time."

Edmond Duranty, *La Nouvelle Peinture*, 1876

"Sisley was wholly wrapped up in his art, in the pride of overcoming nature in that daily battle engaged in by the artist, and the hope that he had recorded on his canvases something of the fleeting beauty of eternal things. "

Gustave Geffroy, *Sisley*

Alfred Sisley: Approaches to a Station in Winter. Pastel.

Alfred Sisley: Snow at Louveciennes, 1874.

"Sinister and beautiful under the clear sky is this familiar landscape . . . The terrible poetry of winter is written in canvases in which Monet has recorded the frozen appearance of air and water, the cold reverberations pulsing under the hardened surface of the river, the numbness of vegetable life suspended in this boreal light, ghostly, frost-bitten trees, funereal poplars, ravaged hills, between the dull sky and the water shining with a metallic light."

Gustave Geffroy, *Claude Monet*

"M. Monet is the most skillful and most daring, M. Sisley the most harmonious and most timorous, M. Pissarro the most real and most naïve," wrote Armand Silvestre in 1874. And indeed, even at the first glance, what is most striking in a picture by Sisley is the harmonious, poetic effect conveyed by his delicate, transparent nuances of gray, pink and light green. Sisley, probably even more than his friends, endured great hardships due to the incomprehension of the public, but endured them with a noble stoicism that compels admiration. His natural reserve, dignity and sensitivity inform his approach to nature, and land, water, reflections and sky, whether blue or overcast, unfailingly enthrall his painter's eye. Like Monet, Pissarro and Renoir, he liked snow effects, but "probably none of them ever matched Sisley's rendering of snow precisely because of the delicacy of the tonal passages, to which his eye was incomparably sensitive. His *Snow at Louveciennes* has pink tones suggestive of optimism, of sympathy for this white cloak overlaying houses and earth" (Lionello Venturi).

Alfred Sisley: Port-Marly, Weir under Snow, 1876.

Claude Monet: The Church at Vétheuil, Snow, about 1878.

Camille Pissarro:
Garden with Trees in Blossom.
Spring, Pontoise, 1877.

Paul Cézanne:
Pissarro going out to Paint,
about 1874. Pencil.

"In front of his canvas, his palette in hand, his colors well arranged to diffuse over his landscape the brightness of the sky, Pissarro forgot everything except the spectacle which his eye had chosen and which corresponded to his innermost feelings. He was a countryman, enamored of the village, the gardens and fields next to the rustic houses, the valley where the stream went by and the river wound away, the road bordered by flowering hedges, the orchard whose apple trees displayed the full-blown grace of pink and white blossoms, the rich yield of red and yellow fruit."

Gustave Geffroy, *Claude Monet*

Louveciennes, Pontoise, Auvers-sur-Oise, these names bring to mind at once the diaphanous light of the Ile-de-France, trees in bloom or under snow, bright skies whether blue or gray, water and its reflections, all the seasons and changing aspects of the countryside which we now see through the eyes of the Impressionists.

While Monet and Sisley loved the variegated reflections of the sky on water and fields or filtering through foliage, Pissarro often preferred village themes. While taking care to embody trees and houses in an organic composition, he succeeded, as in this canvas of *Garden with Trees in Blossom*, in conveying the immediate, exuberant impact of spring by a profusion of manifold clustering touches of color laid in with amazing freedom.

"These landscapes, seascapes, flower pieces and scenes of modern life bring into the dimness of our homes a wealth of light and freshness. One cannot say as much for many other works for which high prices have been paid, and which, sallow and jaded, soulless and tame, bring the sensitive, sincere art lover nothing but yawning boredom."

Philippe Burty, preface to the Hôtel Drouot sale, 1875

William Bouguereau: Nymphs and Satyr, 1873.

Auguste Renoir: Path in the Woods, 1874.

William Bouguereau, one of the most successful Salon painters under Napoleon III and a contemporary—a very hostile contemporary—of the Impressionists, saw nature still peopled with nymphs. This was taken to be a sign of prodigious culture, of far-ranging imagination and technical mastery. Anybody, it was assumed, could paint what he saw around him every day. How ridiculous to go out painting trees and sunspots when the museums were full of the exploits of the gods! Thirty years later, thanks to the Impressionists, landscape was established as perhaps the most admired and highly developed form of painting.

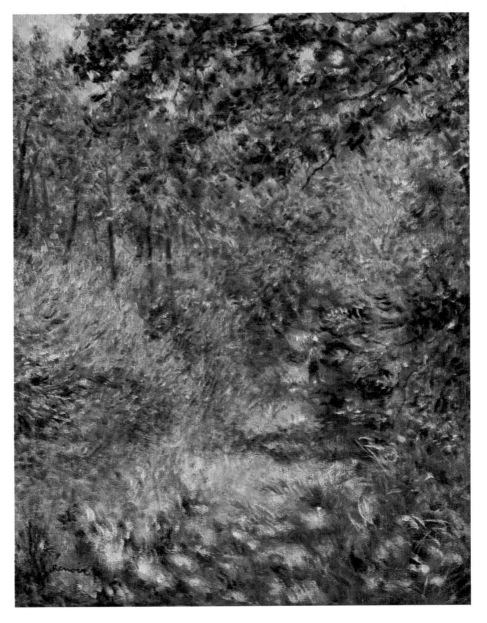

"In the matter of coloring they have made a real discovery for which no precedent is to be found anywhere, neither in the Dutch masters, nor in the bright tones of fresco painting, nor in the light tonalities of the eighteenth century. They have not only applied themselves to that free and subtle interplay of colors which results from the observation of the most delicate values in contrasting or interpenetrating tones. The peculiar discovery of these artists consists in having recognized that tones are *discolored* by intense light, that sunlight reflected by objects tends, by its very brightness, to reduce them to that light-unity which merges its seven prismatic rays into a single colorless flash, which is light itself. From intuition to intuition, they have gradually been led to break down sunshine into its rays and elements, and to recompose its unity by the overall harmony of the iridescences which they spread over their canvases. "

Edmond Duranty, *La Nouvelle Peinture*, 1876

Auguste Renoir: The English Pear Tree, 1885.

Claude Monet: Haystacks, about 1890. Pencil.

What incensed the public of that day was not so much the landscape subjects chosen by the Impressionists as their way of painting. Their determination to catch the passing moment obliged them to work with a speed and freedom that gave their pictures a sketchy, unfinished look; if the fleeting impression was to be caught and conveyed, there could be no question of careful finish.

All the impressionist painters tended, as time passed, to go beyond the mere delineation of the motif towards a purely pictorial expression of it. Witness the contrast between the *Haystack* painted by Pissarro in 1873 and the series of Haystacks painted twenty years later by Monet. With Pissarro, light serves to synthesize the various elements. In connection with a picture of the same period, he wrote to Théodore Duret in 1873: "I shall attempt a field of ripe wheat this summer. There is nothing colder than bright summer sunshine; quite unlike the work of the colorists, nature is colored in winter and cold in summer." But Pissarro did not hold aloof from what he saw: he represented the rick of hay, but also the wagon and peasants. In 1890 Monet began painting a series of haystacks, but with him the subject was "the instant." On October 7 of that year he wrote to Gustave Geffroy: "I'm plugging away, toiling doggedly at a series of different effects (of haystacks), but at this time of year the sun goes down so fast that I can't keep up with it.

I'm becoming so slow a worker, it's maddening. But the further I go, the more I realize the amount of work involved in rendering what I'm after: the 'instantaneousness,' the envelope of things, with the same light pouring in everywhere. More than ever easy canvases tossed off at one go get my back up."

In his *English Pear Tree* of 1885, Renoir in turn gave up the delimitation of specific forms: the figures fade into the shadow of the trees, the road disappears in the grass, the leaves melt into the sky. And the sky is no longer a backdrop but a colored medium infusing everything it envelopes with its constant variations.

Camille Pissarro: The Haystack, Pontoise, 1873.

Auguste Renoir: Path Winding Up Through Tall Grass, about 1876-1878.

Claude Monet: Summer, 1874.

Never did the Impressionists venture on bolder color effects than in their summer landscapes. Between 1873 and 1878 they painted pictures in which an almost miraculous balance is achieved between sensation and creation. Plying a light and resourceful brush Monet and Renoir record all the vibrations of light and try to match on canvas the bloom and vividness of nature.

Each color is directly modified by the one beside it; a given tone appears totally different when it is placed in a certain context. Two greens or two blues lose in intensity when they stand side by side; but the juxtaposition of green with red, its complementary, or blue with orange, steps up their intensity and luminosity. The flowers of the fields provided the Impressionists with the spots of complementary color they needed to enliven their meadows and prairies. Corot muted the sonority of green by surrounding it with ochres and grays, neutral tints with a dimming effect. Monet brightened his fields with poppies, for red sets off green. The theory of complementary colors had been set forth forty years earlier by the chemist Chevreul.

Claude Monet: *Poppies, 1873.*

Claude Monet: *Field of Oats, 1890.*

Claude Monet: *Breakfast in the Garden, 1872-1873.*

Claude Monet: *Gladioli, about 1873.*

Auguste Renoir: *Young Woman with a Dog, about 1880.*

"It takes immense genius to reproduce simply and sincerely what you see in front of you." Edmond Duranty, *Le Réalisme*, 1856

Flowers were a theme which enabled the Impressionists to paint from nature while working indoors. It was a theme which also gave them the opportunity of studying the harmonies and contrasts of pure color. Once they had defined their style, the Impressionists ceased to regard flowers as a still life, but rather as a living specimen of nature herself. A comparison of two flower pieces by Renoir and Cézanne reveals two opposite poles of pictorial sensibility. Cézanne arranges his flowers symmetrically, building up his canvas by an almost geometric assemblage of planes and infusing his flowers with a sense of perenniality; one feels that they will last. Renoir, on the contrary, conveys a fleeting impression; the mirror in which his myriad touches of color are reflected multiplies the lights until they flare up like fireworks.

Auguste Renoir: Arum and Hothouse Plants, 1864.

Edgar Degas: Woman with Chrysanthemums (Madame Hertel), 1865.

Auguste Renoir: Bouquet in Front of a Mirror, 1876.

Paul Cézanne: Bouquet with Delftware Vase, 1873-1875.

The Theme of the Still Life

Paul Cézanne:
Jug and Spirit Stove.
Pencil.

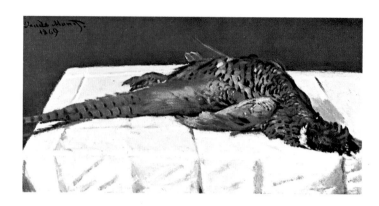

The Impressionists naturally treated the theme of the still life, although at first sight it may seem to have little connection with their main concerns. This type of picture implies a studied preparation, a deliberate arrangement on the part of the painter, but what attracted the Impressionists was the choice of everyday subjects which it offered. Just as their landscapes are devoid of nymphs, so their still lifes generally consist merely of a bird, a fish lying on a kitchen table, an apple, a pitcher of milk or a bowl on a shelf.

The new interest in still life stemmed not only from the persistent influence of the Dutch masters but from the revelation of Chardin, twelve of whose still lifes entered the Louvre in 1869 with the La Caze bequest. Manet carefully built up his still life in the *Salmon* of 1866, assembling noble elements—a fish ready to serve, a chinaware bowl and a fine glass—in a composition in which recession is traditionally suggested by a knife laid slantwise. Monet chose to paint a dead bird on a bare white tablecloth; but the bird was a pheasant with brilliant plumage, therefore a subject still having some prestige. Cézanne, however, was interested only in the geometry of forms uninteresting in themselves—apples, biscuits, a bunch of grapes. Such objects became the pretext for a perfectly autonomous pictorial creation whose overall harmony was untroubled by any specific feature or implication extraneous to the picture itself. The still life entitled *Pot of Flowers on a Table*, painted in the 1880's, is a masterly demonstration of this approach.

Claude Monet: The Pheasant, 1869.

Edouard Manet: Still Life with Salmon, 1866.

Paul Cézanne: The Sideboard, 1873-1877.

Paul Cézanne: Pot of Flowers on a Table, 1882-1887.

"To make of Impressionism something solid and durable like the art of the museums."

Cézanne

Fitful and Fleeting Reflections

Even before 1870 the Impressionists—Monet, Pissarro and Renoir above all—had begun using separate brushstrokes and pure, unblended colors, the better to render reflections on water and to accentuate the glow of light. Zola, speaking of Monet in 1868, pointed out the importance of this technique: "With him, water is alive, deep, above all real. It laps against the boats with little greenish ripples cut across by white flashes; it spreads out in glaucous pools suddenly ruffled by a breeze, it lengthens the masts reflected on its surface by breaking up their image, it has dull and lambent tints lit up by broken gleams."

After 1870 Monet followed up this experiment and used separate brushstrokes not only to represent water but for all his other themes. The complete unity of vision he then attained was made possible by this deliberate restriction to a single technical device. *Sailboat at Argenteuil* is one of the major examples of that unity: light, in its manifold variations, is in fact the sole subject of the picture. The vibrations of the atmosphere, which modify not only the water but the trees, houses and sails, create a new pictorial dimension which compels the spectator to look at the picture with a fresh eye. The symbolist poet Jules Laforgue, writing in 1883, pointed out the novelty of this art: "In a landscape bathed in light, in which people are modelled like colored grisailles, where the academic painter sees only white light outspread, the Impressionist sees it bathing everything not with a dead whiteness, but with a thousand vibrant clashings, with rich prismatic decompositions. Where the academic sees only the outline binding the modelling, he sees the real, living lines, not taking geometric form but built up with a thousand irregular touches which, from a distance, convey life. Where the academic sees things fitting into their regular respective planes according to a framework reducible to a pure theoretical diagram, he sees perspective established through a thousand nuances of tone and touch, through the varied conditions of the air laid out not on a motionless but on a moving plane."

Claude Monet: Sailboat at Argenteuil, about 1874.

Claude Monet

Alfred Sisley: The Flood at Port-Marly, 1876.

"Treating a subject for its tones and not for its own sake, that is what distinguishes the Impressionists from other painters."

Georges Rivière, 1877

Sky and water and the reflections of one in the other, the vibration of colors in sunlight or in the subdued light of overcast skies, these are among the major themes of the Impressionists, of Sisley and Monet in particular. Monet never tired of painting water: "I should like to be always on it or beside it and, when I die, to be buried in a buoy," he once said. The paintings made by Monet at Argenteuil mark a moment of happy equilibrium in his work. Troubles and worries disappeared in the full free exercise of the creative urge, in the conquest of an autonomous art which can only be judged in terms of its own intentions. Thus began a new era in modern painting, which in the exploration of that conquest found its true purpose. From his first seascapes at Le Havre to the Waterlilies at Giverny, Monet never ceased to investigate the essential problem of the relations between the artist's eye, feelings and imagination.

Floods, in which water, sky and land become one and the same element, were a theme treated by Monet, Pissarro and Sisley; they inspired some of the latter's most famous pictures. Octave Mirbeau, in an article in *Le Figaro* in 1892, analyzed what seemed to him to distinguish Sisley's early period of impressionist plenitude from his later pictures: "His very sensitive and responsive nature found itself at home among all the scenes of nature; the impressions it received from them were not very sharp, but they were manifold and vivid... There was more charm than strength in his painting, an innate grace, something quick, dainty and loose, a devil-may-care touch whose appeal was keen and gave to the lack of finish a sometimes exquisite poetry."

Claude Monet: Argenteuil Bridge, 1874.

Claude Monet: Argenteuil Bridge (detail), 1874.

"*The power, the buoyancy, in a word the life that Renoir puts into figures, Monet puts into things; he has found out the very soul of them. In his pictures water ripples, locomotives move, the sails of boats belly in the wind, the very ground and houses, everything in the work of this great artist has an intense personal life that no one before him had discovered or even suspected.*"

GEORGES RIVIÈRE

Claude Monet: The Beach at Trouville, 1870.

Edouard Manet:

Boating, 1874.

Figure Study for "Boating," 1874. Pen and Ink.

During the summer of 1874 Manet and Monet saw a good deal of each other at Argenteuil, a riverside village on the Seine now famous as one of the high places of Impressionism. Won over by the discoveries of open air painting, Manet had by now already begun intensifying and varying his light effects in order to leaven the plastic form of his figures and better integrate them into their natural surroundings. Although he held aloof from the impressionist exhibitions—deaf to the urging of his young friends, he declined to take part in their first show at Nadar's—he admired the work they were doing, especially that of Monet and Renoir. At Argenteuil Manet and Monet began working together in a real community of endeavor and became close friends. Manet then chose typically impressionist themes—sailboats at the waterside, boaters on the river, etc. But while Monet, even when placing the figures in the foreground of his composition (as in *Beach at Trouville* of 1870), handled his picture in terms of light and shadow, with rapid, contrasting touches that caused figures and atmosphere to merge, Manet on the contrary clung to a certain emphasis on form, which he rendered by the heightened intensity of his color. In composing *In A Boat* he hit on a happy and unusual device (one with which Degas also experimented): the scene appears to continue out of the picture, the respective positions of the figures suggesting space even while keeping them in close-up; we have the impression that the boat is gliding before our eyes.

Edouard Manet: Argenteuil, 1874.

"One enjoyed the day, the fatigue, the speed, the free and vibrant out-of-doors, the glittering of the water, the sun flashing over the earth, the shimmering flame of all that dazes and dazzles in these sauntering outings, that almost animal intoxication with life conveyed by a great steaming river, blinded by light and fine weather."

Edmond and Jules de Goncourt, *Manette Salomon,* 1865

Auguste Renoir:
Woman in a Boat, 1877.

Paul Cézanne:
Four People in a Boat,
1870-1875. Pencil.

"To my mind a picture should be something pleasant, cheerful and pretty, yes pretty! There are too many disagreeable things in life as it is for us to contrive still more of them."

Renoir

"Renoir possessed to a rare degree that sense of the modern which is the mark of original artists of all ages. He had a direct vision of life, of figures gathered together, of sentimental conversations, scenes of pleasure and stylish displays, and he was the painter of the free life, passing through it with his youthful fancies and the apparent whimsy of his studious art, that harbored so much in the way of scruples and research. This is the Renoir of suburban enjoyments, of young people embarking for the Cytheras of Bougival, Chatou and Nogent; of Parisian women whose wistful smiles and dreaming gaze make them the Mona Lisas of the boating parties; of outdoor luncheons in which the radiant atmosphere of the fine days, the color of the eyes and the pattern of the smiles evaporate delightfully in the cigarette smoke and the mild excitement of the conversation."

Gustave Geffroy, *Claude Monet*

Argenteuil and the Banks of the Seine

Seen side by side, these two pictures of the same subject, one by Monet, the other by Renoir, reveal at a glance the essence of one of the privileged moments of impressionist painting. At Argenteuil Monet surpassed himself; there, in the mid seventies, "the freshness of his vision gave a matchless, almost magical beauty to the new style" (Jean Leymarie). He was conscious of having mastered the means which enabled him to record on canvas those elements which by definition are impalpable and fleeting: the transparency and vibration of air and water.

The enthusiasm and ascendancy of Monet were such that his friends followed him in this line of research. Renoir often came to paint with him and we find them here at the same hour of the day, in front of the same motif; the riverside with a sailboat about to cast off, while others glide by in the background and ducks paddle in the shallows. With equal ease the two painters convey the enchantment they experienced in front of this motif; but their vision, so similar at first sight, reveals two very different temperaments. Monet has an eye for what one can only call "immediacy." He achieves here an admirable synthesis of light, emphasizing only essential accents, careful above all to render the movement of light with utmost accuracy. "Monet is only an eye, but what an eye!" said Cézanne.

Renoir, on the contrary, surrendered to the charm of the subject and multiplied details (sailboats, ducks, etc.), such was the pleasure he took in the beauty of the scene. He paid no particular heed to lines of construction, but recorded a happy moment with caressing touches of the brush.

Boaters on the Seine at Bougival, painted a few years later, confirms Renoir's marvelous power of turning a picture into a festival of the senses. With bursts of color he transforms earth, water and men into a bouquet of spring flowers.

Claude Monet: *Sailboats at Argenteuil*, 1873-1874.

Auguste Renoir: *Sailboats at Argenteuil*, 1873-1874.

Auguste Renoir: *Boaters on the Seine at Bougival*, 1881.

"It was Argenteuil that was to sharpen Monet's perceptions and to provide the point of departure for the most decisive evolution of his art... From then on, whatever the place in which he went to work, whatever the venture on which he embarked, and he embarked on some that carried him to the very confines of nature and fancy, he had laid down the principle of his artistic language; he went on to enrich its terms, vary its shapes, extend and volatilize its expression, but that language remained his very own."

Arsène Alexandre, *Claude Monet*

"Worries and poverty were left at the entrance to the ball. Always filled with a merry crowd of young people swept up in the dance, the place offered a cheerful scene that Renoir dreamed of representing in a large picture."

Georges Rivière, *Renoir*

Windmills in Montmartre, about 1855. Stereoscopic View.

Auguste Renoir: Le Moulin de la Galette, 1876.

Entrance to the Gardens of the Moulin de la Galette in Montmartre. Photograph.

Auguste Renoir: The Swing, 1876.

On the heights of Montmartre the old Moulin de la Galette still stands just off the rue Lepic. With his friends Lamy, Goeneutte and Georges Rivière, Renoir was one of the habitués of the Moulin, and in order to paint this large picture of it he installed his studio in an old house in the nearby rue Cortot. He worked on the canvas in the afternoon on the spot, where his friends came to pose for him, while in the morning he painted *The Swing* in the garden under his studio window.

Photographs of the period show the Moulin de la Galette as it was then: a popular, countrified, open air dance-hall, charming no doubt in a Paris even then beginning to be overcrowded, but without any particular attractions. Thus Renoir saw it, and it was precisely this ordinary, unaffected air of the place that enchanted him. Lightly and freely handled, the whole picture pulses with life. Bluish shadows and pinkish lights crisscross and interfuse, flickering over faces, leafage, straw hats and the girls' dresses, and dappling the ground in a vibrant interplay of color and light, sun and shadow.

...and Sunday Outings at Bougival

"It was the capriciousness of the Paris weather which, by compelling the painter to abandon certain open air landscapes, prompted him to begin the *Luncheon of the Boating Party*. He was able to carry it through, with the same good luck as when he undertook the *Ball* [i.e. the *Moulin de la Galette*]. These two pictures have sometimes been likened to each other, and rightly so, even though the handling is very different... Some of the color harmonies used in the *Ball* fail to reappear in the *Luncheon of the Boating Party*. What the two pictures do have in common is the spirit in which the artist painted the figures, also the style... The summer of 1880 may be considered an important stage in Renoir's career. it brings to an end the series of scenes depicting the popular life of the Parisians. Thereafter he was rarely if ever to be seen again working at the Moulin, at Bougival or in the Place Pigalle."

Georges Rivière, *Renoir et ses amis*

Auguste Renoir: *The Luncheon of the Boating Party*, 1881.

"*Bal des Canotiers*" (Boaters' Dance-Hall) at Bougival. Photograph.

Auguste Renoir: *Oarsmen at Chatou*, 1879.

F. Lunel: *La Grenouillère*.

"The boating party has had lunch under the awning of the restaurant. The picture was executed on the spot, in the open air. The Seine and its banks, lighted up by the summer sun, give it a glowing background. One finds here the features of the painting called impressionist, common to Renoir and his painter friends. But one also finds here certain characteristics which are his alone. The eye is particularly attracted by the women with whom the boaters have been lunching.

"The men, while they might have been painted less well by another than they were by Renoir, might have had the same character that he has given them. But one cannot imagine these women, as they are here, having been painted by anybody else. They have the free and easy manners one would expect of young women who have lunched and are enjoying themselves with a group of young men, but they also have that graciousness, that roguish charm which Renoir alone could give to women."

Théodore Duret, *Renoir, 1924*

Quai des Grands-Augustins Seen from the Pont Saint-Michel, 1864. Photograph.

Camille Pissarro: The Outer Boulevards, Snow Effect, 1879.

Edouard Manet: Street Pavers in the Rue Mosnier, 1878.

Auguste Renoir: Le Pont Neuf, 1872.

Claude Monet: Boulevard des Capucines, 1873.

Auguste Renoir: The Great Boulevards, 1875.

The Paris Boulevards

Street scenes, full of the bustle of modern life, were a theme that attracted all the impressionist painters, especially Monet, Renoir and later Pissarro. Manet revealed its possibilities with his *Concert in the Tuileries*, the first picture of an open air social gathering. As early as 1865 Monet and Renoir were painting townscapes in Paris, but it was not until 1872 that they focused their eye on the street, with its movement and light, its passing figures and traffic. It is difficult to set up one's easel in the middle of the street or sidewalk, and the painters often worked from an upper window, catching the scene below along a plunging line of sight—an angle of vision that lent itself to dynamic foreshortenings well suited to the subject. Thirty years later, when ill-health kept him indoors, Pissarro painted many views and street scenes from his windows, moving regularly in order to renew and vary his motifs. Renoir and Degas became masters in the art of catching things from an unusual point of focus. Renoir's *Place Clichy* is one of the boldest close-ups in all modern painting: the spectator no longer sees the subject from a distance, but is directly involved with it.

Auguste Renoir: Place Clichy, about 1880.

Boulevard des Capucines with the Grand Hôtel, 1890. Photograph.

The Eye of Degas

"No art is less spontaneous than mine. What I do is the result of thought and the study of the great masters; of inspiration, spontaneity, temperament, I know nothing. The same subject has to be done ten times, a hundred times over. Nothing in art, not even movement, must seem accidental."

Degas

Edgar Degas: Dancer Adjusting her Slipper, 1874. Pencil and Charcoal.

Now I write to ask your pardon for something that often recurs in your conversation and more often in your thoughts: it is for having been in the course of our long art relations, or having seemed to be, *harsh* with you.

I have been so to a singular degree with myself; you must remember it well since you have been led to reproach me for it and to wonder at my having so little confidence in myself.

I was, or I seemed to be, hard with everyone, through a sort of passion for brutality, which came from my uncertainty and my bad humor. I felt myself so badly made, so badly equipped, so weak, whereas it seemed to me that my *calculations* on art were so right. I was sullen with everyone and with myself. I ask your forgiveness if, under pretext of this confounded art, I wounded your very noble and very intelligent mind, perhaps even your heart.

Letter from Degas to the painter A. de Valernes, October 26, 1890

Critical attack did not prevent the Impressionists from holding further exhibitions in 1879, 1880 and 1881, with a final exhibition in 1886. The prime mover in all these exhibitions was Degas. It was not merely that his delicate paintings would have been lost on the vast walls of the Salons, as Zola suggested; we know now that Degas was in desperate financial straits and needed buyers. The collapse of his brother René's affairs in New Orleans had caused the Bank of Anvers to call in its loans to the De Gas Bank. Had not Edgar arranged to meet the indebtedness, disgrace and destitution would have fallen upon the whole family. In Edgar's case this meant selling pictures and the impressionist exhibitions were a convenient means of advertising his work during these years.

Pride prevented Degas from talking about his trouble, though it seems to have been known to the habitués of the Café Nouvelle-Athènes (which had replaced the Café Guerbois as the avant-garde hangout), for George Moore writes: "It is rumoured that he [Degas] has sacrificed the greater part of his income to save his brother who has lost everything in an imprudent speculation in America." But very few people seem to have understood the amount of time and energy absorbed by his prodigious output: he was a recluse of necessity and his defense was misogyny.

Degas had made studies of ballerinas, ballet masters and orchestral players in his youth; but it was not until after his return from America that he began producing pastels and paintings of ballet subjects in great number. The Opera House was still in the rue Le Peletier and he was completely at home in its precincts. "Where the muses meet, they dance," he was fond of saying. Vollard tells a story about a ballet girl who posed for him. "I painted her waking up," Degas said. "There was nothing to be seen but her legs feeling about through the opening of the bed curtains for her slippers, which had been thrown on an oriental carpet. I even remember the reds and yellows. I can see her two green stockings too. I wanted to keep this painting, but it appeared to please the poor girl so much that I gave it to her." He also began modelling ballet girls in wax, working from drawings made in the nude; but, instead of fashioning their skirts in wax, he had a seamstress make tiny delicate frou-frous of silk and satin. He had studied the technique of sculpture and thought it the most suitable medium in which to express profound suffering. He continuously remade his little wax models, regarding them always as inadequate; those few which have survived, and were later cast in bronze, do have about them some unfathomable sadness.

After the old Opera House burned down in 1873 Degas turned to his immediate neighborhood for subjects. In his studio in the rue Victor Massé, says Vollard, there were easels, a tall desk at which he stood to write, a press for pulling lithographs and etchings, tracing after tracing by way of correcting his drawings, and a bath tub. "Once an object found its way into his studio, it never left it, nor changed its position, and gradually became covered with a dust that no flick of the feather duster came to disturb," says Vollard. His servant Zoé dominated his daily life, but had strict orders not to touch anything in the studio. "What an unusual fellow, this Degas," wrote Edmond de Goncourt, "sickly, hypochondriac, with such delicate eyes that he fears to lose his sight and for this very reason is especially sensitive and aware of the reverse character of things. He is the man I have seen who has best captured, in reproducing modern life, the soul of this life." According to the observant Vollard, Degas was wont to complain about his eyesight in order to get rid of visitors.

Calling on Degas one day Vollard saw that he was painting a landscape with his back to the window. "But, Monsieur Degas," said Vollard, "seeing the truth with which you reproduce nature, who would suppose that you do it by turning your back to her!"

"Oh, Monsieur Vollard," said Degas. "When I am in a train, you know, I do now and then put my head out of the window."

In fact, he had pronounced views on "open air" painting, at least as it concerned himself. He had come in time to believe firmly in working from memory, or memory and imagination combined, rather than nature. He could express himself very well, yet he had a profound distaste for intellectualizing. "Of what use is my mind?" he said to Daniel Halévy. "Granted that it enables me to hail a bus and pay my fare. But once I am inside my studio of what use is my mind? I have my model, my pencil, my paper, my paints. My mind doesn't bother me."

According to Vollard Degas never indulged in private gossip, though his darts sometimes transfixed people like butterflies on a cork. "Shy, apparently unsociable, but when nightfall drove him from the studio and he no longer had to defend himself against those who were always ready to disturb him in his work, he could be delightfully genial," says Vollard, who then tells the story of how he once invited Degas to dinner. Held regularly in the basement of his little shop in the rue Lepic, Vollard's dinners were already much talked about in the art world. Here, crowded together among his paintings—his Cézannes, his Renoirs, and many others yet to become famous—his guests partook of some exotic curry, made according to a recipe from the island of Réunion, and the conversation was always lively. Degas had heard about these gatherings and, in accepting Vollard's invitation, laid down certain conditions: he would have only a dry roll without butter, there were to be no flowers on the table, and the dinner must begin punctually at 7.30 p.m. "You lock up your cat, I know," said Degas, "but no one must bring a dog. And if there are women, they must not wear perfume—how horrible are these odors when there are things that smell so good, baked bread, for example..." None more than Degas believed in the necessity for a kind of discipline in all the acts of life, says Vollard.

Among the Impressionists, Renoir understood him best, perhaps. "He found," said Renoir, "a way of expressing the malady of our contemporaries: I mean movement." Nor was Renoir deceived by Degas's acerbity, the range of his irony or the profundity of his prejudices. "Perhaps beneath his porcupine attitude there was a streak of rare kindness," says Renoir. "His frock coat, well-starched collar and top hat concealed the most profoundly revolutionary artist among the young painters."

"Edgar Degas was of middle height, well proportioned, with an air of distinction. He carried his head high without affectation, and when standing and talking with someone he kept his hands clasped behind his back. His dress was plain, with no particular refinement, but without eccentricity or slovenliness, and like all the bourgeois of his time he wore a top hat, but one with flat brims and pushed back a little on his head. He usually protected his ailing eyes against the glare of light by tinted glasses or a pince-nez straddling his rather short nose. His face, with hardly any color in it, was framed by dark auburn sidewhiskers trimmed close, like his moustache and flat hair. Such was Degas about 1875, looking very much like the drypoint portrait which Marcellin Desboutin made of him about that time."

Georges Rivière, *Degas*

Marcellin Desboutin: Portrait of Degas, about 1876. Etching.

No subject could be more characteristically modern than that of the railroad station, and Monet painted some eight or ten pictures of the Gare Saint-Lazare in Paris—the first of his famous series. Turner and Daumier, in very different ways, had already treated the theme of trains. With the other impressionists, attracted by the clouds of steam it threw up, the train was but one of the elements of the landscape; Monet, in 1877, made it the sole theme of his picture.

J. M. W. Turner: Rain, Steam and Speed, 1843.

"The year 1878 saw him paint some pictures of a rather special kind, which fell in well, however, with his analytical study, now increasingly varied and complex, of color effects: I refer to the smoke-filled pictures of the Gare Saint-Lazare. In these canvases, not very numerous but highly characteristic, Claude Monet both exerted and amused himself in recording this eerie scene unfolding in broad daylight, these ghostly shapes of iridescent steam floating and swirling over the machines, between the high cliffs of surrounding houses, which overlook the perpetually shaking departure platforms."

Arsène Alexandre, *Claude Monet*

With his *Railroad* of 1873, Manet had made a timid approach to this theme, suggesting the presence of a locomotive by a cloud of steam. Monet, however, went into the station itself and out onto the platforms, marvelling at what seemed to his contemporaries a noisy, reeking monster devoid of aesthetic qualities and, in its novelty and utility, outraging all the rules of good taste. Monet delighted in this continually changing scene, well lit by the large glass panes overhead and swept by puffs of smoke or steam which, through the play of light and shadow, gave glimpses of unexpected forms. Monet felt that a single picture could hardly convey an idea of the variety of this shifting pageant, and he was thus led to paint a whole series of pictures in the Gare Saint-Lazare, from different angles, at different times of day.

A number of these canvases figured in the group exhibition of 1877, where their novelty and accuracy were pointed out by Georges Rivière, one of the most ardent supporters of Impressionism, in the pages of *L'Impressionniste*, a small magazine he launched for the purpose of defending his friends' work.

1876-1877

Claude Monet: The Gare Saint-Lazare

"Let those who wish to do history painting do the history of their own time instead of shaking up the dust of past centuries."
                                   Georges Rivière.

The Le Havre Train at Médan. Photograph by Zola.

1878

1877

1877

1877

The Suspended Moment

"They have tried to render the walk, motion, hurry and intermingling of passers-by, just as they have tried to render the trembling of leaves, the shimmer of water and the vibration of air drenched with light, just as they have managed to catch both the iridescent play of sunshine and the soft envelope of cloudy skies."

Edmond Duranty,
La Nouvelle Peinture, 1876

Edouard Manet: The Rue de Berne Decked with Flags, 1878.

Edouard Manet: The Rue Mosnier Decked with Flags, 1878.

Claude Monet: The Rue Montorgueil Decked with Flags, 1878. On a flag at the right can be read ▸ *the words: Vive la France. This scene represents the Fourteenth of July celebrations in Paris.*

142

...and Suspended Movement

Horses and dancers were the two subjects by means of which Degas deepened his study of movement. The keenest of observers, he strove to catch the sequence of positions which constitutes movement. On the racecourses he avidly scrutinized the gallop of the horses and the motions of the jockeys, without trying to record with his pencil what the eye is incapable of analyzing but seeking rather to convey the impression they aroused in him. What he perceived was sequence and duration.

All the artists and scientists of this period were keenly interested in the problems of movement and speed. At the very time when Degas was sketching at the Longchamp racetrack, the English photographer Eadweard Muybridge succeeded, after four years of experimentation, in recording on film with a series of cameras the successive movements of a galloping horse. But when Muybridge presented his photographs in Paris in 1881, in Meissonier's studio, the public was skeptical; to convince it, he had recourse to Reynaud's praxinoscope, a disk—the forerunner of moving pictures—on which the snapshots were fixed in sequence and which, when spun around, gave the exact impression of movement.

The first actual projection of moving pictures on a screen, by means of the cinematograph invented by the Lumière brothers, took place in Paris on December 15, 1895.

Edgar Degas: Jockey, 1885-1890. Pencil and Pastel.

Edgar Degas: Four Studies of a Jockey, about 1866. Sepia and Gouache.

Edgar Degas: Horse Races at Longchamp, 1873-1875.

"It is all very well to copy what you see; it is much better to draw what you only see in memory. Then you get a transformation during which imagination collaborates with memory. You reproduce only what has struck you, in other words essentials. There your recollections and your fancy are set free from the tyranny exerted by nature."

Degas

143

The Flash of the Snapshot

"*Degas is one of the few painters to have given the ground plane its due importance. He has done some admirable floorboards...*
"*The ground plane is one of the essential factors in the vision of things. On its nature largely depends the reflection of light. As soon as the painter comes to consider color not as local color acting by itself and by contrast with neighboring colors, but as the local effect of all the radiations and reflections which occur in the picture space and which are exchanged by all the bodies it contains; as soon as he strives to perceive this subtle repercussion and to avail himself of it in order to give his work a certain unity altogether different from that of the composition, then his conception of form has changed. If he goes far enough, he arrives at impressionism.*"

Paul Valéry, Degas, Danse, Dessin

"Drawing is not what one sees, but what one must make others see."

Degas

Edgar Degas:

Dancers in the Foyer, 1879. Pastel.

The Racecourse. Amateur Jockeys beside a Carriage, about 1877-1880.

Dancers in Yellow, 1878-1880. Pastel on Monotype.

Racehorses, 1883-1885. Pastel.

144

"I speak of former times, for apart from the heart it seems to me that everything in me is aging proportionally. And even my heart has something artificial about it. The dancers sewed it up in a pink satin bag, a rather faded pink satin, like their dancing slippers."

Letter from Degas to the sculptor
Albert Bartholomé, January 17, 1886

It was in 1872 that Degas became interested in the theme of the dance. His friend Désiré Dihau, who played the bassoon in the orchestra at the Paris Opera, took him backstage, and he was at once captivated by the blend of the real and the artificial that he found there. While the racecourse had made him attentive to speed, the dance revealed to him all the expressive intricacies of the human figure in movement, constantly maintaining a seemingly precarious equipoise through an endless sequence of wavering postures. Even motionless, the dancer gives the impression of moving, her limbs retaining the tremulous imprint of her exertions. Degas multiplied his studies, continually working them up from accurate observation to the further stage of plastic transposition. In approaching this new subject, he began by painting the dancers at rest and gradually progressed in the late 1870's to the full complexity of their gyrations. But the impression of movement would not be complete if it were not thrown into relief by the glare of the footlights and the arresting foreshortenings of the composition. Degas obtained an incomparable range of spatial effects thanks to the boldness and skill with which he exploited unusual points of view and perspective. With unerring instinct he abandoned the symmetrical arrangements of classical composition for the dynamic, off-center layout of modern picture design in which equilibrium is no longer based on equivalent masses but on the relations and resulting tensions between voids and solids.

In 1878 Degas began doing sculpture as well, not only to spare his eyes some of the strain involved in painting, but also and above all to achieve the ultimate expression of movement implicit in the fully rounded volumes of a static figure.

Edgar Degas:

Ballet Dancer Resting, about 1880-1882. Pastel.

End of the Arabesque, 1877.

Manet: The Bar at the Folies-Bergère

"And since we embrace nature closely, we no longer separate the figure from the background of the apartment or the backdrop of the street. In actual life the figure never appears against a vague, empty, neutral background. But around and behind it are furniture, fireplaces, hangings, a wall that suggests a man's means, his class, his profession....Even his rest will not be a pause, it will not be an aimless, unmeaning pose in front of the camera lens; his rest is as much a part of life as his action is."

Edmond Duranty

Edouard Manet: At the Café, 1878.

Edouard Manet: The Bar at the Folies-Bergère, 1882.

"When I came back to Paris in January 1882, the first visit I paid was to Manet. He was then painting the *Bar at the Folies-Bergère*, and the model, a pretty girl, was posing behind a table loaded with bottles and food. He recognized me at once, shook my hand and said: 'It's a bore, but you must excuse me: I'm obliged to keep my seat. Sit down over there.'

"I took up a chair behind him and watched him at work. Though he painted his pictures from a model, Manet did not copy nature. I realized then how masterly his simplifications were. He was modelling the girl's head; but his modelling was not obtained with the means that nature indicated. Everything was abridged: the tones were brighter, the colors more vivid, the values nearer to each other. It all went to form an ensemble of a tender, blond harmony...

"More people came in, and Manet left off painting to go and sit down on the divan, against the righthand wall. I then saw how sorely he had been tried by illness. He walked leaning on a cane and seemed to tremble. Yet he remained cheerful and spoke of soon being well again. I went to see him again during my stay. He said things like this: 'Concision in art is a matter of necessity and elegance. The man who is concise makes you think; the man who is wordy is a bore. Always modify your work in the direction of concision... In a figure, seek out the main light and the main shadow; the rest will come naturally; it is often very little. And then, cultivate your memory; for nature will never give you anything but information to go on. It is like a railing that keeps you from falling into banality... One must always remain the master and do what is entertaining. Nothing burdensome! Ah, no, nothing burdensome!'"

Georges Jeanniot, *La Grande Revue*, August 10, 1907

Edouard Manet: The Waitress (La Servante de Bocks), 1878.

"The look of things and people has in real life a thousand ways of being unexpected. Our point of view is not always in the center of a room with its two side walls receding towards the back wall; it does not always reduce the lines and angles of the cornices to regularity and mathematical symmetry; nor can it always overlook the unfolding stretch of ground or floor in the foreground; it is sometimes located very high, sometimes very low, losing the ceiling, glimpsing objects from below, cutting across furniture unexpectedly. Our eye, arresting its gaze sideways at a certain distance from us, seems to be limited by a frame, and it sees these lateral objects as if they were cut off by that frame."

Edmond Duranty, La Nouvelle Peinture, 1876

Edouard Manet: Café, Place du Théâtre-Français, 1881.

Edgar Degas: Women on the Terrace of a Café, 1877. Pastel on Monotype.

Auguste Renoir: Small Café, 1876-1877.

Edgar Degas: Absinthe, 1876.

The Café Concerts

"Degas carried into his studies of reality the concern that makes 'classical' artists... A keen desire to elicit the one line which determines a figure, but that figure as found in life, in the street, at the opera, at the milliner's, and even in other places; but, again, that figure surprised in its own peculiar habits, at a particular moment, never without action, always expressive—this, for me, somehow or other sums up Degas. He ventured to combine, he dared to combine, the snapshot and the infinite toil in the studio, to enclose the impression in an elaborate study and the immediacy of things in the continuance of reflective will."

Paul Valéry, *Degas, Danse, Dessin*

"His prodigious skill flashes out everywhere; his resourcefulness, so attractive and so peculiarly his own, arranges figures in the most unexpected and amusing way, at the same time in a way that is always true and always normal. What M. Degas hates most, in fact, is romantic rapture, the substitution of dreams for life, in a word airs and flourishes. He is an observer; he never indulges in overstatement; the effect is always obtained by nature herself, it is never overdone. This is what makes him the most valued historian of the scenes that he shows us."

Georges Rivière in *L'Impressionniste*,
April 6, 1877

Edgar Degas:

Café Singer Wearing a Glove, 1878. Pastel and Tempera.

Two Studies for a Music Hall Singer, 1878-1880. Pastel and Charcoal.

Café Singer in Green, 1884. Pastel.

" A picture is something that calls for as much cunning, trickery and vice as the perpetration of a crime. Go wrong and add an accent of nature . . . "

Degas

Degas was resolutely hostile to open air painting; as early as 1869 he showed a marked preference for the artificial light of theaters, cafés, music halls, laundresses' and milliners' shops. The portraitist became a genre painter; he was less interested in evoking a face than in painting people in characteristic attitudes, in the setting of their daily life and profession. He caught the "professional" movement of his subjects; moreover he caught them from an unusual angle or in an unusual pose that arrests the spectator's attention. Degas was perfectly aware of the importance and novelty of the pictorial design which he practiced and developed. In his definition of the Ideal Studio, he wrote: "Raise steps all around the room in order to accustom the student to draw things from below and from above. Let him paint things only as seen in a mirror

in order to accustom him to hatred of illusionism. In doing portraits, pose the model on the ground floor and have the student work from the first floor in order to accustom him to retaining forms and expression and never drawing or painting immediately."

Degas kept to a limited number of themes, on which he turned out endless variations. He liked to say: "Let me get it well into my mind that I know nothing at all, that is the only way of progressing." He had taken up pastels in 1869, when he was getting interested in rendering the instantaneousness of movement; then in 1878 he worked out a technique combining tempera and pastels which became a favorite medium of his. It enabled him to achieve the purest, most marked effects of color, as well as smoothly blended passages and nervous, spirited linework. Pastels, a quicker technique than oil painting, were also easier on his eyes, which could no longer bear the strain of long working sessions.

Paul Valéry, who knew Degas well and in whom the artist often confided, has written: "However amusing and playful he may sometimes have appeared, his pencil, his pastel crayon and his brush are never employed carelessly. Willpower dominates. His line is never quite as close as he wants it to be. He attains neither to eloquence nor to the poetry of painting; he seeks only truth in style and style in truth. His art may be likened to that of the French moralists: a prose of sharpest outline forcibly enclosing or articulating a new and genuine observation."

Edgar Degas:

Café Concert at "Les Ambassadeurs," 1876-1877

At the Theater, 1880. Pastel.

Café Concert, 1876-1877. Pastel.

The loge is a privileged place from which one can see, and be seen by, the whole theater. The prosperous bourgeoisie of Paris assiduously frequented the theater, the balls, the public entertainments, often dividing its evenings between these and the cafés. Degas painted his first opera pictures in 1867. He began by portraying the musicians in the orchestra, then progressively raised his eyes to the stage, on which his whole attention was soon focused. He loved the make-believe of the theater, where dream and reality were so attractively mingled. He was entranced by the dancers, in whom he found naturalness paradoxically achieved by study and willpower, and whose movements continually assumed unusual patterns as planes were suddenly, violently clipped off against the light and constantly changing perspective effects were opened up. *The Ballet from "Robert le Diable"*, of 1872, is the canvas which marks his return to the theme of the theater. Manet, in his *Masked Ball at the Opera*, produced a nocturnal pendant to his *Concert in the Tuileries*—which Mallarmé had recognized as a work of capital importance—and once again found a glittering subject of characteristic modernity, the pretext moreover for a symphony of contrasting values. As for Renoir, he was less interested in the stage than in the public, in the beauty of women decked in all their finery and basking in the gaze of their admirers and rivals. *The Loge* was the first picture in which he succeeded in eliciting from artificial light the sparkling luminosity of his landscapes, rendered with the same freedom of touch.

Edgar Degas: The Ballet from "Robert le Diable," 1872.

Edouard Manet: Masked Ball at the Opera, 1873.

Edgar Degas: Musicians in the Orchestra, 1872.

Auguste Renoir: The Loge, 1874.

Berthe Morisot: The Cradle, 1873.

Berthe Morisot: Young Woman Seated on a Chair. Pencil.

"Mademoiselle Berthe Morisot, with her double privilege as a woman and a highly gifted artist, is marked out to win over the public and the critics... She is a sensitive colorist who brings everything into a general harmony of whites not easily attuned without lapsing into affectedness..."

Philippe Burty, *La République française*, April 25, 1877

If the critics who singled out Berthe Morisot for special abuse imagined that they could shame this frail young woman into severing her connection with the crazy Impressionists they could not have been more mistaken. Not only did Berthe Morisot contribute paintings to all but one of the eight exhibitions, but she helped finance them and never again exhibited at the Salon.

On the death of her father in 1873 she had inherited a great deal of money and, after her marriage to Eugène Manet, Edouard's brother, a year later, she was a rich woman. She was not, therefore, inconvenienced when one of her watercolors went for 45 francs at the Hôtel Drouot auction in 1875. That summer she and Eugène voyaged to England where she made paintings of the Isle of Wight, the beach at Ramsgate and other lonely nooks on the Channel coast, which she put on the line at the 1877 Impressionist exhibition. Because she lived the opulent life of her class the run of critics made the error of thinking that she was a lady dabbling in art; but not the perceptive Paul Mantz, who wrote in *Le Temps*: "In all the group there is only one impressionist. This is Berthe Morisot. Her painting has all the freshness of improvisation; it is truly the impression, registered by a sincere eye, and loyally rendered by a hand which does not cheat."

When she married Eugène Manet she was thirty-three, an intense, reserved and independent woman. She was approaching forty when her daughter, Julie, was born, for which event she had skipped the fourth Impressionist exhibition. The child made of her a different woman, and a different painter. Eugène rented a house, 4 rue de la Princesse, at Bougival, where they spent the summers, with Berthe ceaselessly sketching her daughter among the trees and flowers of the magnificent garden. Afterwards, when Berthe's niece, Nini, came to live with them, she painted the two young girls in a series of motifs: girls gathering cherries, girls playing hide-and-seek, girl with a hat, girl with a basket, etc. Later there was "Young Woman this..." and "Young Woman that...," all luminous and infinitely tender portrayals of the transiency of youth, indeed of life itself.

In 1883, while Berthe was painting her young girls as they played in the Bois de Boulogne, Eugène built a large villa at 14 rue de Villejust in Paris. Here, against Empire panelling encasing the oils of Edouard Manet, the Eugène Manets were the hosts of a high salon, to which came Degas, Whistler, Puvis de Chavannes, Caillebotte, the Rouarts, Renoir, Monet, Paul Valéry and Stéphane Mallarmé (to whom Victor Hugo had recently written a letter, beginning: "My dear impressionist poet...") and many other celebrities. In Parisian life the power of the salon could hardly be overestimated: the Impressionists had won a bridgehead.

Paul Valéry (who married Nini) says that Berthe was "simple, pure, intimately, passionately laborious, rather withdrawn, but withdrawn with elegance." Renoir said: "She was so feminine she would make Titian's 'Virgin with a Rabbit' jealous."

The day was past when thirty windmills spun their broad vanes on Montmartre hill and the district was the flour and perfume center of the Paris region. But at the top of the rue Lepic there were two old mills still standing, one of which the miller, Debray, had converted

Edgar Degas: At the Milliner's, 1882.

"I must work hard at evening effects, lamps, candles, etc. The point is not always to show the source of light but the effect of light. This approach has immense possibilities today—how can one fail to see that?"

Degas

Edgar Degas: Laundress Seen Against the Light, 1882.

Auguste Renoir: Laundress. Drawing.

into a rustic ballroom. It was a great square hangar with a platform for the orchestra and a raised circular gallery where the customers sat at tables between dances. Colored paper lanterns hung from ceiling and walls; the floor, polished by decades of loose grain, was firm and fast, and there was plenty of room for the quadrilles and polkas and the new flonflon. On hot summer evenings the proceedings were moved out to an adjacent garden where the lanterns were suspended from trees. Dances were held there on Sundays and holidays, 3.00 p.m. to midnight; entrance was 25 centimes for each man and a further charge of 20 centimes for each dance. "Bring your money!" cried the barker as the orchestra started up. Between dances customers were served with a delicious tart, sweet wine and salad. The Debrays were specialists in making these tarts, or galettes, and so the place was called Moulin de la Galette—the Mill of the Tarts.

Renoir went there often in the company of friends, including Degas who at this time was looking for motifs in the café dansants, circuses, music halls and bars. Renoir was inspired to make a picture of the Moulin de la Galette. He saw it as a huge canvas taking in the whole sweep of the dance floor, balconies, orchestra and dancers. His studio in the rue Saint-Georges was far too small for such an enterprise, so Renoir began looking around Montmartre for a convenient working place. In the rue Cortot, in an unfrequented quarter of La Butte, to give Montmartre hill its local name, he saw on a ruinous gateway the notice: "Furnished Rooms To Let." On entering the gateway he found himself in a vast garden with lawns and old trees, all in a state of wild neglect, but with unimpaired views of the northern purlieus of Paris. The house, dating from 1650, had once been a farm; it was a painter's dream of solitude and airy light. Renoir was soon occupying a couple of attic rooms and making use of a deserted stable as a studio. Here were painted *The Swing* and *Nude in the Sun*. (And here, 12 rue Cortot, succeeding generations of artists, including Suzanne Valadon, Utrillo and Raoul Dufy, would also do their best work.) Renoir made several paintings of the Moulin de la Galette, using his friends as models and enlisting their help in carrying the huge stretched canvas to and from the Moulin every day.

As a local identity he helped organize a fancy dress ball at the Moulin to raise funds for the care of the hundreds of children who roamed about the district (the suppression of the Commune had left its widows and orphans, especially in Montmartre and La Villette). There were to be amateur numbers and prizes for the best dancers. Renoir helped make and decorate with velvet ribbons the straw hats (the little *timbales,* as they were called) which were to be given as prizes. The ball was a dazzling success; the special numbers brought down the house, the volunteer bands had the real beat. But the receipts barely covered expenses. At this time, to make the wherewithal to pay for his new quarters, Renoir was painting a society portrait. Georges Charpentier, the successful publisher, was pleased with the Renoir he had bought (for 180 francs) at the Impressionist auction sale in 1875, and had commissioned Renoir to make a portrait of his wife. Every day Renoir was going to the Charpentier mansion in the rue de Grenelle where Madame Charpentier posed for him in her latest Worth gown. Naturally, sitter and painter conversed, and when Renoir told her about their glorious failure to raise money for the orphans, Madame Charpentier offered to create a fund for a day nursery in Montmartre. In later years Renoir was prouder of the fund than of the portraits he painted of the Charpentiers. The connection with the Charpentiers led to an introduction to Baron Bérard of Wargemont Château, near Dieppe, and more portraits of impeccable children and elegant ladies. "I remember Renoir at Wargemont," says Jacques-Emile Blanche, "wearing a funny pointed straw hat with a red band, like oarsmen between La Grenouillère and Bougival, a canvas coat over a shirt without a tie, as he sat beside the coachman, or perhaps it was the butler, on the Wargemont wagonette." Renoir's society portraits had landed him in the Salon and promised to make his fortune. "I believe Renoir is launched," wrote Pissarro. "So much the better. It is hard, the poverty."

In the rue Saint-Georges, where Renoir had his studio before moving up to Montmartre, there was a little crémerie where four or five people could have a good meal very cheaply. Going there often Renoir was soon on familiar terms with the customers, among whom was Aline Charigot and her mother, both of them dressmakers, though working for different houses. They were from Essoyes and rolled their "r's" like Burgundians; Monsieur Charigot, a wine grower, hadn't been heard from since going off to America some years before; but the old farmhouse was still theirs. Aline was one of those blond round girls with very narrow waists; it was not simply that she was pretty, but she was the girl Renoir had always painted. Aline was nineteen, Renoir forty. Renoir became very fond of Aline. "She was like a cat," he once said, "you wanted to rub her back." The banks of the Seine were their favorite strolling place; and they went often to Fournaise's restaurant at La Grenouillère where Renoir painted Aline in a blue dress, petting a pekinese dog, in a picture he called the *Luncheon of the Boating Party*. They visited Essoyes and Aline wanted him to stay and paint there. "To be so isolated one has to be strong," Renoir said. He made a trip to Algiers and was fascinated by the color of the place; Aline was waiting for him at the station when he came back. Aline wanted them to be married, so she could have a child; but Renoir was afraid of children. Just the same, Aline had her child, Pierre, born in 1885. Renoir went on other trips, to Venice, Madrid, etc. Aline was always waiting for him at the station. So, in 1890, they set it up; and it turned out to be one of the most successful marriages any artist ever enjoyed.

Aline held her own among the brilliant people who came to visit Renoir by becoming a wonderful cook; she liked to eat, which was a great help. Her *bouillabaisse* was talked about everywhere. She had been taught to play the piano, as a kind of young ladies accomplishment; but, after hearing Chabrier play one evening, she never touched the piano again. Degas, having seen Aline visit an art show

"At that time Renoir seldom left Paris. While before 1870 he had spent long periods in the villages in and around Fontainebleau forest, after the war he scarcely went beyond the immediate suburbs: Bougival, Saint-Cloud, Louveciennes where his mother lived. Usually he stayed in Paris where he found models more easily than anywhere else."

Georges Rivière, *Renoir et ses amis*

549bis VIEUX-PARIS. - La Butte Montmartre, Cabaret du Lapin Agile (XVIIIᵉ arrᵗ).

Old Paris: The Hill of Montmartre, with the Cabaret of the Lapin Agile (18th arrondissement). Photograph.

Auguste Renoir: The Dance at Bougival, 1883. Pencil.

Auguste Renoir: Dancing Couple, 1883. Pen and Ink.

158

In the Streets of Paris with Renoir

"Renoir's kindliness and good nature ennobled, so to speak, his pictures of ordinary people. In the young girls of Montmartre who usually sat for him, he saw only the grace of youth, the naïveté and ingenuousness of their age, although often enough they were neither pretty nor ingenuous and he knew they weren't."

Georges Rivière, Renoir et ses amis

crowded with over-dressed socialites, paid Renoir a great compliment: "Your wife was a queen visiting a circus." This is how Renoir broke the news to Marie Meunier about the arrival of Jean in 1894: "*Chère Mademoiselle, Un gros garçon. Tout le monde bien portant. Amitiés.*" They were then living at the Château des Brouillards in the rue Girardon in Montmartre where there was a lovely garden, as one can still see. What the art writer called Renoir's "short classical period" had ended there.

Commenting on Renoir's re-found sensuality, Théodore Duret says: "Renoir invested the Parisienne of the second half of the nineteenth century with a certain grace and attractiveness comparable to the charm with which the painters of the eighteenth century endowed the women of another world and another class." The class is noticeable: his paintings of youthful maternity, Aline feeding Jean, etc., reintroduce us to people unseen in paint since the early Flemings. "I like women best when they don't know how to read and when they wipe the baby's bottom themselves," he said. He was reading Rabelais and Villon.

Théodore Duret called the two decades after the War of 1870, "the heroic age of Impressionism." Heroic is probably the word for Monet, Pissarro and Guillaumin who bore penury and public scorn

Auguste Renoir:
Young Woman with a Muff. Pastel.

Cabs in Paris, 1890. Photograph.

159

with fortitude, though not without resort to many stratagems for its relief. In the case of Sisley, as self-effacing as he was deficient in guile, the word is exact in its old chivalrous meaning.

At the Hôtel Drouot sale in 1875 he had sold 21 pictures for a total of 2,445 francs, a little more than 100 francs a picture. This was as high as his expectancy, or his ambition, reached: he thought that if he could get that much regularly for his pictures, he could get by. Alas, he was obliged to sell his later pictures to friends at 25 to 30 francs each. And yet, he was in his best period, his now famous *Flood at Marly* having been painted at this time. In the autumn of 1877 he settled in Sèvres where he painted delicate landscapes, villages under snow, blue and pink reflections on the snow, sometimes a silhouette in black; the quality of softness and silence is there.

Whenever he had a few canvases in hand he would come to Paris and take them to those few dealers who would be willing to look at them. His greatest pleasure were the "impressionist" dinners given once a month by Duret, Caillebotte or Dr. de Bellio at the Café Riche. Here, in a convivial atmosphere, he met Pissarro, Renoir,

The Constancy of Nature

Alfred Sisley: Barges on the River Loing. Lithograph.

Alfred Sisley: Old Thatched Cottage at Les Sablons, 1883. Pencil.

Alfred Sisley: The Provencher Mill at Moret, 1883. Pencil.

Monet, Stéphane Mallarmé and, in 1890, Gustave Geffroy. One does not know how Marie Sisley managed with her two growing children.

In 1880 the Sisleys moved to Moret-sur-Loing, a hamlet dating from the middle ages, near the forest of Fontainebleau. The rest of Sisley's life was devoted to painting Moret, its church, its mills, its street, its bridge and the river Loing flowing placidly below, and always the sky.

"The sky cannot be just a background," he wrote the critic, Adolphe Tavernier. "It contributes, on the contrary, not only to give depth by its planes (the sky has planes like the earth), it also gives movement by its form, by its arrangement, in relation to the effect or composition of the picture. Is there one thing more magnificent, more changing, than that which occurs frequently in summer, I mean blue sky with beautiful erring clouds? What movement, what allure is not there? It produces the effect of a wave when one is at sea; it exalts, it pulls you along. Another sky, later in the evening. Its clouds lengthen, take often the form of furrows, movements which seem to

Claude Monet: Fishermen, about 1882. Pencil.

160

Camille Pissarro: Pasture at Eragny. Print.

Armand Guillaumin: Banks of the River Creuse, 1900. Charcc

The Impressionists were, first and foremost, painters of color and light, and their efforts to render the atmosphere often led them to break up contours; yet they were masters of line who daily practiced the art of drawing. Continually on the move, always in search of new subjects, they filled their notebooks with sketches, jotting down a new motif at their first sight of it and carefully including the precise topographical indications. Light values and accurate linework retained the imprint of their first impression.

be immobilized in the middle of atmosphere, and little by little disappear, absorbed by the setting sun. This one, more tender, more melancholic; it has the charm of things which are going away, and I love it particularly."

The charm of things which are going away: one repeats the phrase like a memorable epitaph.

Of Armand Guillaumin, the road laborer, Dealer Vollard wrote: "Sales dragged even more than Sisley. And yet, what works the painter of La Creuse has given us [from] his easel in his studio in the rue Servandoni!" When Vollard took one of his pictures, Guillaumin said: "Look here, I hope they're not the sort of people who buy just to cover their walls."

Pissarro, settled in Pontoise, was painting landscapes of matchless serenity. Money did, at last, seem within grasp when, at an auction sale in January 1873, five Pissarro landscapes were sold to an anonymous bidder for a total of 2,570 francs. Excitedly Pissarro wrote Duret: "The reactions from the public sale are making themselves felt as far as Pontoise. People are very surprised that a picture could sell for as much as 950 francs; it was even said that this was astounding for a straight landscape." Pissarro's friend Ludovic Piette (who has left us a fine picture of Pissarro at work, his easel protected by an umbrella) wrote: "Now that you are about to acquire a great name—and you certainly deserve it—money, which has such good legs when it comes to escaping the chase of us other poor runners always eagerly after its scent, money, I say, will no longer fail you." Meanwhile, Pissarro had to admit to Duret: "I haven't a penny to bless myself with. [But] I have worked very hard and I hope that this year I shall at last place myself beyond the reach of want, at least during the dead season." He was planning "a biggish picture with people, people out in the open" as soon as he had the money to pay for models. Guillaumin was working by his side, "a capital fellow, I am very fond of him."

A shadow was cast over the Pissarro family when Minette (Jeanne-Rachel) died in 1874 at the age of nine. A portrait Pissarro had made of her a couple of years previously shows her to have been a very pretty and, possibly, a nervous child, for Pissarro's brush has caught her awe-stricken expression as she holds to the pose her father has put her in: to see what has awed her one has only to turn to the patriarchal portrait Pissarro had made of himself a year earlier. A fourth child, Felix, was born about three months later; he was called Titi.

Earlier painters had looked at landscape like artillery officers: it was there, it was cover for God knows what, but it was solid and had to be taken into consideration. Monet changed all that: he saw landscape as an ever-changing chimera.

Duret explains how he went about it: "He begins to paint a landscape in the morning, when the earth is covered with mist, he will note on the canvas the reflected light that the rising sun throws over the landscape and the mist which enshrouds it. And, since he only paints any effect just so long as it actually exists before his eyes,

Gustave Caillebotte: Paris Boulevard Seen from Above.

"In 1875 a newcomer, Gustave Caillebotte, himself a painter, offered the Impressionists financial support which, for some of them, arrived in the nick of time.

"Caillebotte was wealthy, generous, and a man of taste. For the painters he joined he was a loyal friend whose effectual help was always proffered in so delicate a shape that they seemed rather to be obliging him by accepting it.

"He painted with ardor and not without talent. His temperament brought him close to both Manet and Degas, to the former in general tonality, to the latter in choice of subjects. He underwent the influence of realism, or rather of literary naturalism, but he expressed it with a certain naïveté, so that even the most commonplace subjects he chose were not unattractive. He was for Renoir a staunch friend. "

Georges Rivière, *Renoir et ses amis*

if he wishes to record the effect of the rising sun, etc., he will be able to work at his painting for only a brief space of time. He will have to abandon it as soon as the sun has risen above the horizon... he will have to return to it another morning... For him, therefore, the aspect of a landscape has no continuous duration, its color no permanence. The appearance of nature changes with the seasons, the days, the hours of the days and the conditions of temperature and light. His sunshine warms, his snow makes a shadow. "

It seems simple enough to us today. But Duret also tells us the effect a landscape painted to this simple formula had upon the public of his day.

"The aversion, the horror—I cannot find a word strong enough to express the popular feeling—in which his work was held, was such that, with the exception of half-a-dozen partisans, who had more taste than wealth, and were regarded as lunatics, nobody wanted to take the trouble to look at them; and when, by an extra-ordinary chance, they were looked at, they were merely laughed at. "

Thus, Manet, after visiting Monet at Argenteuil in 1874, wrote to Duret: "I found him quite broken down and in despair. He asked me to find someone who would take ten or twenty of his paintings at 100 francs each, the purchaser to choose. Shall we arrange the matter between us, say 500 francs each? Of course, nobody, least of all he, must know. "

But then, a few months later, Eugène Manet told Berthe: "The entire clan of painters is in distress. The dealers are overstocked. Edouard [Manet] speaks of watching his expenses and giving up his studio. " And there were many letters, like that of Monet to Zola: "If I have not paid tomorrow night the sum of 600 francs, our furniture and all I own will be sold and we'll be out in the street. I haven't a single *sou*. "

When a man is desperate he will dare the unthinkable. Shortly after the disastrous second Impressionist exhibition in 1876, Monet had put on his jacket with ruffled lace at the wrists, had taken his gold-headed cane, and had called on the Director of the Western Railroad. "I have decided to paint your station, " he told the Director. The railroaders were flattered. So far as they were aware painting was something reserved to woodland sprites and the myths of ancient Rome. The idea that a painter might wish to depict something as prosaic as a locomotive was a complete surprise to them, as it was, indeed, to many others. When Monet set up his easel at the Gare Saint-Lazare they cleared the platforms, shunted the trains about and halted the locomotive exactly where he wanted it. The result was eight paintings, several of them among Monet's finest, the high lighting of the glass roof, the vapor of the escape valves, providing a fresh and, even today, enchanting vision. The result evidently so encouraged Monet that he decided to remain in Paris and to continue painting the city, its streets and waterways.

As Georges Rivière said: "It was he [Monet] who kept up the courage of his friends in difficult times. With his fighting temperament he was bravely facing attacks like a bull irritated by banderillas, but not frightened by them. "

THE republican victory in the Senatorial elections of October 1877 had taken the monarchists by surprise. Their hope of establishing a regime similar to that of the late Louis Philippe, with the Count of Chambord as titular monarch, had received an irrecoverable setback. In all domains where monarchist sentiment was predominant, notably that of official art, there was a wave of reaction. Suddenly *délaissés* were all those painters whose attitude had been in any way ambiguous towards the Empire, such as Delacroix and, of course, Courbet whose trial *in absentia* had hardly appeased Bonapartist rancor. The prejudice extended to Corot, Daubigny, Daumier, Diaz and Millet, all of whom died between 1875 and 1879, with the result that, when the collectors boycotted the auction sales of their studio stocks, the art market was flooded with their works.

"The culminating point of the reaction," says Professor Lionello Venturi in *Archives of Impressionism,* "came in 1878, on the occasion of the Universal Exposition of that year, when the jury of official artists excluded, not only Manet and the Impressionists, but also Delacroix, Millet, Rousseau, Decamps, Barye, Ricard and Troyon. This was too much... In collaboration with his former clients Durand-Ruel arranged an exhibition of authentic French painting, 1830-1870, showing the finest works of Corot, Delacroix and Courbet which 'opened the eyes' of the collectors."

In these circumstances the Impressionists were obliged to fall back upon their old supporters, none of them overly affluent.

The first dealers who had to do with the Impressionists were the itinerant salesmen who sold them their supplies and sometimes bought their pictures, not necessarily because there was a sale for them, but probably to encourage further purchases of colors, canvas, etc. Of this order was "Father" Martin, a man of many parts, a former stonemason, a onetime choralist, who was buying Jongkind's work when Pissarro, Monet, Sisley and Cézanne began dealing with him; in return, he sometimes bought their paintings. On one occasion he exchanged a small Cézanne and 50 francs against a Monet, a deal Monet was pleased to make because he liked the little Cézanne. Martin bought the two pictures by Pissarro which had been hung in the 1870 Salon, but a year or so later refused any longer to handle Pissarro, because he disliked "the heavy common style and that muddy palette of his." Martin's luckiest break appears to have been his bid of 500 francs for Renoir's *The Loge* at the auction sale following the first Impressionist exhibition.

Of a very different character was "Father" Tanguy, whom Pissarro, Renoir and Monet had met in Fontainebleau forest. As a color-grinder, employed at Edouard's, rue Clauzel, his hands were normally stained black, a circumstance which had caused him to be summarily arrested as a suspected Communard musketeer during the suppression of the Paris Commune. Among those many thousands herded into the concentration camp at Sartory he had been saved by the intervention of Henri Rouart, the amateur painter and engineer who, at the time, was an artillery officer in the same regiment as Degas. A short thickset little man with dark blue eyes and a neatly trimmed beard (Van Gogh made a portrait of him

Paul Cézanne:
Dr. Gachet in the Studio, 1873.
Charcoal.

I have found it [the exhibition of 1876] decidedly interesting. But the effect of it was to make me think better than ever of all the good old rules which decree that beauty is beauty and ugliness ugliness, and warn us off from the sophistications of satiety . . . None of its members show signs of possessing first-rate talent, and indeed the "impressionist" doctrines strike me as incompatible, in an artist's mind, with the existence of first-rate talent. To embrace them you must be provided with a plentiful absence of imagination . . . HENRY JAMES

Auguste Renoir: Portrait of Victor Chocquet, 1876.

Paul Cézanne: Portrait of Victor Chocquet, 1876-1877.

later) Tanguy was now installed in a dingy little room, 14 rue Clauzel, where he sold colors and bought an occasional picture. His views on the new trend were very simple: it was necessary to eliminate "tobacco juice" and to paint "thick," i.e. to use good clean colors and plenty of them. He was suspicious of anyone who asked for a tube of black. "Tell Tanguy to send me some paints," Pissarro wrote his son Lucien. "What I need most are ten tubes of white, two of chrome yellow, one bright red, one brown lac, one ultramarine, five Veronese green, one cobalt . . . " Tanguy and Pissarro liked to talk politics; they were both socialists of a sort. Tanguy had an engaging way of looking closely at a newly acquired painting and looking up at the painter with an expression that might have been that of a loving father. Many of the paintings in his shop had been acquired in lieu of payment of a color bill, which is how he had come to possess Cézanne's *Achille Emperaire*. Cézanne left the keys of his studio with Father Tanguy when he went to Aix in the summer. If a customer wanted a Cézanne painting Tanguy took him around to the studio where the canvases were stacked and let him choose what he liked, payment according to size, forty francs for small canvases, a hundred for the larger ones. There were even some unstretched canvases on which Cézanne had painted several little studies. He left it to Tanguy to cut them up with the scissors for collectors who could not afford forty francs. Later, when Vollard heard about this, he exclaimed: "Imagine, paying a louis and marching off with three little Cézanne apples!" After Tanguy's death in 1894 his stock was put up for auction at the Hôtel Drouot, where four Cézanne landscapes were sold for 145, 175, 275 and 170 francs respectively; two others went for less than 40 francs each. It was on Pissarro's advice that Vollard began buying Cézannes and eventually cornered the market—when there was a market.

In a sense Ambroise Vollard replaced Tanguy as the impressionist dealer, except that, coming much later in their development, he benefited from their increasing recognition. Born on the island of Réunion in the Indian Ocean, the son of a minor French colonial official, he had come to Paris as a young man, frankly seeking his fortune. For a time he had worked in the shop of a fashionable art dealer where he had quickly sized up the possibilities of the trade. He had begun by privately trading art objects among collectors and had then opened a little shop, 4 rue Laffitte. He had won the confidence of many artists by bringing them objects or pictures which his acumen told him would be of particular interest to them. His manner of approach was deferential, usually phrased in the terms of old-fashioned courtesy, yet also rough-edged and bold. He was soon on good terms with Degas, Renoir, Cézanne and Pissarro, whose taste he respected, and (in the not-so-distant future) would have dealings with Gauguin, Bonnard, Matisse, Derain, Rouault, Picasso, Chagall, in greater or lesser degree. An observant recorder of artistic idiosyncrasy, his recollections add much to impressionist lore.

It is Vollard who tells us the sequel to the meeting between Renoir and Victor Chocquet, after the latter had written to Renoir asking him if he would make a portrait of his wife. Chocquet occupied a minor position, a sinecure, in the Finance Ministry and lived with his wife in the attic apartment at 204 rue de Rivoli. He had a small private income and his wife, fifteen years his junior, was in line to inherit a considerable fortune. A passionate collector, who wore rags in order to save money with which to buy paintings, he had managed, by keeping a sharp watch on the auction rooms, to acquire an exceptional collection of Delacroix watercolors and several oils. He had asked Delacroix to paint a portrait of his wife, but the old painter had excused himself on account of eye trouble. Evidently it was *The Loge*, seen by Chocquet at the Hôtel Drouot auction sale in 1875, that inspired him to commission Renoir. At least three portraits of Madame Chocquet were painted by Renoir, one in the manner of *The Loge*, another airy picture of her standing with her back to the attic window (lost, alas, in the ruins of Bremen during World War II).

Renoir was not the kind of man to keep a find like Chocquet to himself and induced Chocquet to buy a little Cézanne from Tanguy. The tactics for circumventing Madame Chocquet's anticipated horror at this purchase, were worked out by Renoir. Arriving at the Chocquet apartment with the Cézanne picture, Renoir shows it to Chocquet. "Oh! What an odd little picture!" cries Chocquet, raising his voice to attract his wife's attention. Then, calling her to him: "Marie, come look at the little painting that Renoir has brought to show me!" Madame makes some polite remark and Renoir omits to take the painting home.

When Madame Chocquet had got to the point of tolerating Cézanne's nude bathers, Chocquet asked Renoir to bring Cézanne on a visit. Cézanne arrives in his usual dress, this time wearing an old cap borrowed from Guillaumin, and launches into his prepared lines.

"Renoir tells me that you admire Delacroix?"

"I adore him," says Chocquet. "Let's look over my Delacroix's together." They begin with the pictures on the walls and end sitting on their knees with Delacroix watercolors spread over the floor and walls. Thus Chocquet becomes a Cézanne enthusiast. And by the exercise of similar tactics he is taken to Argenteuil and introduced to Monet.

Renoir and Cézanne made half-a-dozen finished portraits of Chocquet, all of them flattering when matched beside the sketches for same. After the Chocquets came into their inheritance in 1882 they saw less of Cézanne and Renoir and their interest in impressionist painting diminished. Chocquet's collecting passion turned to eighteenth century objets d'art.

From the time of the first group exhibition the Impressionists had won several valuable patrons who helped them, sometimes indirectly, in their subsequent struggles. Count Armand Doria, who had bought Cézanne's *House of the Hanged Man* after the first exhibition (he later exchanged it for another Cézanne in the possession of Chocquet), was related to Madame Charpentier, wife of the publisher, and it was probably through Doria that Renoir was introduced to the Charpentiers as a portrait painter. Yet another patron was the operatic baritone Jean-Baptiste Faure, who bought one of Monet's *Snow Effects* in 1870 or thereabouts, later became a firm supporter of Manet and Degas, though having a long-lasting

Auguste Renoir: Ambroise Vollard Holding a Maillol Statuette, 1908.

Vollard tells how, when he took the pose for this portrait, Cézanne required of him an absolute immobility: "As soon as he had applied the first brushstroke, and to the very end of the sitting, he treated the model as he would a simple still life." After one hundred and fifteen sittings, Cézanne remarked: "I am not dissatisfied with the shirtfront."

Paul Cézanne: Portrait of Ambroise Vollard, 1899.

Letter from Degas to the singer and collector Jean-Baptiste Faure, March 1877:
My dear Mr. Faure,

I have received your letter with great sadness. I prefer to write to you rather than to see you.

Your pictures would have been finished long ago if I had not been obliged daily to do something to earn money.

You have no idea of the troubles of all kinds that are bearing down on me.

Degas was no doubt alluding to the family business reverses and debts that weighed so heavily on him for many years.

Vincent van Gogh: *Le Père Tanguy*, 1887.

"Tanguy, having become the dealer of Pissarro and Cézanne, saw himself taken up by young unrecognized artists who could find a welcome nowhere else and for whom it was in short a stroke of luck to find themselves under his wing, alongside painters who had already awakened a certain interest . . . His shop was then visited by art lovers in search of low-priced works which were generally despised but in which they divined merit and some promise of future success. These art lovers were joined by the artists themselves, anxious to see each other's works, and they were followed by that nondescript crowd of young people, men of letters or men calling themselves such who inevitably gravitate around artists of any kind. Tanguy's shop, frequented by a group of men with common aspirations, was thus raised to the level of an art center."
                                                                    Théodore Duret

difference with the latter. Faure, on Degas's behalf, bought back from Durand-Ruel six canvases which Degas wanted to re-work. In return for this favor it was formally agreed that Degas would paint four large pictures for Faure. Two of these were delivered in 1876, but Faure had to wait eleven years and to sue Degas for the remaining two; the rise in the value of Degas's work was no doubt at the bottom of the dispute. At a despairing moment in Sisley's life, Faure, at his own expense, took the painter to England where Sisley made a series of pictures of the Thames valley.

There were two doctors among the early patrons of the Impressionists. Dr Georges de Bellio and Dr Paul-Ferdinand Gachet, who had a nodding acquaintance with each other, both acquired important impressionist collections, partly by purchase, but mostly by gift of the grateful owners. Both doctors prescribed medicines for numerous ailing Pissarros and Dr Gachet had the honor of attending Pissarro's mother who lived to be ninety-four. Both were called in by Renoir when his favorite model, Margot, lay dying (they were unable to save her). Both attended Camille Monet and both lent Monet small sums of money. (". . . It is a sad situation to be in at my age," wrote Monet—he was thirty-eight—to de Bellio, "always obliged to beg, to solicit buyers . . . ") De Bellio was at Caillebotte's bedside and later attended Seurat; Dr Gachet was Gauguin's doctor and took care of Van Gogh in his last hours.

Dr de Bellio, a Rumanian, was a gentleman of independent means and a member of the little group which dined at the Café Riche. Dr Gachet was a defiant non-conformist, flamboyant in his manner and dress, but very gentle and sensitive in his personal relationships. He had painted oils in his youth, but had felt the call to medicine. He was much impressed by the theories of Proudhon and liked to hear Courbet discoursing on art at the Brasserie des Martyrs; later he had become an habitué of the Café Guerbois and, still later, of the Café de la Nouvelle-Athènes. He still drew a little and kept an engraving press at his house in Auvers, quantities of paper and copper plates which he freely loaned to his artist friends. In 1882 Renoir might have died of pneumonia but for Dr Gachet's timely attention. He looked after Hortense Cézanne and her small boy. He also attended Berthe Morisot.

Armand Guillaumin had known Eugène Murer as a youth in Moulins. It was an agreeable surprise, therefore, to find him conducting a pastry shop on the Boulevard Voltaire: it meant a free meal from time to time. When Murer expanded his business to include a regular restaurant Guillaumin brought along Renoir, an old hand at shop decoration, who painted garlands of flowers on the ceiling. When Monet, Pissarro and Sisley began dropping in Murer worked out a system by which he accepted a painting in payment for a certain number of free meals. Sisley was particularly grateful: he was actually starving. It was good business for Murer because the paintings, hung in the restaurant, brought a number of literary people to the restaurant and Murer had literary ambitions. Soon there were regular Wednesday dinners at Murer's: Georges Rivière, Cézanne, Father Tanguy, Cabaner, Dr Gachet, even Hoschedé, the dime store magnate, came along. The genius of the pastry department was Murer's half-sister, Marie-Thérèse Meunier, a woman "of fine presence" according to Renoir who, with Pissarro, made portraits of her. To help Pissarro, who was in great need, Murer organized a lottery in which the prize was a Pissarro painting. The winning ticket was held by the kitchen help who asked if she might take one of Mademoiselle Meunier's big cream-puffs instead.

Murer and his half-sister moved to Rouen where they took over the Hôtel du Dauphiné et d'Espagne, one of their advertised attractions being, "A magnificent collection of Impressionist paintings which can be seen any day without charge between ten and six."

A late buyer was Ernest Hoschedé, the wealthy owner of *Au Gagne Petit,* a cut-price department store on the Avenue de l'Opéra, and the publisher of *L'Art et la Mode.* Hoschedé had begun investing in Impressionist paintings around 1876. At the third Impressionist exhibition in 1877 eleven of the Monets were on loan from Hoschedé.

The following year Hoschedé went bankrupt and the court ordered him to sell his collection of paintings. Thus, five Manets, twelve Monets, thirteen Sisleys and nine Pissarros came under the hammer at the Hôtel Drouot. The bids were contemptible, the Monets averaging 184 francs and the Sisleys 114 francs. One Pissarro went for seven francs, another for ten. "The Hoschedé sale has finished me off," said Pissarro, and went off to stay with his friend Ludovic Piette at Montfoucault. So set back were the Impressionists that they postponed their annual exhibition (their fourth) until the following year. At the Salon, which coincided with a Universal Exposition, all the impressionist painters were excluded.

It must have seemed a more than fortuitous break when Madame Hoschedé arranged to rent a house for Monet on the Seine near Vétheuil where Camille could wait out her new pregnancy. When she died there, in 1879, shortly after her delivery, Monet wrote a hasty note to Dr de Bellio, asking him "to retrieve from the pawn shop the locket for which I am sending you the ticket. It is the only souvenir that my wife had been able to keep and I should like to tie it around her neck before she leaves forever." Next morning, as he put the locket in place, Monet found himself looking into Camille's still features, conscious of noting, with a kind of professional interest, the darkening shades in which death and dissolution were registering their presence.

Camille had been nursed in her last hours by Alice Hoschedé, who had arrived at Vétheuil with her six children a short time before. The collapse of the Hoschedé enterprises had brought about her separation from the department store owner. Alice stayed on at Vétheuil, looking after her own and Monet's children. It was one of the worst winters in memory, the frozen Seine and the subsequent floods providing Monet with the motifs for ten paintings. But he no longer had to worry about where the next meal was coming from, nor did he ever again write a begging letter. Alice took over and in 1892 they were married.

Yet, though he lived to be doyen of all the painters of his epoch, Monet never again painted a human face, save his own.

"Cézanne seemed to take to me, we became friends and he asked me to pose for a portrait, in hopes of exhibiting the canvas at the Salon, the 'Salon of Bouguereau,' as he called it, and 'possibly,' he added, 'we may even be awarded a medal!' So for almost three months he came to me nearly every day. During this time he produced what is, though unfinished, one of his finest works. The library, the papers on the table, the little plaster cast by Rodin, the artificial rose which he brought in at the beginning of the sittings, everything is first-rate, and there is of course also a figure in this setting painted with such meticulous care... The face, however, he only sketched out, and he would always say: 'I'm keeping that for the end.' Alas, the end never came!"
Gustave Geffroy, *Monet*

Paul Cézanne: Portrait of Gustave Geffroy, 1895.

167

*Impressionism achieved something
more than a technical advance.
It expressed a real and valuable
ethical position. As Count Nieuwerkerke
correctly observed, it was the painting
of democrats. Impressionism is the
perfect expression of democratic
humanism, of the good life which was,
until recently, thought to be within
reach of all.*

KENNETH CLARK

I N 1879 President MacMahon had resigned, thus tacitly admitting that there was no longer any possibility of overthrowing the Third Republic or of restoring the monarchy by constitutional means. Jules Grévy, a Liberal, was elected in his place and his personal action during the next seven or eight years did much to bring about the lasting effacement of the executive. As President of the Republic, Grévy contented himself with exercising a "magistrative influence" in bridging successive coalition governments. Thus, while cabinets came and went, the right of dissolving a government fell into desuetude and the atmosphere of national crisis vanished from French government. The function of President no longer attracted "personalities" and at the same time the power of the Assembly to destroy a government was reduced, a system which finally gave France government stability such as she had not had before, or has had since. In August 1884 two significant sentences were written into the republican constitution: (1) "The republican form of government cannot be the subject of a proposal for revision," and (2) "members of the families which have reigned over France are ineligible to be presidents of the Republic." A general amnesty for Communards and other political offenders was declared; the *Marseillaise* became the official national anthem, and Bastille Day, July 14, a national holiday. In 1881 the government, recognizing the existence of abuses, delivered the organization of the Salon des Arts into the hands of the artists themselves who were empowered to elect their own jury and to establish their own standards for the admission of works of art.

The Impressionists had won their battle. They had succeeded because they had paralleled (in fact, were a part of) a social revolution which, at great cost, but also to the greater glory of France, had accomplished that most difficult of all transitions, the passage from authoritarian dictatorship to democratic republicanism. They had yet to enjoy the fruits of victory and, if this was to be slow in coming, so was the reform of public taste, deformed by thirty years of pretension. The trend, however, was already noticeable in the accounts at Durand-Ruel's: whereas in 1880 Durand-Ruel had paid out a total of 10,000 francs to Sisley, Pissarro and Degas, in 1881 he paid out a total of 71,000 francs to the same three artists, plus Renoir and Monet.

Renoir was already making plans for the reform of the Salon des Arts. He had abandoned the Impressionist group exhibitions after 1877 when his society portraits had been shown at the Salon. "There are in Paris," he had said, "fewer than fifteen collectors capable of liking a painter outside the Salon. There are eighty thousand who will not even buy a nose if it is not of the Salon." Sisley had quit the group and Monet had weakened; both felt that the group exhibitions tied them to Durand-Ruel when they might be doing business with his competitors. The sixth group exhibition in 1881 was held without the participation of Renoir, Monet, Sisley, Cézanne and Caillebotte, leaving of the original Impressionists only Degas, Morisot and Guillaumin. With this in mind Renoir drew up plans for a reorganized Salon, divided into four sections, each section limited to one thousand works, each with its own jury. These he reserved for (1) members of the Institute, (2) foreigners, (3) historical and genre painters, (4) naturalists and impressionists. To his surprise and disappointment no one was interested. The Salon had ceased to be an issue; as he would discover within a few years, the whole field of art was about to be fragmented into a score of new and, even for Renoir, radical tendencies. The Salon would be left to ossify in obscurity.

"I did not go to either Oxford or Cambridge, but I went to the Nouvelle-Athènes. What is the Nouvelle-Athènes?... The Nouvelle-Athènes is a café on the Place Pigalle. Ah! the morning idlenesses and the long evenings when life was but a summer illusion, the grey moonlights on the Place Pigalle where we used to stand on the pavements, the shutters clanging up behind us, loath to separate, thinking of what we had left unsaid, and how much better we might have enforced our arguments... How magnetic, intense, and vivid are these memories of youth! With what strange, almost unnatural clearness do I see and hear... I can hear the glass door of the café grate on the sand as I open it. I can recall the smell of every hour. In the morning that of eggs frizzling in butter, the pungent cigarette, coffee and bad cognac; at five o'clock the fragrant odour of absinthe; and soon after the steaming soup ascends from the kitchen; and as the evening advances, the mingled smells of cigarettes, coffee, and weak beer. A partition, rising a few feet or more over the hats, separates the glass front from the main body of the café. The usual marble tables are there, and it is there we sat and aestheticized till two o'clock in the morning..."

Thus, George Moore, the Irish novelist, reconstructs the Café de la Nouvelle-Athènes which had replaced the Café Guerbois as the favorite haunt of the avant-garde intellectuals and artists in Paris

Gatherings at the Café de la Nouvelle Athènes

In the seventies the Café Guerbois was superseded by the Nouvelle Athènes as the artists' meeting place. Situated in the Place Pigalle, it was familiarly known as the Café of the Intransigents, after the Impressionists had taken to meeting there at the time of the first group exhibition in 1874. Degas painted his *Absinthe Drinkers* at the Nouvelle Athènes, taking as his model the engraver Marcellin Desboutin, who was one of its legendary figures. All the Guerbois regulars now betook themselves to Place Pigalle—Manet, Degas, and the critics Duranty, Duret and Burty. Others joined the group: Georges Rivière, Forain, Henri Guérard, Zandomenghi, Jean Richepin, Villiers de l'Isle-Adam, Armand Silvestre, Charles Cros, the musician Cabaner, and also George Moore who has so well described the Nouvelle Athènes in his *Confessions of a Young Man*. Renoir dropped in regularly, but Monet, Pissarro, Cézanne and Sisley, all living in the country, only came occasionally.

"The habitués of the Nouvelle Athènes, as they were in 1874 and later, formed the first sympathetic public that the Impressionists had met; from there was launched the propaganda that was to provide them with a phalanx of partisans" (Georges Rivière).

The Café de la Nouvelle Athènes in Montmartre, 1906. Photograph.

during the late seventies and early eighties of the last century. The café's other distinction was that it had a picture of a dead rat painted on its ceiling. Here came Renoir, sometimes Pissarro, and such people as Duranty, Cabaner, Castagnary, Daudet, Nadar, Gambetta and, of course, Manet and Degas, as Moore informs us:

"At that moment the glass door of the Café grated upon the sanded floor and Manet entered. Although by birth and by art essentially a Parisian, there was something in his appearance and manner of speaking that often suggested an Englishman. Perhaps it was his dress—his clean-cut clothes and figure. That figure! those square shoulders that swaggered as he went across a room, and the thin waist; and that face, the beard and nose, satyr-like shall I say? No, for I would evoke an idea of beauty of line united to that of intellectual expression—frank words, frank passion in his convictions, loyal and simple phrases, clear as well-water, sometimes a little hard, sometimes, as they flowed away, bitter, but at the fountain-head sweet and full of light. He sits next to Degas, that round-shouldered man in suit of pepper-and-salt. There is nothing very trenchantly French about him either, except the large necktie; his eyes are small, and his words are sharp, ironical, cynical. These two men are the leaders of the impressionist school. "

Manet had become a celebrity, besieged by interviewers, writers, dealers, fashionable ladies and gentlemen. He welcomed them all to his new studio on the ground floor of a luxurious building, 4 rue

Around Manet, Esteem and Admiration, the Smile of Women and Flowers

Edouard Manet: Spring (Jeanne Demarsy), 1882. Print.

Edouard Manet: Woman's Head. Red Chalk.

Stéphane Mallarmé, Méry Laurent and Manet (seated) photographed in 1872.

Stéphane Mallarmé (standing) and Renoir (seated) photographed by Degas.
In the mirror, Madame Mallarmé and her Daughter.

"Nothing less resembled Degas's *deliberately hard* character, direct to the point of brutality, than Mallarmé's *deliberate* character... Nothing less resembled Degas's brilliant intransigence, his judgments rendered with implacable banter, the summary and sarcastic executions which he never withheld, his always perceptible bitterness, his terrible variations of mood, his outbursts, than Mallarmé's smooth, agreeable, delicate, delightfully ironic manner.

"I think Mallarmé stood in some awe of this character so different from his own.

"As for Degas, he spoke in the kindest terms of Mallarmé, of the man above all. The work seemed to him the fruit of a mild madness which had come over the mind of a marvelously gifted poet. "

Paul Valéry, *Degas, Danse, Dessin*

Saint-Pétersbourg. It had been a *salle d'armes,* or fencing arena, a spacious room with a high beamed ceiling and panelled walls, still dominated by the referee's rostrum, with a silk curtain hiding the former armory; tall windows and balconies overlooked the rue Mosnier, on one hand, and, on the other, the Pont de l'Europe which crossed the new railroad to the Gare Saint-Lazare. Every time a locomotive steamed past—a thrilling sound, then—the whole building shook. Manet had installed a piano, a Louis XV console, a Japanese tapestry decorated with flower and bird designs, some chairs and settees upholstered in green plush. "Otherwise," says Charles Toché (as reported by Vollard), "everything was of monkish simplicity, not a useless piece of furniture, not a knick-knack, but everywhere the most brilliant studies on the walls and easels... on the mantelpiece, a plaster cat with a pipe in its mouth. "

He had affairs with beautiful and notorious women, such as Nina de Villard, of whom he made a remarkable portrait he called *The Black Cat,* and Méry Laurent, the former mistress of Dr Evans (the American dentist who had helped smuggle the Empress Eugénie to England when the Commune broke loose).

Manet had been in bad health for several years. The disease which he had contracted in his youth, possibly on his trip to Rio de Janeiro, had been but superficially cured. In the late seventies Manet had begun to display the symptoms of locomotor ataxia and ulceration of his left foot, neither of which yielded to treatment.

When he could no longer stand before his easel he took a villa at Rueil, near Versailles, where there was a flower garden which he painted from a wheel-chair after the brilliant manner of the Impressionists. Meanwhile, his childhood friend, Antonin Proust, had been appointed Minister of Fine Arts in a cabinet formed by Gambetta. Proust began by buying for the nation a series of paintings by Courbet and by recommending Manet for the Legion of Honor. President Grévy objected, but was overruled by Gambetta in accordance with the executive powers of the Assembly. From Capri, where he was painting, Renoir wrote to Manet: "I... salute you as the painter beloved by everyone, officially recognized... You are the happy fighter, without hatred for anyone... and I like you for that gaiety maintained even in the midst of injustice. "

Exhibited at the Salon of 1882 *Bar at the Folies-Bergère* was coldly received by public and critics, including the ferocious Albert Wolff, to whom Manet wrote, saying: "I shouldn't mind reading while I'm still alive the splendid article which you will write about me once I am dead. " Officially nominated Knight of the Legion of Honor when the Salon closed, Manet was congratulated by, among others, Count Nieuwerkerke, to whom he tartly replied that had the Count conferred the honor he might have made his fortune by this time, whereas now it was too late to compensate for twenty years' lack of success.

To his friend Proust, Manet said: "The fools. They were forever telling me that my work was unequal. That was the highest praise they could bestow. Yet it was always my ambition to rise—not to remain at a certain level, not to remake one day what I had made the day before, but to be inspired again and again by a new aspect of things, to strike frequently a fresh note. Ah, I'm before my time. A hundred years hence people will be happier, for their sight will be clearer than ours today."

In April 1883, Manet's left foot was gangrenescent. The surgeons were of the opinion that amputation was necessary. Dr Gachet, who was in attendance, protested vigorously and there was an argument on the merits of homeopathic treatment as against surgery. Manet agreed to submit to surgery and his leg was amputated. He died on April 30, 1883.

Just before dying, Manet had told Antonin Proust: "This war to the knife has done me much harm. I have suffered from it greatly, but it has whipped me up... I would not want that any artist should be praised and covered with adulation at the outset, for that means the annihilation of his personality."

When Duret began preparing for a posthumous exhibition of Manet's work in 1884, he was refused the use of the galleries of the Ecole des Beaux Arts by Professor Kaempfen, the director, who told Duret that he was surprised at the request as in his opinion the artist was nothing less than a revolutionary. Jules Ferry, minister of public instruction, overruled Kaempfen and the exhibition was a grand success. According to the memoirs of Durand-Ruel who, with Georges Petit, organized the sale of Manet's studio effects, all the paintings were sold, mostly to new collectors, for a total sum of 116,637 francs. At the Universal Exposition, five years later, Manet was ranked among the masters of the century. *Olympia* put on view, attracted special attention and a fund was started to purchase the painting for the Nation.

"Do you remember," Degas said to George Moore one day, "how Manet used to turn on me when I wouldn't send my paintings to the Salon? He would say, 'You, Degas, you are above the level of the sea, but for my part, if I get into an omnibus and someone there doesn't say, "There, Monsieur Manet, how are you, where are you going?" I am disappointed, for then I know that I am not famous.'"

Degas was remembering the incident happily: Manet was now famous.

One of Degas's earliest admirers was a young American girl who had bought one of his pastels in a little shop in Paris and, without knowing anything about the artist, had liked it so much that she had bought others, paying less than a hundred francs for some. Mary Cassatt had decided that she wanted to be a painter and had set about realizing her ambition in a thoroughly businesslike manner, first studying at the Pennsylvania Academy of Fine Arts (1864 to 1865), then going to Italy where she had copied Correggio and other masters. Arriving finally in Paris, her painting had been accepted by the Salons, 1872 to 1876, but on being rejected in 1877, she had joined the Impressionists.

She had already met Degas, for whom, says George Biddle, the American painter, "she had a veneration. What he felt was actually her law and standard... I have never seen a great and successful artist who so ungrudgingly acknowledged the debt to an earlier and lifelong influence..." Born in Allegheny City, Pennsylvania, May 22,

Mary Cassatt

"I cannot bring myself to admit that a woman draws so well."

Degas speaking of Mary Cassatt

Mary Cassatt came of a wealthy Pittsburgh family and spent much of her childhood in Europe. After some early training at the Pennsylvania Academy of Fine Arts in Philadelphia, she studied art in Paris shortly before the War of 1870. She copied the masters at the Louvre and took a keen interest in the new work of Manet and the Impressionists. After her meeting with Degas, who came to her studio in 1877, she began taking part in the group exhibitions. She bought impressionist pictures herself and encouraged her friends and relations to do so; in this she rendered a signal service to her new friends. Although she was a great admirer of Degas, her own work has an incontestable originality, a highly personal note of feminine intimacy. Her sensitive pictures of mothers and children, both in oils and etchings, have a charm to which Degas and the others warmly responded. In a letter to his son Lucien, Pissarro wrote in 1893: "Miss Cassatt is holding a very fine exhibition of paintings at Durand-Ruel's. Her work is very good indeed!" Degas often took her as model, sketching her as she walked through the galleries of the Louvre with a catalogue in her hand, or at the milliner's trying on hats.

Mary Cassatt soon became the Impressionists' most effective agent in the United States. Durand-Ruel and later Vollard often called upon her services; knowing the material difficulties of her painter friends, she never refused her help. In his *Souvenirs d'un marchand de tableaux*, Vollard pays tribute to her selfless generosity and her repeated exertions in favor of Monet, Pissarro, Renoir, Cézanne and Sisley.

Edgar Degas: Mary Cassatt in the Louvre, about 1879. Pencil.

Mary Cassatt: Feeding the Ducks, 1895. Color Etching.

Mary Cassatt: Woman at her Toilette, 1891. Drypoint and Aquatint.

1844, Mary Cassatt was the daughter of a wealthy Pittsburgh banker and a sister of Alexander J. Cassatt, President of the Pennsylvania Railroad. When in 1876 Degas explained to her the difficulties which had brought Durand-Ruel to the verge of bankruptcy, she had been able to arrange a loan which set the art dealer on his feet again and enabled him to recommence dealing with the Impressionists.

Mary Cassatt was, it seems, the model for a series of pictures which Degas made of women trying on hats at the milliner's, which reveal her fringe of chestnut hair and pert well-cut features, large competent hands and narrow waist. Pissarro left canvases which she would try to sell at her tea parties. "It was with a sort of frenzy that generous Mary Cassatt labored for the success of her comrades, Monet, Pissarro, Cézanne, Sisley and the rest," says Vollard, "But what indifference where her own painting was concerned! What an aversion to 'pushing' her own work in public. One day at an exhibition, they were arguing for and against the Impressionists. 'But,' said someone, speaking to Mary Cassatt, without knowing who she was, 'you are forgetting a foreign painter that Degas ranks very high.'

'Who is that?' she asked in astonishment.

'Mary Cassatt.'

'Oh, nonsense!' she exlaimed without false modesty."

She went out painting with Renoir, who noted that "she carried her easel like a man." Over a glass of cider, she told Renoir: "There is one thing against your technique: it is too simple. The public does not like that." Renoir was flattered. She criticized Monet for his lack of "mentality," but commissioned him to paint her brother, the railroad magnate (and detested the result). Her friends Louisine and Henry Havemeyer listened to her advice and the Havemeyer collection in the New York Metropolitan Museum is the result.

It was largely due to Mary Cassatt's influence and financial backing that Durand-Ruel decided to hold an exhibition of Impressionist painting in New York. Leaving his gallery in Paris to the direction of his son Joseph, he left for New York in March 1886, accompanied by his son Charles, with three hundred canvases by Millet, Manet, Monet, Renoir, Sisley, Pissarro, Degas, Whistler, Morisot, Boudin, Guillaumin, Forain, Seurat, Signac, et al. According to the New York *Daily Tribune* seven to eight pictures were sold within two weeks and the critics were disarmed by the number of important collectors among the buyers. The show lasted two months and was a success. In his memoirs Durand-Ruel says that the American art dealers had not opposed the exhibition, taking it for granted that it would fail. But when Durand-Ruel made arrangements for a second exhibition to open at the end of 1886 he encountered difficulties with the U.S. Customs, and was obliged to postpone it until 1887.

"Without America, I was lost, ruined, through having bought so many Monets and Renoirs," Durand-Ruel said years later. "Two expositions there, in 1886-1887, saved me. The American public does not laugh, it buys—moderately, it is true; but, thanks to it, Monet and Renoir could continue to live; and since then, as everyone knows, the French public has followed suit."

Pissarro's Influence on the Younger Generation

It was through the banker Gustave Arosa, a collector of modern pictures and Gauguin's godfather, that Pissarro met the future painter of the South Seas. Gauguin at that time, in the late 1870's, was a prosperous stockbroker and an amateur painter. Pissarro took him in hand and guided his efforts, and the two men often worked together at Pontoise after 1879. From 1879 on, Gauguin took part in all the group exhibitions. After suffering heavy losses in the stock market crash of 1882, Gauguin gave up his stockbroking job and in 1883 made up his mind "to paint every day." He then lived with Pissarro for a time; the two self-portrait drawings date from this period and mark the culminating point of their friendship and of Pissarro's influence on Gauguin. Thereafter they drifted apart, and in 1886 Pissarro wrote to his son Lucien: "Hostilities continue more and more among the romantic Impressionists. They get together quite regularly; Degas himself comes to the Café. Gauguin has again become very intimate with Degas and often goes to see him—curious, isn't it, this reversal of interests! Gauguin has forgotten the snubs of last year at the seaside, forgotten his sarcasms against the sectarian Degas, forgotten what he told me often enough about the egoism and common side of Guillaumin. And I was naïve enough to defend him stoutly against them all." The honest Pissarro looked askance at the pushing and unscrupulous ambition of his former friend; and Gauguin, for his part, could not forgive Pissarro for his conversion to Pointillism.

Said Renoir: "We perhaps owe it to the Americans that we did not die of hunger."

Each year, 1879 through 1882, there had been an Impressionist exhibition, usually in the rooms of empty houses that had just been built or were being reconditioned in the more frequented streets. In 1883, March through June, there had been an exhibition in the Boulevard de la Madeleine where each month had been devoted to a different artist, first Monet, then Renoir, Pissarro and Sisley. In the liberal atmosphere of the consolidated Republic there were suddenly many more painters using bright colors and unorthodox composition, who were classed, or classed themselves, as impressionists. Max Liebermann in Germany and Wynford Dewhurst in England were painting in the impressionist manner. Paul Signac, a young Parisian hardly out of his teens, had been making impressionist paintings of great promise. Apart from its technical innovations, the sheer vigor and unorthodoxy of the Impressionist movement had given encouragement to a number of young painters of great originality. Paul Gauguin had worked with Pissarro in Normandy and, after a number of experiments in the impressionist manner, had developed his own powerful style. Georges Seurat had taken impressionist theory a step further into what was called "pointillism," a deviation which had captured Pissarro's interest. Odilon Redon had been so far liberated from convention that he could indulge his own particular fantasy in painting, in a way that enchanted the prosaic Guillaumin. Where were these young painters to go, if the Impressionists did not take them under their wing? The question caused a schism among the foundation members of the movement. Degas, supported as always by Berthe Morisot, was prepared to expand the exhibition to include almost any new painter, causing Monet to mutter, "The little clique has become a great club which opens its doors to the first-come dauber." Pissarro was anxious to take in Signac and Seurat. Sisley felt that they should maintain their exclusiveness. Gauguin, who had exhibited with the Impressionists, 1879 through 1882, was also against opening the exhibitions to "nullities and pupils of the Ecole."

Camille Pissarro:
Self-Portrait, 1888.
Pen and Ink.

Gauguin and Pissarro:
Self-Portraits Side by Side, about 1883. Drawings.

Camille Pissarro: Crouching Peasant Woman, 1878-1881. Charcoal.

Vincent van Gogh: Woman Gathering Grass. Drawing.

Georges Seurat: The Stone Breaker. Drawing.

Thus, in 1886, when it was decided to hold the eighth Impressionist exhibition, Monet, Renoir, Sisley and Caillebotte abstained and there was a heavy representation of Degas protégés, as well as Pissarro's young friends Seurat and Signac. In the circumstances it was decided to drop the word "impressionist" and the show was simply advertised as "Eighth Exhibition of Paintings." It was their last exhibition; it was the end of an epoch.

As it turned out, the sensation of the Eighth Exhibition was Seurat's pointillist painting *A Sunday Afternoon on the Island of La Grande Jatte*. It was a huge canvas and Seurat had had to use a ladder to get to its upper part. He had conceived a painting on the scale of the old masters, but carried out in a radical technique. The subject was a stretch of the Seine river bank, with some forty objects in view, people, animals, canoes, etc. Form and color were rendered by hundreds of thousands, perhaps millions, of small dots or points of different colors. His friend Signac describes Seurat at work: "Confronting his subject, Seurat, before touching his panel with paint, scrutinizes, compares, looks with half-shut eyes at the play of light and shadow, observes contrasts, isolated reflections, plays for a long time with the cover of the box which serves as his palette, then, fighting against matter as against nature, he slices from his little heap of colors, arranged in order of the spectrum, the various elements from which to form the tint best designed to convey the mystery he has glimpsed. Execution follows on observation, stroke by stroke the panel is covered."

As a youthful student, Seurat had discovered in the library of the Ecole des Beaux Arts two books which had provided him with the theoretical basis for a new approach to painting. The first was Chevreul's *The Law of Simultaneously Contrasting Colors* (1839), a

By the time Van Gogh arrived in Paris, in March 1886, the impressionist movement had lost its cohesion: each painter had branched off on a distinct path of his own, orienting his expression in accordance with the personal outlook of his maturity. "So it was," wrote Lionello Venturi, "that in 1885 Renoir marked his return to linear form, Pissarro realized his neo-impressionism, Monet predetermined the Fauve manner and Sisley approached it. All had lost that perfect balance between the natural impression and the chromatic imagination which had created the impressionist style."

Pissarro, in subscribing to the Pointillism of Seurat, who was twenty-nine years his junior, defied the tradition which has it that the elder men should influence the younger generation. Even in holding that the painter's art should be based on the conquests of science, the Post-Impressionists faithfully reflected the life and preoccupations of their time, and they sought to renew their means of expression by carrying their color discoveries to their ultimate consequences. By way of a new conception of form, the drawings of Pissarro, Van Gogh and Seurat reveal the same truthful rendering of the everyday gestures and attitudes which had so keenly interested Millet thirty years before.

Theo Van Gogh, who had acquainted Vincent with the Impressionists, followed the development of Pissarro's art and that of the other Impressionists, whose pictures he sometimes sold in the gallery where he worked. On September 5, 1889, Theo wrote to his brother: "There is old father Pissarro who after all has done some very fine things lately, and in them one finds those very qualities of rusticity which show at once that the man is more at ease in a pair of wooden shoes than in polished boots."

Camille Pissarro: Charing Cross Bridge, London, 1890.

treatise for tapestry weavers on the optical effects of differently dyed wools when woven side by side. The second was Charles Blanc's *Grammar of the Arts of Design* (1867) in which the author held that "color, which is under fixed laws, can be taught like music." From this it was but a step to the theory of vibration and James Clerk Maxwell's rotating disc of merging colors. In this way Seurat had arrived at the concept of "optical painting" or "chromoluminarianism." Already a skillful draftsman Seurat had abandoned line as a means of achieving definition and had begun drawing in tone, reaching a point where form was reduced to an abstraction. In 1882 he was painting pictures using separate touches of the brush in different colors which fused with an extraordinary luminosity at a certain distance. He divided a color, say orange, into its component parts, red and yellow, and put these latter colors side by side on the canvas, instead of mixing them. Seurat had, in effect, carried "impressionism" to its logical conclusion.

Georges Seurat was uncommunicative, solitary in his habits and totally absorbed. It was unfairly said of him that he was afraid that someone would steal his technique. He wore a long, narrowly

In 1886, at the eighth and last impressionist exhibition, Pissarro showed his first pictures in the pointillist style. He was enthusiastic about the art of Seurat, based in part on the scientific observations of the physiologist Charles Henry. By 1891 Pissarro had come to realize the dangers of "scientific painting" for a sensibility as keen as his, and he confided to Georges Lecomte: "One must yield to one's painterly instinct, one must be humble before nature... The desire to interpret it must not make one lose the close, direct contact with it... Reasoning and science run the risk of blunting our sensations... I am happier and it seems to me that I go further, now that I express with greater freedom what I see and feel."

In February 1892 a large Pissarro exhibition was held at the Durand-Ruel gallery. It was a great success and from now on Pissarro's financial worries were over. But eye trouble gradually forced him to give up working out of doors and he took to painting town views from windows.

"M. Seurat, a highly gifted artist, was the first to take up and apply the scientific theories, after making a thorough study of them. I have done no more than follow him... What we are seeking is a modern synthesis by means based on science, on the theory of colors discovered by Chevreul, and following the experiments of Maxwell and the measurements of N.O. Rood. For the mixture of pigments we substitute the optical mixture. In other words: the breaking down of tones into their constituent elements. Because the optical mixture gives rise to much more intense luminosities than the mixture of pigments. As for the execution, we regard it as of no account, it is quite unimportant. In our view, it has nothing to do with art, originality consisting solely in the character of the design and the vision peculiar to each artist. "

Pissarro, letter to Durand-Ruel,
November 6, 1886

Georges Seurat: Courbevoie Bridge, 1886-1887.

Georges Seurat: Bathers at Asnières, 1883-1884.

New Lines of Research and Experiment

"So do not believe that I would artificially maintain a feverish state, but know that I am in the middle of a complicated calculation, resulting in canvases turned out one after the other at high speed, but calculated long *in advance*. And so when they tell you that this has been done too quickly, you can reply that it is they who have looked too quickly."

Vincent van Gogh, letter to Theo, summer 1888

Vincent van Gogh:
The Fourteenth of July in Paris,
1886-1887.

Paul Gauguin: *Landscape at Le Pouldu, 1890*

Vincent van Gogh: *View from his Window in Rue Lepic, Paris, 1886-1887. Drawing.*

"How do you see that tree? It's greenish brown? Well, put on some green, the finest green on your palette. And that shadow—rather blue, isn't it? Don't be afraid to paint it as blue as possible."

Gauguin to Sérusier, 1888

During his stay in Paris, from 1886 to 1888, Van Gogh met Gauguin, through Emile Bernard, and conceived a great admiration for him. The impressionism of 1874, which had not yet won over the public, was already being left behind by these eager young men who met together in the cafés of Montmartre and aspired to go much further than their elders in the handling of color. Seurat was showing the way towards a certain abstraction in which the artist's purpose was not so much to interpret light reflections as to recreate them through his knowledge of the scientific facts of color. By way of Pointillism Van Gogh discovered the possibilities of pure color, and the practice of divisionism soon led him to adopt a broad, spontaneous brushstroke better suited to his temperament. In his street scene with fluttering flags and bunting, he already goes beyond color-light towards that purely emotional use of color which was to reach its climax in the canvases painted in Provence, beginning in the fall of 1888. Gauguin too, by the time he joined Van Gogh at Arles in October of that year, had reached the decisive stage in his evolution, developing a harmonic palette and creating a poetic, symbolic, indeed musical color image.

The Salon Painters and the Independents

While the Salon jury continued to be uncompromisingly hostile to the Impressionists and their followers, the "official glories" nevertheless felt the need to modernize their style by a few borrowings from the palette of the open air painters, for taste was moving now in the direction of *la peinture claire*, painting in bright colors. Degas sarcastically remarked: "They come to the Impressionists to clean up their palette." Following the massive refusals pronounced by the Salon jury in 1884, the Société des Artistes Indépendants was formed under the chairmanship of Odilon Redon, for the purpose of holding independent exhibitions. This Society took over the name initially used by the Impressionists, and for the next twenty years the new trends of art were revealed annually at the Salon des Indépendants. The first exhibition was held in a wooden shed in the Tuileries in 1884: there Seurat showed his first large composition, *Bathers at Asnières*, which gave birth to Pointillism.

trimmed beard which helped to give the impression that he had, in the words of one acquaintance, "a Christ-like head," and of another that he possessed "the delicate yet massive profile of Assyrian kings." He took no part in conversation unless it concerned questions of art, and then he would speak with an authority that was final. He lived a monkish life in a small room and studio in the Boulevard de Clichy where, according to Signac, he had a narrow bed facing a stack of unsold canvases, while in the studio there was a red divan, a few chairs, a little table heaped with books and magazines, paints, a tobacco pouch. On the walls there were little paintings by Guillaumin and other friends and, covering almost one entire wall, *La Grande Jatte*.

It has been reported that Pissarro, on seeing *La Grande Jatte* for the first time, was dumbfounded. He was immediately captured by the pointillist or optical technique; it was so very close to his own, and it appealed to his intellect, his "logical positivism," as it were. He had decided to adopt it and urged his son Lucien, also painting at this time, to do likewise. The shortcomings of the technique were dramatically demonstrated a few years later at an exhibition at which pointillist paintings by Seurat, Signac, Camille Pissarro and Lucien Pissarro were exhibited together. Observers found it impossible to distinguish one man's work from another's, especially as the signatures were also in dots. After devoting four years to pointillism, Pissarro went back to his old manner of painting, leaving the field to Seurat. "I do not blush for having been conquered by his method,"

Fernand Cormon:
The Victors at Salamis,
1887. Print.

William Bouguereau
Among his Works.
Photograph.

said Pissarro, "I blush for not having sold a certain number of my paintings."

Just how serious this failure to sell paintings, impressionist or pointillist, was for the Pissarro family at this late stage of Camille's career, is indicated in a letter Julie Pissarro wrote to her son Lucien in the autumn of 1887. "Your poor father," said Julie, "is really an innocent, he doesn't understand the difficulties of living. He knows that I owe 3,000 francs and he sends me 300, and tells me to wait! Always the same joke. I don't mind waiting, but meanwhile one must eat. I have no money and nobody will give me credit. I paid off a little of the debts here and there, but it is so little that they don't want to give me any more credit. What are we to do? We are eight at home to be fed every day. When dinner time comes, I cannot say to them, 'Wait'—this stupid word your father repeats and repeats. I have used up anything I had put aside. I am at the end of my tether and, what is worse, have no courage left. I had decided to send the three boys to Paris and then to take the two little ones for a walk by the river. You can imagine the rest. Everyone would have thought it an accident. But when I was ready to go, I lacked courage. Why am I such a coward at the last moment? My poor son, I feared to cause you all grief, and I was afraid of your remorse. Your dear father wrote me a letter which is a masterpiece of selfishness. The poor dear man says that he has reached the top of his profession and doesn't want to prejudice his reputation by having an auction sale or by pawning his pictures. Not to prejudice his reputation! Poor dear. What repentance for him if he should lose his wife and his two little ones! To uphold his reputation! I think he doesn't know what he is saying. My poor Lucien, I am terribly unhappy. Goodbye, shall I see you again, alas?"

Up to 1870 Cézanne had obeyed his virile imagination; his subjects were literary, pathetic or erotic; he painted with a heavy impasto. Even his friends were critical; of his *Afternoon in Naples*, Zola said: "How can you abide such painting?" During the two years he had spent at Auvers after the war, Cézanne had come under Pissarro's influence and had changed his fiery execution for a calmer one, based on the impressionist coloration. Pissarro, who compensated for the lack of visual imagination by an extraordinary perception of nature, had warned Cézanne against his "romanticism."

Cézanne had exhibited at the first Impressionist exhibition in 1874, but had abstained from the second in 1876 because it was held at Durand-Ruel's gallery. After the attacks on the third exhibition and the auction at the Hôtel Drouot he did not again exhibit with the Impressionists. He was not, in fact, an impressionist painter, in the sense that Pissarro, Monet and Sisley gave to the term. It was his character and outlook, his iconoclasm and irascible temper, which brought him among the Impressionists. "He looked like a porcupine," says Renoir, using one of his favorite literary images. "His movements seemed restricted, as though he was encased in some invisible shell—his voice too. He articulated words carefully in his strong Aixois accent, an accent which went with the reserved but exquisitely

Cézanne: The Solitary Pathfinder

Cézanne Painting at Aix-en-Provence, January 1904. Photograph taken by Maurice Denis accompanied by Emile Bernard.

Cézanne's Studio at Aix-en-Provence. Photograph.

According to Lucien Pissarro, it was at his father's house in Pontoise that Cézanne painted this *Still Life with a Tureen*. So, though it is usually dated to about 1883-1885, it may have been begun in the late seventies; the pictures in the background, moreover, can probably be identified with certain works by Pissarro, one, the landscape on the left, of 1873, the other, the *Chickens* in the center, of 1877.

The year 1877 is a key date in the history of Impressionism: it was the year of their third group exhibition, held in the rue Le Peletier and openly called now, in spite of Degas's objections, the Exhibition of the Impressionists. For Cézanne, this marks the moment when he began to break away from Impressionism. After the 1877 exhibition he took part in no further manifestations of this kind, though he repudiated neither Impressionism nor, even less, the friendship connecting him with his old comrades. But, more clearly than the others, he saw how wide was the range of possible development implicit in Impressionism and realized that the happy balance of possibilities achieved by then could not be maintained indefinitely.

The lesson Cézanne had learned from Impressionism was a vital one, and it was Pissarro more than anyone else who helped him to assimilate it. He had learned to build with color masses, in terms of intense and luminous volumes, and he had learned to place objects without reference to the traditional rules of perspective. This was a necessary preliminary in his quest for the monumental aspect of images. From now on he subjected images to the corrective control of his mind, going about it with a diligence that testifies both to his humility and to his perfect awareness of the goal before him. He brightened his colors and boldly contrasted them; he intensified his brushwork in order to give the maximum thickness and solidity to objects. From this time on, and to an increasingly marked degree, he imposed precise geometric forms on objects and arranged them on multiple, dislocated planes. He still started out from his *petite sensation*, as he called it; this, in his impressionist period, had been the focal point of his researches; now he realized the extent to which it had to be elaborated on in order to reflect it adequately in his own mind.

Thus did Cézanne lay the foundations of all modern painting.

Paul Cézanne: Still Life with a Tureen, about 1883-1885.

Cézanne: Rigor of Design and Vision

Paul Cézanne: Portrait of the Artist's Wife, about 1883-1886.
Pencil and Black Chalk.

In 1882 Cézanne returned to Aix and settled there for good. His native Provence provided him with a purer, steadier light than the Ile de France, the neighborhood of Aix with starker, better defined, more sharply structured landscapes. Here he could work longer on the same motifs, his scrutiny undisturbed by sudden gusts of wind in the leafage or the continually shifting clouds of northern skies. He dreamed of "doing Poussin over again from nature," by which he meant reconciling the demands of perception with those of order and harmony. Day in, day out, he scrutinized his motifs; with the same perseverance he sought to give duration to fleeting sensations.

polite manner of the young provincial. Yet his restraint would give way sometimes and he would come up with his two famous insults, 'Eunuch' and 'Blockhead.' He was suspicious. He was a lone wolf. But he shared their [the Impressionists'] ideas and hopes. He had faith in the 'judgment of the people.' The whole problem was a way of getting one's work shown, of forcing the doors of Monsieur Bouguereau's Salon."

After almost two years in Auvers (living without papers, as Dr Gachet discovered) Cézanne found lodgings in the rue de Vaugirard for Hortense and his small son and returned to Aix. He told his mother of his liaison, but was afraid to tell his father, in case the old man (he had retired from the bank, very rich) flew into a rage, stopped his allowance and perhaps disinherited him. Hortense who spent much of her time reading novels (she had previously been employed to bind them) did not seem to mind the frequent separations which were her lot during the next eight or ten years. Cézanne was very fond of her and his small son and wrote to her almost daily when absent. She seems to have been a plain sensible woman whose most treasurable quality may have been her capacity to sit still while Cézanne painted her. This was no mean feat, for, as Duret says, "His canvases, which appeared so simple, demanded a large, often an enormous, number of sittings." (Vollard, who posed on a chair precariously perched on a packing-case, counted ninety sittings, after which Cézanne regarded the portrait as still far from finished, being satisfied only with "the triangle about the waistcoat.") Since Cézanne made at least a dozen portraits of Hortense, it seems fair to say that she was a woman of a certain patience; not only in her function as model, but in her whole life. For Cézanne's determination to keep his father from learning of Hortense's existence created a curious dichotomy in their lives. He had now a fine studio on the top floor of Jas de Bouffan, his father's mansion near Aix, and liked nothing better than painting its vineyards, chestnut trees, barns, and bathing pool. ("Painting nudes on the banks of the Arc is all I could wish for," he said once.) But always he had to tear himself away to return to Hortense and the boy. At one point he brought them south with him and put them in lodgings at Marseilles, borrowing funds from Zola in order to do so, and walking the eighteen miles from Aix to Marseilles, and back again, to see them. But Hortense did not much care for provincial life, preferring, during his absences, gay Paris. They were married finally, in 1886, when young Paul was already fifteen years of age. Six months later his father died and only then did Cézanne discover that his parent had, many years before, settled his considerable fortune equally on his three children, as a means of avoiding death duties. He had known of his son's liaison with Hortense, either through his wife or by opening his son's mail, and had not let that matter interfere with his plan. Thus Cézanne had been a rich man for longer than he knew. One is left with the impression that the supposed readiness of Cézanne's father to disinherit his son was largely fictitious or imagined on his son's part, but had provided him with a reasonable excuse for arranging his domestic life in a manner suited to his moody temperament. That

"My picture of L'Estaque is like a playing card. Red roofs against a blue sea. If the weather is favorable I may be able to see this through to the end... But there are some motifs which would require three or four months' work, which could be done, for the vegetation doesn't change. It consists of olive trees and pines which keep their leafage. The sun is so tremendous that objects seem to me to be silhouetted not only in white or black, but in blue, red, brown, violet. I may be wrong, but this seems to me to be the exact opposite of modelling."

Cézanne, letter to Pissarro, July 21, 1876

Paul Cézanne: Self-Portrait, 1881-1884. Pencil.   *Paul Cézanne: The Sea at L'Estaque, 1882-1885.*

Paul Cézanne: Boy with a Red Waistcoat, 1894-1895.

"*Making out the model, and the realization of it, is sometimes a very slow process for the artist. Whatever the master you may prefer, this should be no more than an orientation for you. Otherwise you will only be an imitator. With any sense of nature at all, and a few happy gifts, you should be able to make your own way... Believe me, once your feelings are aroused, your own emotion will in the end emerge and win its place in the sun. Get the upper hand, have confidence. What you must make yourself master of is a good method of construction. Drawing is only the configuration of what you see.*"

Cézanne, letter to Charles Camoin, December 9, 1904

It seems impossible to subordinate so precise a linear design to so rigorous a composition and so dense a coloring. Yet Cézanne succeeds in reconciling contraries: the objective study of nature and the mathematical laws of harmony, the accidental and the eternal. This almost miraculous balance is the fruit of hard work doggedly pursued. First of all, the painter scrutinized his model, sizing it up in all its implications, however provisional; with a fine pencil he laid in the contours, following the imperceptible movement of his immobilized subject, working repeatedly at the contours in order to bring out the expression of volumes. In the second phase, he subordinated the particular to the general and merged detail into the whole, but without effacing its presence. The least movement of the observer modifies the point of view; Cézanne did not feel entitled to arrest the movement of the world, to reduce it to the fixity of a "snapshot" taken at random. He tried to open his forms by repeated passages of color applied at different times, and so giving rise to contrasts from which he elicited that impression of durability and continuity which defined his style. Each form in the motif before him had to be fully worked out and defined, and at the same time to suggest a further range of possible transformations. Cézanne did not "record" the real world but compelled it to yield up its different possibilities of being and seeming.

"Go to the Louvre. But after you have seen the great masters reposing there, you must hasten out again and quicken within you, through contact with nature, the instincts and sensations of art that reside within us."

Cézanne, letter to Charles Camoin, September 13, 1903

Paul Cézanne: Card Player, 1890-1892. Pencil.

Paul Cézanne: Card Players, 1890-1905.

187

Paul Cézanne: Les Grandes
Baigneuses, 1898-1905.

Paul Cézanne: Bathers,
1883-1887. Pencil.

One must "marry the curves of women to the shoulders of hills," Cézanne liked to say to his young friend Joachim Gasquet. This dream of the plenitude of correspondences had obsessed him for twenty years. He tackled the theme in the *Grandes Baigneuses* during his impressionist period; and in his later years he painted several fully realized versions of it. The subject and size of the composition did not permit him to work in the open, but in this studio composition he found the opportunity to summarize and complete all the experiments made from nature, subjecting them now to the requirements of pure painting, the language of forms and colors.

"I proceed very slowly, nature as it offers itself to me being very complex; and improvements are always called for. One's model has to be looked at closely and rightly felt; and then it remains to express oneself with distinction and force.

"Taste is the best judge. It is rare... The artist should ignore opinion that is not based on the intelligent observation of character! He should keep aloof from the literary spirit, which so often draws the painter away from his true path—the concrete study of nature—and leads him astray in intangible speculations."

Cézanne, letter to Emile Bernard,
May 12, 1904

Paul Cézanne: Rocks at Bibemus, 1898-1900.

The *Cabanon de Jourdan* is Cézanne's last landscape; he was working on it when caught in a rainstorm. Marie, Cézanne's sister, wrote to his son Paul on October 20, 1906: "Your father has been ill since Monday... He was left exposed to the rain for several hours, and brought home on a laundry cart; two men had to carry him up to his bed. The next day, early in the morning, he went into the garden to work on a portrait of Vallier [his gardener], under the lime tree, and came in dying."

Paul Cézanne: Le Cabanon de Jourdan, 1906.

Cézanne photographed by Emile Bernard at Aix in 1905.

Hortense evidently acquiesced in this tacit arrangement says much for her good sense and possibly her own need of freedom.

It was Pissarro who urged Vollard to take up Cézanne. Their first meeting is described thus by Vollard: "Cézanne greeted me with outstretched hands. 'My son has often spoken of you. Excuse me for a little while, Monsieur Vollard, I am going to rest a moment before dinner. I have just come back from my motif. Paul will show you the studio.' The first thing that struck me as I set foot in the studio was a huge picture of a Peasant pierced full of holes with a palette knife. Cézanne used to fly into a passion for the most absurd reasons—sometimes for no reason at all—and was wont to vent his anger upon his canvases. "

Vollard describes Cézanne's studio: "On the floor lay a big box stuffed full of watercolor tubes; some apples, still 'posing' on a plate, were in the last stage of decay; near the window hung a curtain, which always served as a background for figure studies or still lifes; lastly, there were pinned on the walls engravings and photographs, both good and bad, chiefly bad, representing *The Shepherds of Arcadia* by Poussin, *The Living Bearing the Dead* by Luca Signorelli, several Delacroix's, *The Burial at Ornans* by Courbet, *The Assumption* by Rubens, a *Cupid* by Puget, some Forains, *Psyche* by Prud'hon, and even the *Roman Orgy* of Couture. "

Paul Cézanne: La Montagne Sainte-Victoire, about 1900. Pencil and Watercolor.

As with any active civilization there were moments of grave anxiety in the middle years of the Third Republic. The long struggle for secular education had its bad moments and the threat of a modern-style military dictatorship which seemed to grow with General Boulanger's popularity (among other things he introduced an order permitting the wearing of full beards in all ranks of the army) was considerately ended by his own hand. During all such crises the old prejudice against the Impressionist surfaced.

Such was the situation in 1894 when Gustave Caillebotte died of cerebral paralysis in his forty-sixth year, bequeathing his incomparable collection of impressionist paintings to the Nation: eighteen Pissarros, sixteen Monets, nine Sisleys, eight Renoirs, seven Degas's, five Cézannes and four Manets—sixty-seven canvases in all. Twenty years earlier, when Renoir had praised one of Caillebotte's canvases (depicting a group of house-painters at work) Caillebotte had blushed and had said: "I try to paint honestly, hoping that some day my work will be good enough to hang in the antechamber of the great room where the Renoirs and the Cézannes hang." Someday it would, but that day was still far off, even for the Renoirs and the Cézannes.

The gift was attacked in the press and some political pressure was brought to bear to have it rejected. It was said at the time that Caillebotte had bought the works which no one else would buy in order to help his friends financially, a manifest canard since Caillebotte's collection included Renoir's *Moulin de la Galette*, Monet's *Gare Saint-Lazare* and Pissarro's *Red Roofs* and many other equally distinguished paintings. In fact, Caillebotte was so ashamed of the low prices he had paid for his Renoirs that, just before dying, he had invited Renoir to take any picture he liked from his collection by way of compensation (Renoir took a Degas which he later sold). Some years ago the Louvre administration conducted its own inquiry into the circumstances surrounding the rejection of twenty-nine of the paintings bequeathed by Caillebotte, only to discover that the records were far from complete. In his account of the shabby treatment accorded the Caillebotte bequest Germain Bazin, incumbent Chief Curator of the Louvre, says: "Placed in the foreground of events curators are too often judged by the public as being responsible for situations over which in fact they have not sole control. An official, generally speaking, is only responsible to public opinion for his mistakes. The credit for success always goes to someone higher up the ladder."

The people "higher up the ladder" in 1894 were politicians. Consideration of the Caillebotte bequest ran parallel with the court martial of Captain Alfred Dreyfus on the charge of having delivered secret military information to the Germans, and his sentence to degradation and imprisonment for life on Devil's Island. The wave of anti-Semitism (Dreyfus was an Alsatian Jew) which swept France at this time did not leave the Impressionists unscathed. Vollard, for example, reports Degas turning his favorite model out of his studio with the words: "You're a Protestant! You all go hand in hand with the Jews for Dreyfus." On the other hand Monet (with Marcel Proust and Anatole France) signed the petition against the violation of

French School: View of a Room in the Luxembourg Museum, Paris, about 1880.

They [the Impressionists] refused to find in what philosophers call "external" reality a means or a symbol; they loved life itself and were rewarded with a copious gift of the very stuff of it. This unpretentious and unpremeditated paganism is, unless I mistake, what has endeared and still endears them to so many sensitive people who, as a rule, care little for painting.

CLIVE BELL

"J'Accuse...!" Letter from Emile Zola to Félix Faure, President of the French Republic, published in "L'Aurore," January 13, 1898.

On December 29, 1889, Pissarro sent the dummy of a book entitled *Les Turpitudes sociales* to his niece Esther Isaacson, who lived in London. It is still unpublished. It contains a cover page and twenty-eight drawings in which the artist attacked the social evils of his time. He said of it: "I do not think that I have gone beyond the expression of the truth." The four drawings reproduced here were captioned as follows:
(1) The first drawing represents a poor old philosopher. Thinking that it had really happened, he gazes ironically at the great sleeping city. He sees the sun rise radiantly and looking intently sees written in luminous letters the word ANARCHY. The Eiffel Tower tries to hide the sun from the philosopher's gaze, but it is not yet high enough and wide enough to screen from view the star that sheds its light upon us. This philosopher represents time, for he has an hourglass beside him; the sands will soon run out and he will turn it over to begin a new era. This, as you see, is symbolism!

procedure in the trial of Dreyfus, after Zola had exposed the military frame-up in his famous article *J'accuse*. Nothing proves that the Impressionists were directly affected by the Dreyfus affair; but is it too much to say that the climate of acceptance was bad for radicalism of any kind? The fact that a major part of the Caillebotte bequest were paintings by Camille Pissarro cannot have escaped the attention of the politicians who, we now have it on good authority, sometimes override the judgment of the Curator: how are we to interpret their rejection of eleven paintings by Pissarro, when all the Degas's are accepted, other than in terms of exacerbated prejudice?

Coming in the later years of his long struggle for recognition the Dreyfus Affair, in all its aspects, profoundly disturbed Pissarro. But his reaction was characteristic: "All the sadness, all the bitterness, all the unhappiness, I forget them and I even don't know them in the joy of work."

A notable omission in the Caillebotte bequest was any representative work by Berthe Morisot. Caillebotte had not collected her paintings, which were neither as easily nor as cheaply acquired as those of the other Impressionists, probably because they were not to his taste. Berthe Morisot's position in society continually obscured her reputation as an artist; critics usually ignored her, or treated her as a dilettante. Yet, after Pissarro, she was the most consistent exhibitor at the Impressionist exhibitions, taking part in all of them, save that of 1879 (when she was pregnant). Stéphane Mallarmé who, says Théodore Duret, literally worshipped Berthe, exerted himself on her behalf with the result that one of her paintings (*Woman at the Ball*) was hung in the Luxembourg gallery. It was one of her last satisfactions. She had never quite recovered from the death of her husband, Eugène Manet, in 1892; frail and of a delicate constitution, she died, March 2, 1895, in her fifty-fourth year. The news was a great blow to Renoir who was working beside Cézanne on a landscape when he received the telegram informing him of her death. He folded his easel and hurried home. Of all the friends and companions who had been with him in the struggle for recognition Berthe Morisot was the one with whom he had kept most closely in touch. "What a curious thing is destiny!" he was moved to say sometime later. "A painter of such pronounced temperament, born in the most severely middle-class surroundings which have ever existed, and at a period when a child who wanted to be a painter was almost considered the dishonor of the family! And what an anomaly to see the appearance in our age of realism of a painter so impregnated with the grace and finesse of the eighteenth century; in a word, the last elegant and 'feminine' artist that we have had since Fragonard, with the additional something of the 'virginal' that Madame Morisot had to such a high degree in all her painting." She was, of course, a direct descendant of Jean-Honoré Fragonard.

The "Monarch of the Skies," as Corot had called Eugène Boudin, died at Deauville, August 8, 1898, at the age of seventy-four. Wynford Dewhurst, who saw him shortly before his death, says that he resembled an old sea pilot, with a healthy ruddy complexion, white beard and keen blue eyes. He bequeathed his paintings to the people of Le Havre where they may now be seen in the municipal gallery. Jongkind had predeceased him by seven years, dying in a condition of mental instability, due to drink and depravation.

Since 1890 Alfred Sisley had been exhibiting with the Société Nationale des Beaux-Arts, an anti-Salon group, without having made a significant sale. In May 1897, François Depeaux, a French industrialist, persuaded Sisley to accompany him to London and undertook to buy whatever landscapes he should paint there. For four months Sisley painted the English and Welsh countryside, with, however, a noticeable change in the quality of his painting, which appeared to have become somewhat metallic. In October 1898, Marie Sisley died and Sisley's own life expectancy was running out. That year, Pissarro wrote to his son Lucien: "Sisley they say is gravely ill. This one is a beautiful, a great artist. I've seen works by him of a rare amplitude and beauty, among others *The Flood*, which is a masterpiece." Sisley died of cancer of the throat at Moret-sur-Loing, January 29, 1899. He was sixty. Just before dying he had called on Claude Monet to commend his children to Monet's care. "Of all the great Impressionists," writes Vollard, "the Master of Moret never even knew the most modest living... He endured his disease with courage, displayed to the end an optimism nothing could impair. After his last operation he said, 'I am suffering even more than before, but I know that it is going to cure me. I am seeing pink butterflies.'"

Three months after Sisley's death a sale of his works was held for the benefit of his children. Dealers and collectors competed for the twenty-seven canvases, which realized a total of 112,320 francs, almost as much as Sisley had earned in his life. Shortly afterwards the dealers Josse and Gaston Bernheim began buying up his work. At a public sale, March 1900, fourteen Sisley pictures excited great interest and *The Flood*, declared to be a masterpiece, was sold to Count Isaac de Camondo for 43,000 francs (Sisley had sold it for 180 francs). From that date the value of Sisley's works rose steadily.

The people of Moret-sur-Loing raised a monument to Alfred Sisley: the first Impressionist painter to be so commemorated.

Fame came to Pissarro in the twentieth century. But, already in 1890, two pictures brought, for him, very high prices: *Entrance to the Village of Voisins* was sold for 2,100 francs and *Rocquencourt* for 1,400 francs. He was finally being given a place in the important collections.

"Pissarro was a delightful man," says his biographer, Adolphe Tabarant, "and so profoundly human that any wrong done to another man angered him like a personal offense. You could not set eyes on him without being impressed by the simple majesty of his countenance, on which there was never a hint of hardness or disdain. His eyes, from which he suffered so much, were magnificent, and they smiled as his lips smiled, putting at ease whoever came to see him. Certainly a look of sadness would sometimes gather in those eyes of his, true artist's eyes, so deeply in love with the beauty of things, but that would be when he was alone and beset, as he often

(2) Misery in a top hat. Poor old musician, he walks home, worn out, from a café concert at Grenelle where he earns his 30 *sous*, at midnight, in rain, snow, wind, and old, old! What misery! He had believed in his genius, had dreamed of glory!

(3) Nothing to eat. This rough sketch is the first idea of a drawing I wanted to do over again. I have preferred to put it in as it is; its tragic brutality, its churlish execution, is more telling than a polished drawing.

(4) The crust of bread. Have you never passed in front of one of those shady-looking houses where bourgeois philanthropy, not feeling very sure of itself, ignominiously lurks and doles out to the starving a crust of bread which it has stolen from them?

was, by manifold anxieties... When we became acquainted in 1890 he was beginning to invest himself with that aureole of serenity which lent added charm to his gracious senescence. Dressed entirely in black velvet, he presented a fine appearance... Worthy of being painted by Rembrandt in the fur-trimmed cloak with which the Dutch master invests his Rabbis, his learned Doctors and his burgomasters, he looked inexpressibly venerable with his fine regular features, his big oriental eyes so full of light, his beard in which advancing years were snowing their white flakes, his beautiful hands exhibiting the delicacy of a master of the brush..."

On his way back from Durand-Ruel's gallery Pissarro would often stop for a chat at Vollard's shop in the rue Laffitte. "The first thing that struck one was his air of kindness, of sensitiveness and at the same time serenity, a serenity born of work accomplished with joy," says Vollard. "And yet, what a life of vicissitude was his. He suffered poverty and he had a great many children... looking at those landscapes that exhale the very scent of the fields, those quiet peasant women bending over their cabbages, those placid goose girls, who would guess that most of these canvases were painted during the period of the artist's worst calamities... With what openness of mind the old man judged his fellows, Cézanne, Renoir, Monet! He was interested in all the experiments that were now exercising the artists."

Success made Pissarro work harder than ever before. He visited England, Belgium, the Channel ports, Burgundy, finding new motifs in all these places. When an eye infection, without impairing his vision, forced him to give up open air painting he began working from hotel windows. Muffled up against the cold he painted a series of Paris street scenes, snow scenes and the bridges of the Seine in winter. One day he caught a cold and was put to bed. He developed prostate trouble, lay in pain for a month and died on November 12, 1903, in his seventy-third year.

Five months after his death Durand-Ruel held a comprehensive exhibition of his works (178 canvases, etchings and engravings) which sold for prices ranging from ten to twelve thousand francs each.

The last of the group to enjoy public favor was Paul Cézanne. In 1895 Vollard had bought some two hundred Cézanne canvases for between eighty and ninety thousand francs, and thereafter became his principal dealer. The canvases which filled Vollard's little shop in the rue Laffitte still confused the public. "Tell me, Monsieur Vollard," said one of his serious customers, "why does good painting have to be so ugly?" When Chocquet's collection was put up for sale, after his widow's death in 1899, the Cézannes brought good prices, for the first time. In 1900 Maurice Denis painted a picture, exhibited at the Champ de Mars, which he called *Homage to Cézanne*: Bonnard, Degas, Redon, Roussel, Sérusier and Vuillard are shown gathered around one of Cézanne's pictures. The following year Cézanne tactfully let it be known that, while he would not think of making any request or of taking any steps himself, he would readily accept

Camille Pissarro: Market Scene. Print.

any decoration that might be conferred upon him in recognition of his merit. Roujon, the then director of the Beaux Arts, was approached with a view to persuading him to recommend Cézanne for the Legion of Honor. The request met with a peremptory refusal. The Director declared himself ready to decorate any other Impressionist, especially Claude Monet, who, however, was precisely the one who refused to be decorated; but to decorate Cézanne he regarded as tantamount to repudiating the principles of his office.

Although he had suffered from diabetes for some time, Cézanne stubbornly refused to modify his habit of work and continued to paint in the open in all weathers. Caught in a storm while working in the fields he kept on working under a steady downpour for two hours before starting out for home. He collapsed on the road and a passing laundry-wagon picked him up and the driver took him home. His old housekeeper chafed his arms and body to bring back the circulation; he recovered consciousness and was put to bed, but remained feverish all night long. On the following day he rose as usual and went into the garden to work on the portrait of an old sailor. In the midst of the sitting he fainted and the model called for help; he was put to bed and never left it again. After receiving the last sacrament, he died October 22, 1906. He may be said, says Duret, to have died with his brush in his hand. He was sixty-seven.

A time came when Degas lost touch with modernity, as, for example, not liking the telephone. "You mean when it rings you answer it?" he said. "Like a servant!" He was also bored with talk about the "painting of the future." Shown some Seurats at an exhibition, he turned round abruptly and pointed out a picture hanging nearby, and said: "Why shouldn't *that* be the painting of the future?" It was a picture by the Douanier Rousseau.

In 1912 his house in the rue Victor Massé, in which he had lived for twenty years, was sold and the new owner decided to pull it down. Degas looked for another house, equally old-fashioned, and found one in the Boulevard des Batignolles. Vollard remembers Degas saying to him: "A man should marry. You don't know what the solitude of old age is like, Vollard." "Why, then, have you never married?" said Vollard. "Oh, with me, it's different. I was too afraid of hearing my wife say after I had finished a painting, 'That's a pretty thing you've done there'."

One day in 1916 Daniel Halévy, who had known Degas since childhood, wrote in his diary: "I hear that Degas is ill—the bronchial tubes as always." Halévy went to his bedside. "It is a bare room, new, with no past. Degas, immobile in bed, greets me with a kind word or two... At a given moment the nurse comes and straightens the pillow. Her short sleeve is transparent. All of a sudden Degas seizes her arm in both hands with more strength than one would have believed possible. He places her right arm in the light that shines from the window. He looks at it with passionate concentration. How many women's arms has he looked at like this and, so to speak, spied on in the light of his studio? I had been thinking that his strength had been exhausted, but here he was, still working."

The First Cézanne Exhibitions at Vollard's

"At Vollard's there is a very full exhibition of his work. Some still lifes of an amazing finish, some things incomplete, but really extraordinary in their savagery and character. I believe this will be little understood."
Pissarro, letter to Esther Isaacson, November 13, 1895

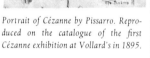

Portrait of Cézanne by Pissarro. Reproduced on the catalogue of the first Cézanne exhibition at Vollard's in 1895.

Catalogue of the second Cézanne exhibition at Vollard's in 1898.

Maurice Denis: Homage to Cézanne, 1900.

"In 1901, as a token of admiration for the painter of the Sainte-Victoire, Maurice Denis was to paint one of his most moving pictures: the *Homage to Cézanne*, which can be seen in the Luxembourg Museum. Represented in the center of this canvas is a dish of fruit, a copy of a famous piece by Cézanne which belongs to Gauguin. On the left of the composition is Sérusier, the theorist of the group, holding forth before his friends: Denis, Ranson, Vuillard, Bonnard, Roussel, together with Odilon Redon and Mellerio. I too have the honor of figuring in the picture."
Ambroise Vollard, *Souvenirs d'un marchand de tableaux*

Degas died on September 27, 1917, in his eighty-third year. An American Expeditionary Force had just landed in France, for the first time.

Degas left a fortune of eight million francs which his brother René Degas, sometime cotton broker of New Orleans, inherited with all his other effects. When the sale of the studio was being arranged René discovered a series of brothel scenes in the portfolios and, "out of respect for the artist's reputation," destroyed about seventy of them, much to the disgust of Vollard, who thought "these little masterpieces would have served brilliantly to prove how much Toulouse-Lautrec owed to his old master." Renoir regretted that the work of Degas's last years was so little known, for better reasons: "If Degas had died at fifty he would have been remembered as an excellent painter: it is after his fiftieth year that his work broadens out and that he really

Degas and the Shattering of Form

In later years Degas's eyesight began to fail him, but he worked on in the oncoming night, intent on striking out a few more flashes of light and movement. He gave up oils for pastels, a readier technique and one quite as rich in color possibilities. But he despaired of achieving all he had dreamed of. He had doubts about himself and judged himself with poignant severity. To his old friend Bartholomé he wrote: "I am going to go downhill fast and come rolling out somewhere wrapped up in a lot of bad pastels." To Henri Lerolle he wrote: "I have made too many plans, now I'm in a jam, power-less. I'm all at sea. I thought I had plenty of time, I never lost hope of taking up again one fine day, in spite of my eye trouble, what I had failed to do or was prevented from doing amidst all my worries. I piled up all my plans in a closet whose key I kept by me always, and I have lost that key…"

Edgar Degas: Dancers in Yellow, 1903. Pastel.

Edgar Degas:

After the Bath, about 1895.
Pastel and Watercolor.

After the Bath. Pastel.

Like his old comrades Monet, Renoir and Cézanne, Degas had arrived at the height of his maturity: his forms opened up, his colors found a new brilliance, his gestures an unexpected freedom. The truth is that in 1900 the Impressionists remained as revolutionary as in 1874. Their way of seeing had won out, but the public was disconcerted by their shift of emphasis now from the delineation of natural phenomena to pure expression. Their pictures no longer reflected the world: they were identified with its pulsing color and life.

"I doubt if any painter has ever interpreted woman so delightfully. Renoir's light and rapid brush gives grace, suppleness, abandon, it makes flesh transparent, colors cheeks and lips with the blush of pink. Renoir's women are enchantresses. If you take one home with you, she will be the person you take a last look at on going out and the first look on coming in. She will take a place in your life." Théodore Duret, *Les Peintres impressionnistes*

Auguste Renoir: Gabrielle with Jewelry, 1910.

Impressed by Raphael and the Renaissance art he discovered during his trip to Italy in 1881, Renoir turned back to relearn the lesson of Ingres; he sharpened his line and firmed up his modelling. It was not so much a modification of the sensation as a matter of technical research and more studied handling. By 1890, and even before, he was again painting with free, fluid strokes of the brush, and the female nude became his favorite subject. His "classical crisis" brought him back to certain time-honored themes, like Bathers. His renewed study of line and composition helped him forward to a new harmony between more powerful forms and more resonant and sensuous colors.

Auguste Renoir:
Three Bathers, 1883-1885. Pencil.

Auguste Renoir: Bathers in a Landscape, about 1915.

becomes Degas." Not all the lithographs of the "Maisons Closes" disappeared in what Vollard calls "the hecatomb," for the cunning dealer appears to have been able to save those which he had used, or intended to use, as illustrations for his limited editions.

When René Degas died a few years later the Degas fortune was the subject of litigation between the several branches of the Musson-Degas family for many years, it being finally split among the heirs of the third generation.

The Renoirs spent a part of the year at Essoyes, Aline's birthplace, an old peasant house with thick walls, surrounded by a garden planted with fruit trees. "Why should I go to Paris at all?" said Renoir. "I don't want central heating when I have a good wood fire to sit by. The butter here is perfect and the bread better than any you can get in Paris. And then there is the good little country wine..." Gabrielle had entered his service as model and part-time help; and his third son, Claude, was born at Essoyes in 1901. Someone at Essoyes had a bicycle—still a novel vehicle—and Renoir must needs ride it about. He fell off and broke his right arm.

He had already been treated for rheumatism; and he had developed partial atrophy of a nerve in the left eye, as a result of catching cold, so that his face had taken on a fixed expression which startled people. His arm was a long time healing; he developed arthritis and from then on it was a constant fight against illness. He taught himself to paint with his left hand and did not stop working. Meeting Vollard at the entrance to the hospital one day, Madame Renoir said: "Excuse me, the operation has been delayed until tomorrow. I'm very much in a hurry, my husband sends me to buy a box of colors. He wants to paint the flowers I brought for him this morning." Afraid of leaving his family destitute, his output was enormous, and all of it sold.

He was a famous painter. In 1899 his painting *At the Grenouillère* had sold for 20,000 francs and a few years later his portrait of Madame Charpentier would go for 84,000 francs. But when in 1900 he was made Knight of the Legion of Honor, he wrote to Monet apologizing for having accepted the order. Pissarro laughed at him.

His "rheumatism" drove him south during the winters and in 1908 he had a house built at Cagnes, near Nice, which he called "Les Collettes." When World War I broke out he went to live there permanently. His sons Pierre and Jean were both seriously wounded in the war, Pierre suffering a shattered arm, Jean being shot in the leg and only just escaping an amputation. Unlike many others, caught up in its horrors, Jean had no illusion about it being the last great war. In June 1915, Aline Charigot died at Cagnes.

Gabrielle carried on, but Renoir still made his own bed every morning, lit the fire and swept the studio. "I can't stand having anybody about me but women," he was wont to say. He hated corsets and high heels and had strong ideas about the way society was going. He let Claude's red hair grow long because he liked to paint it and also (according to Claude) because he thought that it would protect his head if he fell. He kept his palette as clean as a new coin and washed

Renoir at Le Cannet Returning from a Painting Expedition. Photographs, 1901.

"I haven't a moment's respite, but I mustn't complain. So many men at my age can work no more, but I can still paint."

Renoir

"Just as it was, when Renoir finally settled there (about 1907), the property of Les Collettes was a pleasant place to live, with its well-lighted house surrounded by greenery, the great olive trees with their gnarled trunks cracking open and looking like gray stone, and many orange trees... The profusion of plants, running everywhere, with the variety of their shapes and colors, brightened up the park where for the most part Renoir preferred to let nature take its course. From the terrace of Les Collettes the view extends far out to sea, embracing the area between Cap d'Antibes and the Italian frontier... 'In this marvelous region,' Renoir said to me, 'one seems to be beyond the reach of misfortune, one lives here in a softly padded atmosphere.'"

Georges Rivière, *Renoir et ses amis*

Auguste Renoir: Self-Portrait in a White Hat, 1910.

Auguste Renoir: Landscape, about 1910.

View of Cagnes from Renoir's House, "Les Collettes." Photograph.

his brushes himself every day. His hands became terribly deformed, with stiff joints, causing the thumbs to turn inwards and his fingers to bend towards the wrists. Indoors he wore a cap and a polka-dot English scarf; he had a long white beard and thick white hair. He received visitors, but was often irritated by their asininities. Eliminating the word "artist" from his vocabulary, he called himself a "workman painter." He died in his sleep of a ruptured blood vessel, December 3, 1919, in his seventy-eighth year. He had painted up to the day of his death. A picture of anemones was on his easel.

Thanks largely to Mary Cassatt's financial backing, both of the Impressionist exhibitions and of Paul Durand-Ruel in his critical years, there were now rooms exclusively devoted to the works of Sisley, Renoir, Monet and Pissarro at the Durand-Ruel galleries. In his old age Paul Durand-Ruel liked to talk about the early days of the Impressionists. He remembered very clearly the auction sale at the Hôtel Drouot in 1875 when the painters had been publicly abused and their works knocked down for nominal sums, selling only because of the handsome frames Durand-Ruel had put around them. "And your revenge?" asks Gustave Coquiot, interviewing him for *L'Excelsior*.

"It is complete!" replies the old art dealer. "A painting that I had recovered for 110 francs was sold much later for 70,000 francs in a public sale. Another, bought for 50 francs, was resold I don't know how many times—all amateur collectors repeatedly lose their heads—and brought 100,000 francs last time."

Renoir said of Durand-Ruel: "He transferred the art business from the domain of decoration to that of speculation." Nor was that the end of it. Many of the canvases he sold at what seemed to him fabulous prices cannot be bought for millions today. Some, alas, being worth far more than their weight in gold, spend a great part of their life in bank vaults.

Paul Durand-Ruel died in 1922 at the age of ninety.

Armand Guillaumin had inherited Daubigny's old studio on the Quai d'Anjou in the Ile Saint-Louis and bought his colors from Donnet on the Quai des Orfèvres. He had his own economical method of preparing and stretching his canvases. In 1868 he had worked beside Pissarro painting window blinds. After the war of 1870 he painted in the Auvers district for almost ten years. He was Dr Gachet's good friend; Gauguin bought his pictures and wrote Pissarro from Tahiti, saying that "a place was owed to Guillaumin" in the monthly meetings of the Impressionists. Théo Van Gogh also bought his pictures and Guillaumin was Vincent's friend in his last days. Eugène Murer, his fellow Auvergnat, expresses a contemporary opinion of Guillaumin: "His work remained always a little violent, somewhat shocking and often maladroit [but] his tenacity, his true love of nature gave him a certain mastery." However, "his use of color was exaggerated and lacking in suppleness and the charming quality of Sisley." He was not a pretty painter. He painted the bridges and roads he had worked on; he found subjects in laundry barges on the Seine, in tanneries and factories and had a fondness for chimney

The Large Drawing Room in Paul Durand-Ruel's Apartment at 35, rue de Rome, Paris, seen from the door of the small drawing room.

Letter written by Claude Monet from Giverny, December 1, 1883:

Dear Mr. Durand-Ruel,

...I should like to be able to reply that all your panels are finished, but unfortunately I cannot bring off what I'm after, though taking a great deal of trouble. All the big ones are done, and that is the main part; I have even done two extra ones in case one or two fail to harmonize with the whole. But to get to the end of these six panels, how many of them have I had to obliterate! Over twenty, perhaps thirty. I am busy with the small ones now and I hope this will go better, although the ones I have finished will have to be done over again. As for the other pictures, I shall soon have finished retouching them. I long to see all this out of the way, as I haven't done any open air work from nature for ages. I am glad to hear that what I sent you has been successful, but personally I am finding it harder and harder to satisfy myself and I begin to wonder if I'm going mad or if what I do is no better and no worse than before, but it is simply the fact that I have more trouble now doing what I used to do quite easily. However, I think I am right in being more particular . . .

stacks and the effects caused by smoke in the air. He was the first suburban painter.

He had never pretended that his art placed him above the ordinary moral obligation to provide for his wife and children; he had always worked for his living, but like many workers he sometimes tried his luck in the State Lottery. In 1891 a ticket he had bought in the Crédit Foncier paid off a hundred thousand francs. A free man from that moment he spent the rest of his days wandering about the French countryside painting the landscape he loved as violently as he liked. He outlived all the other Impressionists, dying in June 1927, at the age of eighty-six.

Guy de Maupassant has left us a charming picture of Claude Monet stumping across the grassy fields above the cliffs at Etretat, followed by a procession of children—his own and Alice's—carrying his easel, paintbox and various canvases. It was Monet's practice to work on five or six paintings at once, switching from one canvas to the other according as the weather changed. Says de Maupassant: "I have seen him thus seize a glittering shower of light on the white cliff and fix it in a flood of yellow tones which, strangely, rendered the surprising and fugitive effect of that unseizable and dazzling brilliance. On another occasion he took a downpour beating on the sea in his hands and dashed it on the canvas—and indeed it was the rain that he had thus painted..."

In 1883 they had rented a house at Giverny from an old peasant called Singetot. On the Seine, roughly half-way between Paris and Rouen, it became their home and studio. In good weather the family, Alice's six and Monet's two, ate at a trestle table under a large canvas awning they called "the tent." Alice saw to it that there was always plenty to eat and Monet became quite stout, took to smoking cigars and was something of a bon vivant (he once ate a gross of oysters at a sitting). He made a garden with bowers and flowering shrubs and converted a streamlet into a "Japanese water garden," in which he planted tubs of water lilies. The walls inside the house, according to Vollard, were covered with the work of other painters, "paintings which have been lying about a long while in shop windows," Monet explained to Vollard, as he bought a Cézanne to add to the collection. Dewhurst, who went to Giverny to see Monet, describes him as a short sturdy figure with a long bushy beard, cropped hair (he was going bald) and blue eyes. He wore a soft khaki hat, lavender-colored silk shirt open at the neck, drab trousers tapering to the ankles and there secured by large horn buttons, a short pair of cowhide boots, altogether, says Dewhurst, "an appearance at once practical and quaint." Dewhurst tells a story about Monet painting a huge oak tree standing out in bold relief against a ruddy cliff in the Creuse. After having made a number of studies, his work was interrupted by three weeks of bad weather, fog and rain. When he returned to the site the tree was in full bloom, completely enveloped in buds. Monet called on the mayor of the village who organized a working party which removed every single leaf from the tree, after which Monet continued his painting where he had left off.

Fire at the Durand-Ruel Gallery, New York, 1898. Photograph.

On March 17, 1898, a fire broke out in the premises of the Durand-Ruel Gallery at 389 Fifth Avenue, New York. In the midst of the general panic, the firemen coolly rescued the pictures, bringing them out through the windows.

Impressionist Exhibition at the Grafton Galleries, London, in 1905, organized by Durand-Ruel. Photograph.

Monet's "Home Port" at Giverny

Monet's House and Garden at Giverny. Photographs.

"After having ranged over the banks of the Seine for twenty-five years, from Le Havre to Paris, and again from the embankments in front of the Louvre down to the estuary, Monet all of a sudden found the chosen spot. One might almost say, remembering how often he had been on the move, that this tireless explorer of places and colors had, till then, yet to find his home port.

"He found it at Giverny.

"There in a rustic house, later enlarged and enriched into a comfortable villa, he settled down in 1883."

Arsène Alexandre, *Monet*

When Alice died in 1911 Monet's unhappiness was such that it was thought that he would never paint again. The following year he was found to be suffering from a cataract which the surgeons said could not be removed for many years yet. His spirits were somewhat revived by the marriage of his son Jean to Alice's daughter, Blanche Hoschedé. And then Monet's old friend Georges Clemenceau, who had been France's wartime Premier, had the idea of commissioning Monet to make a huge painting for the oval room of the Orangerie in the Tuileries.

The representation of Nature, as indicated by Dewhurst's story of the defoliated oak tree, had long ago lost its importance for Monet. He had reached the point where the subject of his picture, the Doge's Palace in Venice, the haystacks of Normandy, was a kind of habitual drill he went through in order to produce a picture whose interest surpassed these familiar objects. He repeated the experiment with the façade of Rouen Cathedral, as seen from the window of the little curiosity shop called "Au Caprice" on the northwest side of Cathedral Place. The geometrical Gothic of the Cathedral face provided him with a convenient composition for a series of paintings, each of which lived within itself. This was in the true line of the great forward movement which the Impressionist Revolution had released half a century before. This was Twentieth Century painting.

No sooner had Monet and his friends successfully flouted the canons of official art, back in the days of the Second Empire, than a regiment of artists had charged forward to exploit the breakthrough. The Pointillists and the Post-Impressionists had been followed by the Fauves, the Nabis and the Dadaists, the Cubists, the Symbolists, the Realists and the Surrealists, the Futurists and the Purists, the Expressionists and others, all advancing, overtaking each other, mingling, mixing, borrowing, quarrelling. One has only to think of the names of the painters who had taken up the brush after Monet's famous *Impression*: Seurat, Signac, Redon, Gauguin, Van Gogh, Henri Rousseau, Ensor, Toulouse-Lautrec, Bonnard, Valadon, Vuillard, Matisse, Rouault, Dufy, Marquet, Villon, Van Dongen, Vlaminck, Picabia, Derain, Léger, Picasso, Braque, Utrillo, Modigliani, Delaunay, Gris, Chagall, Ernst, Soutine, Masson, Miro ... Men had come from Russia, Spain, Holland, Italy and many other countries to take part in the French renaissance of painting, the greatest in modern times, the defiant and original tone of which had been set by the Impressionists.

The paintings which Monet now began for the oval room in the Orangerie were in the forefront of this movement. Though recognizably water lilies, darkened pools of them, wall flowing into wall, they were as close as art had come at this time to pure abstraction. For a man of eighty-six, already suffering from rheumatism and occasional bouts of malaria, the result of working in all weathers in wet, and often swampy, places, the effort was enormous. He carried through to the last great canvas, collapsed, and died, December 5, 1926. The *Nymphéas* were unveiled to the world six months later.

Would that other contemporary revolutions were as productive, or could be so beautifully commemorated!

Claude Monet: Poplars at Giverny, Sunrise, 1888.

The Poplars

"Between our eye and the appearance of figures, seas, flowers, fields, the atmosphere in fact interposes. The air visibly bathes each object, shrouds it in mystery, wraps it in all the colors, bright or muffled, which it has carried along before meeting that object."

Octave Mirbeau, preface to the Monet exhibition
at the Georges Petit Gallery, Paris, 1889

After settling at Giverny in 1883, Monet began to look with an even more searching eye at the familiar motifs that he came upon every day. Light had long played the leading part in his painting. Now he felt the need to record it in all its variety; he was no longer content with an instantaneous "shot" taken at random. Observing the same motif at all hours of the day, he was led by degrees to the idea of doing sets of pictures. His aim was to fix with scientific accuracy the modifications of reality caused by the chromatic variations of the atmosphere. For him, the poetry of nature lay in light. The *Haystacks* became his first series of paintings on the same theme: hour by hour, day by day, in canvas after canvas (some thirty of them still exist), he recorded the subtlest variations of light playing over the field before him.

The *Haystacks* were exhibited at Durand-Ruel's in May 1891, the series of *Poplars* in March 1892. "They are studies of the same landscape during the mild weather seasons, at different times of day," wrote Gustave Geffroy. "A stretch of meadowland, a bend in a narrow stream, three trees in front, and the continuation behind of the frail sinuous colonnade of these poplars crowned with their moving capital of green tufts, this is the subject chosen by the landscapist to write a new poem to the glory of the earth and light."

One series led to another, and this method of work was well suited to this period of Monet's life, now that eye trouble kept him more and more at home. He also tried to render his sensations on larger canvases, better suited to the broader scope of his motifs. Working on the same landscape motif in the neighborhood of his studio, he was able to carry out with him, at each session, several large-size canvases. While remaining as responsive as ever to light, he also maintained his sense of design and fitness. To Marcel Pays, interviewing him for *L'Excelsior* in 1920, he said: "You are not an artist if you haven't got your picture in your head before executing it, and if you aren't sure of your craft and composition... Techniques may vary... Art remains the same: it is at once a volontary and a sensitive transposition of nature."

The Cathedrals

Claude Monet:
Rouen Cathedral: Tour d'Albane, Early Morning, 1894.

"My stay here goes forward, which is not to say that I am anywhere near finishing my cathedrals. Alas, I can only repeat that the further I go the harder I find it to render what I feel; and I tell myself that the man who says he has finished a canvas is arrogant indeed. Finished means complete, perfect, and I work on hard without advancing, seeking and groping for my way, without achieving very much, except to tire myself out."

Claude Monet, letter to Gustave Geffroy, March 28, 1893

"What specifically should delight us in this many-sided world is the restless vibration of life that quickens the sky and the earth and the sea, and all nature teeming and all nature inert. Well, this moving wonder of every hour which meets our eyes in all the pageantry of this luminous planet, this changing miracle which ceases only to engender further miracles, this intensity of life which comes at us from man and beast, but which also comes at us from grass and wood and stone, all this festival the earth lavishes upon us unwearyingly."

Georges Clemenceau, *Justice*, May 20, 1895

"My strong point is knowing when to stop. No painter can work more than half an hour on the same motif in the open air if he wants to remain faithful to nature. When the motif changes, you must stop."

Claude Monet

Claude Monet:

Rouen Cathedral, West Facade, Sunlight, 1894.

Rouen Cathedral, Sunset, 1894.

206

London and Venice

"*Claude Monet no longer captures light with the joy in conquest of one who, having seized his prey, holds on to it with clenched hands. He conveys it as the most intelligent of dancers conveys an emotion. Movements fuse and combine and we do not know how to break them down again. They are so smoothly interconnected that they seem to be but a single movement, and the dance is perfect and complete as a circle.*"

Octave Mirbeau, preface to the exhibition of
the Venice series, Bernheim Gallery, Paris 1912

Claude Monet: *London, Effect of Sunlight in Fog, 1904.*

"Hard at work, I have not been able to write to you, leaving it to my wife to give you our news. She must have told you how enthusiastic I am over Venice. Well, my enthusiasm only grows, as does all the unique light of this place. I am saddened by it. It is so beautiful! But I must make the best of it ... I console myself with the thought of coming back next year, for as yet I have only been able to make a tentative start. But what a pity I didn't come here earlier when I was young and bold and would stop at nothing! No matter, I am spending delicious moments here, almost forgetting that I am an old man." Claude Monet, letter to Gustave Geffroy, December 7, 1908

Claude Monet: *The Ducal Palace, Venice, 1908.*

The Grand Canal, Venice, 1908.

Palazzo da Mulà, Venice, 1908.

Claude Monet:

Water Lilies with the Japanese Bridge, 1899.

Water Lilies at Giverny, 1905.

Wisteria, 1919.

Monet (right) at Giverny with Georges Durand-Ruel and Madame Joseph Durand-Ruel. Photograph.

Clemenceau (left) and Monet (right) on the Japanese Bridge in Monet's Garden at Giverny. Photograph.

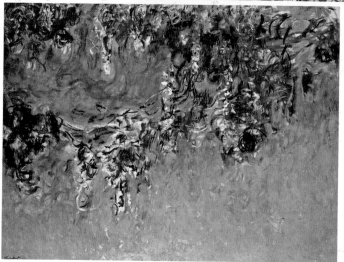

"At Giverny he created an unusual garden by deflecting the course of a stream, the Epte. He obtained a small pool whose water was always clear; he surrounded it with trees, shrubs, flowers, of his own choosing, and he adorned the surface with water lilies of various colors which blossom in the spring, amid their broad leaves, and remain in bloom all summer. Over this flowered water, a light wooden bridge, in the style of Japanese bridges; and in the water, among the flowers, the whole passing sky, all the air playing among the trees, all the movement of the wind, all the nuances of the hours, the still image of surrounding nature. "

Gustave Geffroy, *Claude Monet*

"I have taken up again some things impossible to do: water with grass waving at the bottom . . . It is a beautiful thing to see, but trying to paint it is enough to drive you crazy. Yet I keep tackling things like that."

Claude Monet,
letter to Gustave Geffroy, June 22, 1890

Monet's Water Garden at Giverny. Photograph.

Monet photographed by Sacha Guitry.

Taken up in 1890, the theme of water, of pools mirroring sky and vegetation, absorbed Monet for the rest of his life. These aquatic landscapes span almost forty years of his career. To them he devoted what strength he had left in old age. His knowledge of the subject was so thorough that he ended by identifying himself with it. With a free handling of color and a boldness of design unmatched by any painter until many years later, he wholly assimilated himself with what he simultaneously observed and recorded. On August 11, 1908, he wrote to Geffroy: "Know that I am engrossed in my work. These landscapes of water and reflections have become an obsession. It is beyond the strength of an old man like me, and yet I am determined to render what I feel. I have destroyed some . . . I have begun some afresh . . . and I hope that something will come of such strenuous efforts." Each moment and effect which he studied in his water garden and recorded on canvas is like a cross-section of the teeming life of the world.

"You can produce masterpieces otherwise by memory, by the science of composition, but you will not produce these particular masterpieces, which are quite equal to the others and which express something never yet expressed to this degree: the magnificent poetry of the passing moment, of continuing life. Impressionism, wrongly considered to be a hasty study of details, is precisely the reverse. I shall never weary of repeating it: Impressionism is a synthesis of universal being, sur-prised at a certain point and during a certain state of its evolution. Many painters have attempted that syn-thesis, but they have left it in the form of a sketch, for want of the powers of perception which Claude Monet has, and which have made him realize that the same fleeting minutes recurred almost identically, and that he could extract from them on the spot the résumé and composition which others, with the help of theories, pursue in the studio."

Gustave Geffroy, *Claude Monet*

Claude Monet: Belle-Ile. Brittany. Pencil.

"The Magnificent Poetry of the Passing Moment"

"This juxtaposition of color spots was thought to be easy because it seemed vaguer than a good design carefully laid in, as taught by the schools. In reality the impressionist technique is terribly difficult... It took the prodigious powers of Monet and Renoir for it ever to be imagined that their art was an easy matter! It called for a refined sensibility and a complete science of color. A picture painted in this way does not allow of any retouching... The eye recomposes what the brush has dissociated, and one perceives with amazement all the science, all the secret order that has presided over this accumulation of color spots, which seemed to be thrown on in a furious shower. It is a veritable piece of orchestral music in which each color is an instrument with its own distinct part, and in which the hours, with their various tints, represent the successive themes. Monet is the peer of the greatest landscapists in his understanding of the character of each particular place studied; therein lies the supreme quality of his art."

Camille Mauclair, *L'Impressionnisme*, 1903

Claude Monet: The Water Garden at Giverny.

"For the rest, what do forms matter? What does the subject matter? What does the landscape itself matter that one is trying to paint? What do these elements matter, these prodigious masses ceaselessly contending? M. Monet knows that in fact there is only one real thing, and that is light. He knows that without it 'everything would be shadow,' everything would remain shrouded in chaotic night. It is light that is all-powerful, that magnifies forms, brings out their beauty, renews their luster, metamorphoses their appearance, displaces their contours and quickens them; it is light that peoples the world with its intangible finery, and decks it in a poetry ceaselessly renewed and everlasting."

Georges Grappe, *L'Art et le Beau*

LIST OF ILLUSTRATIONS

INDEX OF NAMES AND PLACES

List of Illustrations

215

INDEX OF NAMES AND PLACES

PRINTED BY
IRL IMPRIMERIES RÉUNIES LAUSANNE S.A.

PRINTED IN SWITZERLAND